THE TRAGIC DAYS
OF
BILLY THE KID

THE
TRAGIC DAYS
OF
BILLY THE KID

BY

FRAZIER HUNT

MAPS BY ROBERT N. MULLIN

HASTINGS HOUSE PUBLISHERS

NEW YORK

Library of Congress Catalog Card Number: 56-8120

Published simultaneously in Canada by
S. J. Reginald Saunders, Publishers, Toronto 1

Printed in the United States of America

TO
THE MEMORY OF
LT. COL. MAURICE GARLAND FULTON
(1877–1955)

unrivaled authority on the Lincoln County War, who
generously supplied many of the documents, letters and
newspaper accounts herein published for the first time.

And to two other friends
ROBERT N. MULLIN
and
J. EVETTS HALEY

Western scholars and researchers, without whose unself-
ish aid and encouragement this volume would never have
been completed.

"Billy the Kid must remain wholly the most unaccountable figure in frontier history."
—ARTHUR CHAPMAN

THE TRAGIC DAYS
OF
BILLY THE KID

PART ONE

The Little Grub-Line Rider

I

A number of years ago Arthur Chapman, the Western poet who wrote *Out Where the West Begins,* explained, "Billy the Kid must remain wholly the most unaccountable figure in all frontier history."

For three-quarters of a century he remained exactly that —the victim of the myths which had surrounded and captured him.

Hundreds of articles, radio and TV shows, stories, books and motion pictures have been written around this unique young man. Unfortunately none of the writers had access to more than a small part of the hidden source material which would have cleared away the fabulous tales and obscure half-truths and brought into clear focus the real Billy the Kid and the great days he lived.

For the first time the fully documented facts have now been brought together. They comprise a great mass of letters, newspaper accounts, official reports and word-of-mouth recollections.

1

And so it is that with the death of the legend of Billy the Kid there comes to life a warm and friendly human being, authentic and accountable. . . .

It was time the Kid pulled out to another part of the country and lay low for a while.

The "law" was after him. There might even be a reward posted at this very moment for his capture.

Somewhere in the Burro Mountains of southwestern New Mexico near the Arizona line where he was hiding out, he had come across the newspaper that carried the verdict of the coroner's jury. He'd killed a man, all right.

There it was in cold type. He must have read the item several times when he found it in a stray copy of the Arizona *Citizen,* dated August 22, 1877.

In the first sentence his name was given as Austin Antrim, but a little way down it was changed to "Henry Antrim, alias Kid." As a matter of fact, he had been known around Silver City and the neighboring area as both Henry and Billy Antrim, as well as the Kid and Henry McCarty, which was his real name. The item read:

> Austin Antrim shot E. P. Cahill near Fort Grant on the 17th inst. and the latter died on the 18th. Cahill made a statement before death to the effect that he had some trouble with Antrim during which the shooting was done. Deceased had a sister, Margaret Flanegan, in Cambridge, Mass., and another, Kate Conlon, in San Francisco. He was born in Galway, Ireland, and was aged 32. The coroner's jury found that the shooting "was criminal and unjustifiable, and that Henry Antrim, alias Kid is guilty thereof." The inquest was held by M. L. Wood, J.P. and the jurors were M. McDowell, George Teague, T. Mc-Cleary, D. M. Norton, Jas. L. Hunt and D. H. Smith.

It was certainly a hand-picked jury. The Kid knew most of the six men and they were friends of Cahill's. It was logical for him to assume he would receive the same harsh treatment from a regular jury if he were caught and tried for murder.

Long after the event an old army scout and well-known frontier character, Gus Gildea, gave an account of what occurred and it appeared in the Tucson *Citizen* of January

31, 1931. Gildea's statement can be accepted as substantially accurate:

It was in the Fall of '77 when I first met Billy the Kid. He was an easy going, likeable youth, still in his teens. I was scouting at Fort Grant then, when Billy came to town, dressed like a "country jake," with "store pants" on and shoes instead of boots. He wore a six-shooter stuck in his trousers.

The blacksmith frequented George Adkin's saloon. He was called "Windy" because he was always blowin' about first one thing and then another. I don't recall the rest of his name. Shortly after the Kid came to Fort Grant, Windy started abusing him.

He would throw Billy to the floor, ruffle his hair, slap his face and humiliate him before the men in the saloon.

Yes, the Kid was rather slender, with blue eyes and fair hair. The blacksmith was a large man, with a gruff voice and blustering manner.

One day he threw the youth to the floor. Pinned his arms down with his knees and started slapping his face.

"You are hurting me. Let me up!" cried the Kid.

"I want to hurt you. That's why I got you down," was the reply.

People in the saloon watched the two on the floor. Billy's right arm was free from the elbow down. He started working his hand around and finally managed to grasp his .45.

Suddenly silence reigned in the room. The blacksmith evidently felt the pistol against his side, for he straightened slightly. Then there was a deafening roar. Windy slumped to the side as the Kid squirmed free and ran to the door, vaulted into the saddle on John Murphy's racing pony and left Fort Grant.

When I came to town the next day from Hooker's ranch, where I was working, Murphy was storming and cursing the Kid, calling him a horse thief, murderer and similar names. I told him he would get his horse back, for the Kid was no thief.

In about a week one of Murphy's friends rode into town on Cashaw, Murphy's horse, saying the Kid had asked him to return the animal to the owner.

It is fairly well established that the Kid rode that night of the killing to the Knight ranch and stage station near the Arizona-New Mexico line, where he had stopped once before when he was in trouble. The Knights were family friends. Knight for a time had run a butcher shop in Silver City where the Kid's stepfather, William H. Antrim, had worked off and on.

There are several accounts as to just what the boy did during the next three or four weeks after the killing of the blacksmith. It is probable that he kept away from the main trails, stopping for a night or two at various isolated little ranches and mining camps where a stranger was always welcome and no questions asked. Within a few days he sent back the horse he had borrowed.

There is a stubborn tradition that he fell in with Jesse Evans and one or two of his thieving gang from the Rio Pecos country of Lincoln County, two or three hundred miles to the east. He may even have joined up with Evans in a little horse-lifting lark here around the Burro Mountains, not far from Silver City. The Evans gang had ridden back to Lincoln County by the time the boy started for Mesilla, the sleepy Mexican county seat of Dona Ana County on the Rio Grande, forty miles north of El Paso.

The Kid certainly didn't look the part of a killer. He wouldn't be eighteen for another two or three months, and he had to stretch a little to bring himself up to five feet, eight inches tall. He weighed only a trifle more than 130 pounds, but he was fairly heavy-boned and wiry, although his hands and feet were unusually small. There was a resilience about his slender figure that made him almost immune to ordinary hardships.

His two upper teeth were prominent but this did not disfigure him. Rather it seemed to add to the peculiar charm that gave him an unusually attractive personality. His light-brown hair was a little on the wavy side, and his blue-gray eyes at times could turn cold and deadly. And he was experienced in frontier ways and fully qualified to take care of himself.

Fundamentally he was good-natured and of a happy, carefree disposition, and there are proofs galore of his genuine kindness of heart to old people and to children, and to the lowly *pobres* (the poor ones) whose language he could speak so beautifully. There is no single authentic case of his ever having abused a native New Mexican. Instead, there is ample evidence that he was as one with them, a fact which was to have a great influence on his short and tragic life.

2

It is strange that the early years and family background of this unusual boy are wrapped in mystery so absolute that no amount of research has ever been able to penetrate it. Within a year and a half after Billy's death, a singular Massachusetts-born tramp-printer and inebriate newspaperman by the name of Ash Upson, living at the time in Roswell in the Pecos Valley, undertook to write, under Sheriff Pat Garrett's signature, a small biography called "The Authentic Life of Billy the Kid." The roving Ash apparently had boarded for a time with the boy's mother in both Santa Fe and Silver City and obtained from her certain facts regarding the lad's early years. Later they were to be fattened by the printer's own fertile imagination.

The various youthful adventures concocted and elaborately described by Ash Upson in the Garrett book have long been accepted as gospel facts. Yet the first valid date and incident in the early days of the Kid's life was unearthed as a result of the research of Robert N. Mullin and Philip J. Rasch almost eighty years after the event took place. Their findings blew to bits many of the accepted "facts" which clearly were the creations of Upson's romantic imagination.

In both the "Book of Marriages" of Santa Fe County, New Mexico, and the records of the First Presbyterian Church in the capital, there was found a notation of the marriage on March 1, 1873, of William H. Antrim and Mrs. Catherine McCarty, performed by the Rev. D. F. McFarland. Among the witnesses were the bride's two sons, Henry McCarty and his older brother Joe McCarty. It is the boy Henry McCarty, later known to the world as Billy the Kid and William H. Bonney, with whom this study is concerned.

The stepfather was a good-natured wanderer who was a sort of jack-of-all-trades but was surely a master of none. At times he worked variously as a miner, semi-professional gambler, odd-job man, and helper in the Knight butcher shop. Born on December 1, 1842, at Huntsville, near Anderson, Indiana, he was thirty years old when he married Catherine McCarty. He had enlisted in the 54th Regiment of Indiana Volunteers in Indianapolis in April, 1862, and for some unknown reason was honorably discharged three or four months later.

Shortly after the marriage the family moved from Santa Fe to the new mining community of Silver City, far down in the mountainous country in the southwest section of New Mexico. It was a long journey by stagecoach, for no railroad had as yet penetrated the Territory. Here Catherine developed what was known as "quick consumption." For the last months of her life she was a pathetic bedridden invalid, her days and nights racked with fits of coughing, and her heart filled with constant worry over what would happen to her two boys when she left this world. There can be no question of the date and circumstances of her passing. In its weekly issue of September 19, 1874, the Silver City *Mining Life* carried the following item:

> Died in Silver City, on Wednesday, the 16th inst., Catherine, wife of William Antrim, aged 34 years.
>
> Mrs. Antrim with her husband and family came to Silver City one year and a half ago, since which time her health has not been good, having suffered from an affection of the lungs, and for the last four months she has been confined to her bed. The funeral occurred from the family residence on Main Street, at 2 o'clock on Thursday.

Authenticated testimony of neighbors and friends furnish ample proof of the gentle care and affection that the smaller boy Henry gave to his dying mother. The memory of her suffering and death marked the few remaining years of his own life with a sense of fatalism and a feeling of the futility of man's struggle against his fate. This he had learned, as well, from the native New Mexicans who understood and sympathized with the boy.

The great-heartedness of the frontier people saw to it that the two orphan boys were not left entirely to the inadequate efforts of the stepfather. He did his best to hold together his little family, but he had no way of controlling the wilder boy, now turning fifteen. Henry's education was swiftly completed in the barrooms and gambling halls and tough spots of the mining town.

For a time the Truesdells, who ran a boarding house and hotel in Silver City, gave the boy his room and board for helping in the kitchen and the dining room. More than once in later years the proprietor remarked that Henry was the only boy who ever worked for him who never stole anything. He was not really a bad boy but only a wild one, Mr. Truesdell always insisted.

But the motherless, homeless boy seemed to have a good many things against him. There was the question of his name, an ambiguity which didn't seem so important at the time yet must have given him a feeling of instability and a complete absence of family roots. It was not the lack of one name that bothered him; it was the fact that he had too many names.

Many people in Silver City learned that his real name was Henry McCarty and they called him that. At times he was also known as Henry Antrim, which was a combination of his own given name and the surname of his stepfather, William H. Antrim. It wasn't long, however, until he was generally referred to as Billy Antrim and Kid Antrim, then as the Kid—later as Billy Kid, and in the end as Billy the Kid.

It was a full two years after he had left Silver City and when he was in grave trouble over the killing of the blacksmith that he began to use the formal name of William H. Bonney; obviously the William H. was borrowed from the given name of his stepfather. No one knows from whence came the surname Bonney. It was an accepted formula of the frontier for a man on the dodge to use an alias, and when he felt he needed one the boy very probably simply hand-picked and adopted William H. Bonney.

More than a quarter century later, in 1902, Henry H. Whitehall, famous sheriff of Grant County, New Mexico, who had known the Kid intimately, corroborated the facts regarding the boy's true name in an interview in the Silver City *Enterprise:*

> Early in his career he changed his name to Billie Bonney in order to keep the stigma of disgrace from

his family. Billie's right name, you know, was Henry McCarty.

There is eternal mystery, likewise, surrounding the generally accepted date and place of his birth: New York City, November 23rd, 1859. Both are based largely on the somewhat questionable authority of Ash Upson, who despite his itching foot seemed to find true inner solace and satisfaction in the lonely and dangerous desert mesas and distant mountains of the Rio Pecos land of eastern Lincoln County. In all, the odd, old fellow remained there a full fifteen years. Fact and fancy seemed mixed in equal proportions in the mind of this near-genius, who was as soaked in the poetry of Shakespeare and the romantic novels of Scott as he was in frontier rotgut.

It is reasonable, however, to accept the above birthplace and date, for certainly Billy would now and again have referred to these innocent facts. There is a strong belief that his father died in New York City and that the mother, possibly for health reasons, then moved west and remarried.

Slightly over a year after the death of his mother, when the boy was just under sixteen and living at the home of a Widow Brown, an incident occurred that was to affect the future course of his life. The good lady, worried over the report that the lad was mixed up with a no-good loafer in a small theft, enlisted the help of Sheriff Whitehall. The sheriff, likewise believing that a good scaring might help the motherless boy, took him to Squire Givens who solemnly sent him to the town jail to think over his minor crime until he could be bailed out and the coming session of the Grand Jury could pass on his case.

That week's issue of the Grant County *Herald* carried an item which apparently marked the end of the affair:

> Henry McCarty, who was arrested on Thursday and committed to the jail to await the action of the Grand Jury upon the charge of stealing clothes from Charley Sun and Sam Chung, celestials, sans cues, sans Joss sticks, escaped from prison yesterday through the chimney. It's believed that Henry was simply the tool of "Sombrero Jack," who done the stealing whilst Henry done the hiding. Jack has skinned out.

The boy made a beeline that night for the Truesdell home, where he had first lived following the death of his mother. Mrs. Truesdell let him in and fixed up a place for him to sleep. Before sunup that morning she gave him some of her own son Chauncey's clean clothes, shared with him the little money she had in her purse, and put him on the early buckboard for the stage station at the Knight ranch, over near the Arizona line. Without doubt she pleaded with him that he must be a good boy for the sake of his dead mother.

The supposition is that he soon drifted on from the hospitable Knight ranch, and for the next year rode the grub line of the cow outfits, mining camps and frontier army posts, doing odd jobs and picking up what passed for a living. Certainly he completed his education in the fine art and science of gambling and in handling cattle and horses, and stood high on the frontier Honor Roll as a Master of the Colt and Winchester. He learned how to make camp and cook, and how to survive in a harsh land and under a cruel sun.

How far he drifted or what troubles he may have stumbled into will never be known, but it is fully established that he killed the blacksmith Windy Cahill on the edge of Camp Grant, Arizona, on the night of August 17, 1877. With the sure instincts of a homing pigeon he probably rode east that night to the friendly Knight ranch, across the line in the Territory of New Mexico. For a time he kept clear of the more used trails, and it may well be that he indulged in the pastime of accompanying the Jesse Evans toughs in the little horse-stealing expedition already referred to.

The bright picture Jesse Evans painted of the excitement and profitable adventure to be found in the lawless land of the Pecos country next to the Texas line made a strong impression on the boy's imagination. So it was that on a September day he jogged over the rough mountain trails eastward to the Rio Grande and the little county seat of Mesilla, a day's horseback ride above El Paso and the Mexican border. From here he could pick and choose his next stop.

It was pleasant for him to hang out around the sunny *plazas* and little adobe *tiendas* and bars of Mesilla and the nearby towns, which were still almost totally native Mexi-

can. Since his own youth in the winding dirt streets and
narrow alleys of Santa Fe, he had spoken Spanish as if it
were his mother tongue.

There hadn't been much of the old Mexican life in the
brash mining towns and army posts where he had been
for the larger part of the three or four years since his family left Santa Fe. He must have missed the gentle, friendly
atmosphere of these old Rio Grande settlements with
their *mañana* philosophy and their sense of fatalism and
their slow-paced existence.

On a Friday in this late September of 1877 the Mesilla
Valley *Independent* carried an item in the right-hand
column of Page 1, under the heading *Grant County Items*
which the boy surely must have seen:

> On Monday last, three horses belonging respectively
> to Col. Ledbetter, John Swishelm and Mendoza,
> were stolen from Pass' coal camp in the Burro Moun-
> tains. On learning the fact Col. Ledbetter and Swis-
> helm went out to the camp and trailed them in on
> the road at Apache Tahoe. Sometime on Tuesday the
> party of thieves, among whom were Henry Antrim,
> were met at Cooks Canyon by Mr. Carpenter. Tele-
> grams have been sent to Sheriff Barela at Mesilla, and
> we hope to hear of the arrest of the thieves and the
> recovery of the horses.

It was the name Henry Antrim and that last sentence
about the telegram having been sent to Sheriff Barela at
Mesilla that caught the Kid's eye. Many people still called
him by that name and if he were picked up now the
charge of horse stealing might be pushed aside so that he
could be extradited to Arizona and tried for the murder
of Cahill. In all probability a jury hand-picked from among
the dead blacksmith's friends would slip the friendless
little punk a one-way ticket to the gallows.

If Jesse Evans hadn't already ridden off for Lincoln
County the Kid would probably have gone to him for ad-
vice. It was general knowledge that in New Mexico a well
organized group of lawyers and politicians called the Santa
Fe Ring was deeply interested in the profitable army and
Indian contracts and controlled the political power of the
backward territory. Its leading figure was an extraordinary
Missourian named Tom Catron. The slouchy, heavy-shoul-

dered, rather generous lawyer lived in Santa Fe and was Federal Prosecuting Attorney.

The Ring's representative at Mesilla was the Prosecuting Attorney of the Third Judicial District, comprising the three southern counties of Lincoln, Dona Ana and Grant. He was a giant Tennesseean named Col. W. L. Rynerson, who had walked overland in the Gold Rush to California. In 1861 he had joined up with the Union Army and the California Column that marched east to the Rio Grande, and helped hold New Mexico for the Union. Big and blustering, he was loyal to the hard men who played his game but remorseless to those who opposed him and the Ring.

It was easy for Rynerson to control the sheriff and, with the help of a friendly judge, to rig a jury and secure an acquittal even in a clear-cut case of murder. Only a few months before the Kid's arrival in Mesilla this exact thing had happened to the notorious Jesse Evans. But Evans was now on the Pecos, more than 200 miles eastward in Lincoln County, and consequently he could not intercede for the Kid.

Obviously it was time the homeless boy made tracks. It was only forty miles south to the Mexican border and the town of Juarez, then known as Paso del Norte. It would be easy enough for him to jog down the river road, cross over to Old Mexico, and lose himself in the vast reaches of Chihuahua.

But a young fellow on the dodge would be almost as safe if he struck out east for the distant Pecos. No sheriff would follow him there. And once he reached the far side of Lincoln County he could hang out with the Jesse Evans gang or at the cow camp of Jimmy Dolan of the old Lincoln firm of L. G. Murphy & Co., which had long stood in with the Santa Fe Ring. The Kid had already met the foreman of the Pecos ranch, a salty Virginian named Billy Morton.

It took him only a minute to roll up his few personal belongings in a blanket and tie them on the back of the low cantle of his old Mexican saddle. They and the clothes on his back were his sole possessions, along with his pony and his secondhand Colt and ten-dollar Winchester. Never in his life would he own more of this world's goods.

The thing for him to do now was to get out as quickly

as he could. He was in grave danger of arrest, and there was not a moment to lose.

3

Mesilla was hardly awake when the Kid jogged over to the ford at nearby Las Cruces and crossed the Rio Grande. The trail ran on east up the long, western slope of the Organ Mountains that lay back a few miles from the river. The climb was a dreary, tiresome one, and now and again the boy pulled up his pony to let him blow. He was in no hurry.

It was late afternoon when he topped the Pass, and there before him spread a whole new world of beauty and color, with a promise of wild danger that thrilled him deep inside. The setting sun was at his back and before his eyes he saw this vast, lonely emptiness begin to glow and come alive.

At the foot of the long eastern slope lay the great, desolate Tularosa Basin, fifty miles wide and extending north and south as far as he could see. Below and to the left stretched a sea of white gypsum sand, now turning into delicate pinks and rose colors as the rays of the red sun began to play on it. And beyond on the distant horizon lay the vague outlines of an interminable string of mountain ranges that formed the western barrier of Lincoln County. Narrow gaps led through these ramparts and made the trails that led into the vast, isolated country beyond. Swift mountain streams sang their way down the widening canyons and gave the magic of life to the little irrigated farms and ranches.

These tiny rivers of Lincoln County bore beautiful names—the Bonito, the Ruidoso, the Hondo, the Feliz, the Peñasco, the Seven Rivers. All of them tried to reach the Pecos to the eastward; save in the late springtime when the rains came, few of them made it. The high desert plateau bordering the Pecos valley was too thirsty for most of them. Near their sources in the mountains to the west lay the Mescalero Apache Reservation and Fort Stanton, and the sleepy county seat of Lincoln. Far to the east stretched the Valley of the Pecos.

This Pecos country, and the sixty miles or so beyond the reddish, sluggish river to the Texas line, was the homeland of John Chisum, the fabulous cattle king, and of the cow camp of the old Murphy firm now run by tough Jimmy Dolan and Billy Morton—and the hide-out of the thieving Jesse Evans gang. Yet this was only a part of great Lincoln County, limitless, isolated, deadly, and now gripped in a bitter feud that could lead only to open warfare and wholesale killing.

It was straight into this land of wild danger and excitement that the slender young boy with the bad start in life was heading.

As he topped the high San Agustin Pass and looked down on the thrilling scene, he could not possibly have conceived the wonderful adventures and the tragic days that lay ahead for him.

The Kid rode into Lincoln County at the high moment of change which sooner or later came to every western frontier: the moment of growing-up; the moment when lawlessness and disorder, and crooked courts and illegal "rings" were finally compelled to give way before the forces of law and order, and the phenomenon called progress.

It is probable that the boy could not remember ever having seen a train or having heard the clanging bell of a locomotive. No single foot of railroad had as yet entered the whole of the almost limitless Territory of New Mexico. The defeat of the Confederacy a scant dozen years previously had sent the transcontinental roads of steel across northern lands, and New Mexico and Arizona had been sentenced to remain in their deadly isolation and backwardness.

But the Kid would have known at least something of the history and background and general lay of the land of this alluring Rio Pecos country, two hundred miles to the east of the Rio Grande. The vast area had been left to the raiding Apaches and Comanches during the long generations of the Spanish and Mexican rule. The American conquest of 1846, followed by the Civil War, had brought in a few bold cattlemen. It was the attraction of their herds and the isolated security offered to outlaws, which a decade later served as a magnet to the gunfighters and killers run out of western Texas and Indian Territory, Colorado, Arizona and even old Mexico. Sprawling Lincoln County, and particularly the Pecos River area, was a haven to them—as it was shortly to be for this homeless boy.

Apparently he missed the hangout of Jesse Evans and first appeared at a tiny settlement called Seven Rivers where a number of little streams emptied themselves into the Pecos. For some days he rode the grub line of the small ranchers of the neighborhood, visiting the Jones and Beckwith and Johnson families. He may have racked on north as far as the two-building cow-town of Roswell, stopping off for a meal or two at John Chisum's open house below the trading post. He probably met the rather solidly built Texan whose light blue eyes humorously looked out of their nests of crow's feet at a world which Uncle John neither feared nor ever quite permitted to dominate him. His heavy-pointed mustaches adorned his large, generous mouth and his weather-beaten face marked him as a man who had spent years in the saddle.

Certainly most of the gossip the boy heard was a bitter indictment of the cattle king, and wise as he was to frontier range conflicts he must have seen that a desperate feud between the small ranchers and the big Chisum had long been in the making. It was about to reach the killing stage.

For almost as far back as he could remember he had heard a good deal about this old Pecos cow man. Just as every school boy in New Mexico had been taught that Lincoln County was the largest county in the United States—stretching 150 miles east and west and 170 miles north and south—so did they all know that John Chisum was the biggest cow man in the world. His Fence Rail brand and his Jingle Bob ear crop marked more than 60,000 longhorns, not counting the latest calf crop. What the boy didn't already know about Chisum the little ranchers along the Pecos, who had long helped themselves to his mavericks and unbranded calves, now filled in for him.

Chisum had come into this Pecos country from Texas in 1866, the year after Charles Goodnight and Oliver

Loving had broken the western trail from the great Texas reservoirs of longhorns to the fattening ranges far to the north. Save for an old-timer named Tom Patterson and one or two other fearless settlers, Chisum had been the first to graze the million and more acres of open, free range along the river. Once he had bought out Patterson's original Bosque Grande buildings, 30 miles or so north of the future cow town of Roswell, he could claim all this middle river country as his own by right of discovery and occupation.

He was a strange old bachelor, fifty-six years old at this particular time, and in all his life he had never carried a gun, save only when the Apaches were loose. At branding time he ran two or three roundup wagons and crews on each side of the Pecos, combing the country far back from the river. There would be as many as eighty or ninety cowboys on his payroll and they would ride a range that stretched for a hundred miles up and down the Pecos. For a full decade Old John had fought Apaches and white thieves and a harsh, relentless Nature which sent against him droughts and floods, scorching heat and blinding blizzards, loneliness and eternal danger—and yet never was able to break his tough, stubborn spirit.

A scant two years before the boy's advent on the Pecos Uncle John had transferred most of his holdings to the firm of Hunter & Evans, bankers and cattlemen of St. Louis. At the same time he left his old Bosque Grande headquarters and migrated some thirty-five miles on down the Pecos to South Springs and a square thick-walled adobe building that could resist attacks by Indians and white men alike. Here he started to breed up a small head of grade cattle he had reserved for himself, while he continued to gather and start north the thousands of head he had sold to the outsiders.

Chisum's small southern neighbors, airing their grievances to the Kid, made no bones about how they felt Old John had long hogged the range, holding the best streams and springs and water holes and controlling all the grazing land around them. His hard-riding, gun-toting cowboys had for years pretty well protected his interests. But when he had sold out to the St. Louis bankers for better than a quarter-million dollars they felt they were justified in squaring up for the past by helping themselves to the beef of the new owners, blotching the brands and disposing of the stolen stock at half price or even less to the Murphy-Dolan firm. This Lincoln outfit, with its newly established cow camp on the Pecos, at various times had contracts to supply beef to both the army post of Ft. Stanton and the Mescalero Apache Reservation on the western side of Lincoln County. Even the legitimate little Pecos settlers resented the fact that Chisum had agreed to stay on as manager of the absentee proprietors.

But the Kid probably heard a certain amount of criticism against the intrusion of the professional thieves and killers of the Jesse Evans type who had recently ridden into the Pecos country to enjoy the rich pickings. However, a common cause allied the small ranchers and the professional thieves when it came to the festering trouble developing between prosperous old Chisum and Jimmy Dolan, who was buying the stolen beef. Likewise, they were both on the same side in their antagonism to Chisum's two friends and colleagues in Lincoln town, the lawyer, A. A. McSween, and a rich, young English newcomer named John Tunstall.

It probably didn't take the Kid long to figure out that the old-fashioned cattle feud was spreading out beyond the valley of the Pecos and swiftly turning into a dangerous war between two groups of powerful men, with the business and political control of Lincoln County as the prize. As against the ambitious Chisum-McSween-Tunstall trio there had been built up a tight group of small Pecos ranchers and the professional thieves, with Jimmy Dolan of Murphy & Co. backed to the hilt by the Santa Fe Ring of politicians and government contractors.

The connecting link between the Santa Fe Ring and this Pecos group was the once powerful mercantile firm of L. G. Murphy & Co. Its former head, Major Murphy, had come from Wexford County, Ireland, and had migrated to America as a young man. After serving a hitch in the regular army, he took his discharge in New Mexico, and when the Civil War broke out he was given a commission in Kit Carson's famous First New Mexico Volunteers, and finally mustered out as a Brevet Major. He immediately joined up with German-born Lt. Col. Emil Fritz, and the two built a store and served as unofficial post traders at Fort Stanton, in western Lincoln County.

The firm had established a branch at the *placita* of Lincoln, eight miles to the northeast, and in 1873 trouble developed between the post traders and the government. The $8,000 which the army paid for the Murphy building at the post, immediately went into the construction of a great store and headquarters at the west end of Lincoln known as "The House."

To continue the involved story: "The House" had just been completed when Lt. Col. Emil Fritz developed a serious illness and decided to visit his old home at Stuttgart, Germany. Along about this same time he brought his sister from Germany and a brother and his family from Pennsylvania, and settled them on a rich irrigated farm on the Rio Bonito, eight miles east of Lincoln. When he died in Germany in 1874 he left an insurance policy of $10,000, besides his interest in the firm.

This insurance policy and the dead hand of the old soldier were to exert a singular influence on events soon to break, and eventually affect the life and fortunes of the Kid.

2

It was a large order for the boy, riding the friendly grub line along the Pecos, to understand all the ramifications that made up the background of what was soon to be known as the Lincoln County War. He had probably been visiting two or three weeks among these hospitable but violently anti-Chisum ranchers when he rode over to the dugout and corrals of the Jesse Evans gang of thieves.

They most certainly were in high glee when the Kid dropped in on them. There can be no question but that they boasted of what they were about to do to old John Chisum, and the smart-aleck lawyer McSween in Lincoln who was playing Chisum's game. And they were utterly contemptuous of the young Englishman John Tunstall. To them he must have appeared as a rich remittance man, who was about ready to be plucked. It was a pretty safe prophecy that he would end up with his papa's money all spent and a bullet hole through his head.

Following his visit to the Evans gang the Kid pointed on across the Pecos to the Dolan cow camp to see Billy Morton. It is quite possible that Jimmy Dolan might have been in the camp when he stepped down from his horse. At least the boy would have learned all about the attractive, quick-tempered and resourceful cattle dealer and businessman who at thirty was a full dozen years the Kid's senior. Jimmy Dolan had been brought to America from Ireland when he was five and at twelve started clerking in a dry-goods store in the East. At fifteen he enlisted in the Union Army and at the end of the war reenlisted and was sent to New Mexico. He took his discharge at Fort Stanton, New Mexico, and promptly went to work for the post traders, L. G. Murphy & Co. Gradually, as Major Murphy drank more and more of his own bar whiskey, Jimmy Dolan took over power and authority, until by 1877 he was in actual control of the various enterprises of the firm.

Whether Dolan was at the Pecos cow camp when the Kid rode in is a matter of small concern: the important thing is that within a few days the Kid had some sort of quarrel or violent misunderstanding with the tough Virginian, Billy Morton, who ramrodded the outfit and was several years older than the little grub-line rider.

Certainly the Kid had found neither the Pecos nor Billy Morton nor the tough professional thieves of the Evans gang to his liking. So he simply rolled up his few belongings in his blanket, tied it behind his saddle, tightened the cinch and took off. It was the most important decision he had made in his young life.

It was late in the fall when he pulled up at George Coe's little ranch in the sweet valley of the Rio Ruidoso, seventy miles or so northwest of the Dolan cow camp, and ten miles below Lincoln and the Rio Bonito. George was only a little older than Billy, and he most certainly welcomed him. After the supper dishes were washed, it's dead sure that George got down his fiddle and they had a little music. The Kid surely sang a ballad or two, or maybe even some old hymns or possibly parodies on them. George, who was just a country boy from Iowa, could play almost anything from "Turkey-in-the-Straw," to "Silver Threads Among the Gold."

In these first days on the Rio Ruidoso the Kid could hardly have understood the hidden danger that permeated even this lovely, secure valley of western Lincoln County. After all, he and his host were only young boys who liked to sing a little and go to native New Mexican dances together, and hunt deer and bear and wild turkeys.

But it wouldn't be long until they would be hunting men.

3

Within a matter of a few days after the Kid's arrival he met George's cousin, Frank Coe, and a number of the small ranchers scattered along the mountain stream. Most of them were on the hook to the Murphy store in Lincoln, and Jimmy Dolan had crowded them pretty hard. When John Tunstall opened his competitive store in Lincoln the majority of these small fry left "The House" and traded with him. For the most part they were brave and experienced, and handy with horses and guns, and they had an elemental sense of justice.

In a way, Dick Brewer was their natural leader. He lived a couple of miles down the river from George Coe's place, and he was a frank and decent man, still reflecting the strict upbringing of his Wisconsin pioneer home. His own ranch buildings and corrals served as a sort of halfway stopping place for men and animals traveling to and from Lincoln to Tunstall's ranch on the Feliz, forty miles across the rolling, hilly country to the southeast.

Dick Brewer undoubtedly introduced the Kid to the young Englishman John Tunstall, who by now had assumed the role of patron and supporter of these hard-pressed valley ranchers in central Lincoln County. Billy had never seen anyone quite like this tall, slender, romantic Englishman, with his small blond mustache and his funny way of talking. He had recently turned twenty-six and he was as natural and straightforward as anyone the boy had ever known.

Tunstall had spent three years in Victoria, British Columbia, in a mercantile business partly owned by his father, and then had gone south to California in search of a sheep ranch to buy. But ranch land was no longer cheap there, and he came to New Mexico. The family fortunes in England had gone into somewhat of a slump and this only son was ambitious to recoup them as swiftly as possible.

Maybe it was because the attractive young Englishman

and the Kid were both sort of misfits and newcomers that
they seemed to understand one another so well. Each was
a distinct individualist, asking no favors, standing on his
own feet, brave and fearless. Yet they had come from the
opposite ends of the world; the one a definite product of
the free and lawless frontier; the other the personification
of all the codes and restraints and gallantries of British
wealth and training.

Years later Frank Coe wrote in an El Paso paper of one
of the first meetings of the oddly assorted pair:

> He [Tunstall] saw the boy was quick to learn and not
> afraid of anything, so when he hired him he made
> Billy a present of a good horse and a nice saddle and a
> new gun. My, but the boy was proud—said it was the
> first time in his life he had ever had anything given to
> him.

It was a dangerous step the Kid made in turning against
the Jesse Evans gang and the crowd of pro-Dolan ranchers
along the Pecos, and allying himself formally with John
Tunstall. He must have fully understood that he would
be branded as a traitor who had been bought off by fancy
gifts and promises. He knew, too, that his life would be
in danger from this moment on.

But he now had a job after his own heart. Riding alongside Tunstall, working cattle on the Feliz range and making himself generally useful on the long trail between the
new store in Lincoln and the ranch headquarters, he
probably had never been so happy in all his eighteen
years. He finally had a boss who suited him to a T.

The chances are that he hadn't been working for the
Englishman more than a week or so when he was introduced to the third member of the Chisum-Tunstall-Mc-
Sween trio that was making it so hot for the Jimmy Dolan
interests. The Kid likely was anything but impressed with
A. A. McSween when he first met him in his rambling
10-room adobe home just west of the Tunstall store in
Lincoln. At the same time he probably met the attractive
and vivacious Susan McSween and her sister and family
who were living in one wing of the big home. "Judge"
Shield had recently arrived from Kansas to help the lawyer in his swiftly growing law practice.

A slender, narrow-shouldered, rather sallow-complexioned man of thirty-two, McSween was certainly not the regulation frontier type. A sparse and drooping mustache hung down from his upper lip like a small inverted horse-shoe. His mop of dark hair topped a high, bulging fore-head, and his black eyes were alert and piercing and there was much of the reformer about him which seemed a natural inheritance from his stern Presbyterian back-ground.

Born in eastern Canada, he had for a time studied for the ministry, but shortly he had migrated to the American mid-west and, turning to law, had graduated from St. Louis University. He started practice in Eureka, Kansas, by 1875, but his asthma, plus a driving ambition to suc-ceed, sent him to the tiny county-seat town of Lincoln here at the eastern edge of the Capitan Mountains. Its single street paralleled the swift-flowing Rio Bonito, and on below the village the narrow canyon widened and the valley was dotted with rich little irrigated farms. At this time Lincoln had less than 400 inhabitants, most of whom were native New Mexicans, but it was by all odds the largest and most important settlement in all of vast Lin-coln County.

Shortly after he first came to Lincoln McSween was re-tained by the brother and sister of Col. Fritz to collect the $10,000 insurance policy, payment of which had been held up by the company. McSween journeyed to New York and hired a firm of experts who made the collection in full but charged a fee of $2,851.06 for their services. Mc-Sween promptly took out his own fee, and a large expense account, but delayed handing over the amount which re-mained to the beneficiaries.

Apparently there was also some question as to just who should receive the money. The insurance company had first disallowed the claim on the basis of a "death from consumption" clause in the policy, but the family denied that Col. Fritz had suffered from tuberculosis and the in-surance was finally paid.

For a while the Murphy & Dolan store had used the young lawyer to handle their foreclosures and collections involving the small farmer-ranchers of both the Rio Bonito and the Rio Ruidoso valleys who had been caught in the trap of "The House." Finally the firm asked McSween to defend some of the Pecos cow thieves in suits brought against them by the big cow man John Chisum. McSween refused and soon he was working for Chisum, pressing the very cases he had been asked to defend.

Some time after McSween had decided no longer to continue as the firm's attorney, he wrote out a report which read in part:

> Lawrence G. Murphy and Emil Fritz doing business under the style of L. G. Murphy & Co. had the monopoly of the sale of merchandise in this city and used their power to oppress and grind out all they could from the farmers, and to force those who were opposed to them to leave the country. For instance the farmers would buy merchandise from them at exorbitant prices and were compelled to turn in their produce in payment thereof at prices that suited L. G. Murphy & Co., and if a farmer refused to do so, he was subjected to intimidation and the whole judicial machinery was used unwittingly to accomplish that object. The result was that L. G. Murphy & Co. were absolute monarchs of Lincoln County and ruled their subjects with an oppressive iron heel.

From a half dozen sources the Kid learned that McSween had been in Lincoln a little more than a year when he journeyed to Santa Fe on a legal matter and there met the tall, slender young Englishman in search of a ranch. He sang the praises of Lincoln County and urged Tunstall to go to Lincoln town and then ride on east to the Pecos and talk with wise, old John Chisum. The result was that in early 1877 Tunstall decided not only to establish a cattle ranch some forty or fifty miles southeast of Lincoln, but to build a large store in the village, with one end to be used as a bank, and to go hammer and tongs after the mercantile business that had for the past several years been exclusively in the hands of L. G. Murphy & Co.

At a sheriff's foreclosure sale in Lincoln the lawyer McSween bought in for Tunstall 400 head of cows belonging to the widow of Bob Casey, who had been a prosperous farmer and rancher east of Lincoln and had been killed in a fight over eight dollars he owed in wages. Both McSween and Chisum advised the young Englishman to establish his ranch at the headwaters of the Rio

Feliz where Casey had built a ranch cabin and corrals but on which he had neglected to file a claim.

Within twelve months the Senior Tunstall in England sent his son four installments of $5000 each; John had established the ranch, built the store in Lincoln, stocked it with goods that he personally chose in St. Louis, and was now driving to the wall the old Murphy firm, already deeply mortgaged to Tom Catron in Santa Fe.

So it was that at the exact time the Kid drifted into the Ruidoso and Bonito sections of Lincoln County, the conflict had changed over from a mere cattle feud into a much larger and far more deadly war of survival. The lawyer McSween and the rich young Englishman now were challenging the very existence of the old Murphy-Dolan-Ring crowd. It was obvious that it was to be a war to the finish with no quarter given or asked.

It was now middle December, 1877, and the Kid had been working some weeks for the generous and kindly young Tunstall. He could hardly have missed the latest gossip concerning McSween and how he was suddenly finding himself in deep water because he had not paid over to the brother and sister of Col. Fritz what remained of the $10,000 insurance policy, after the various fees and expenses had been deducted. It apparently was McSween's contention that there was still some question in his mind whether there might not be other heirs in Germany.

A few days before Christmas the lawyer and his attractive wife started for Las Vegas, roughly 150 miles to the northeast of Lincoln. They made the trip with John Chisum, and the three arranged to start the following day by stagecoach for the railhead at Trinidad, Colorado, and then proceed to a business conference at St. Louis concerning Chisum's ranch affairs.

Shortly before the McSweens left Lincoln, Jimmy Dolan rode off to Mesilla, county seat of Dona Ana County and the permanent headquarters of Judge Bristol of the Third Judicial District. Mrs. Emilie Scholand, sister of the deceased Col. Fritz, was also at Mesilla at this particular holiday time, it being generally understood that she expected McSween to meet here for a final settlement of the Fritz insurance matter. Hearing of McSween's departure for the north, Dolan at once urged Mrs. Scholand to file embezzlement charges against McSween. The matter was turned

over to the firm of Catron & Thornton, of Santa Fe, who
were tied into the powerful Santa Fe Ring. An indictment
was secured against McSween and he was arrested and
roughly handled shortly after his party boarded the stage
at Las Vegas for Trinidad, Colorado.

McSween was granted a change of venue to Lincoln
County, but until the court convened there in April of
1878, he was to be held in the custody of Deputy Sheriff
Barrier of Las Vegas. Only Judge Bristol at Mesilla, on the
Rio Grande, could grant him freedom on bail.

At the same time John Chisum, the big Pecos cattleman, was likewise served with papers in Las Vegas by the
Catron & Thornton firm, and taken to the city jail. The
arrest had to do technically with Chisum's refusal to de-
clare his financial standing in a suit involving the col-
lection of an old and questionable court judgment against
him. He now elected to remain in jail rather than obey
the court order.

Certainly the arrest of McSween and Chisum could be
considered almost as a great twin victory for the Dolan-
Ring side. Two of their three most hated enemies in Lincoln County had been brought to heel and humiliated by
the Santa Fe Ring lawyers in a single day's work. Young
Tunstall would be next.

The Kid certainly was familiar with this sudden disastrous turn of events by the time McSween showed up at
Lincoln with his guard, the deputy-sheriff from Las Vegas.
A day or two later Tunstall explained to the boy and
the other men working for him that he had decided to
accompany the lawyer on the dreary and somewhat dangerous 150-mile ride on west to Mesilla, the seat of the
District Court. He would call in at the Federal Land
Office at nearby Las Cruces and expedite the matter of
the survey of his Rio Feliz ranch. He had already put up
$600 in cash to start the work.

The Kid must have been genuinely disturbed when
Tunstall rode off alone with the unarmed McSween and
the latter's brother-in-law Shield, with the deputy-sheriff
from Las Vegas trailing along. Billy certainly would have
liked nothing better than to have accompanied them on
the long ride, a pistol on his hip and a Winchester in his
saddle boot, handy-like under his left knee.

Tunstall seemed incapable of realizing the very real

danger he was now facing. But the Kid, uncanny in his insight and fully alert to the desperate ways and means of the frontier, must have been distinctly uneasy when his boss rode off so gaily.

3

The Kid must have heard all about the letter Tunstall
wrote to the Mesilla *Independent* shortly before the Englishman rode off for the Rio Grande with McSween. Certainly if there was such a thing as a man writing out his
own death warrant this was it.

For some months past Tunstall and McSween had been
considering how they could make the most damaging use
of a check signed by McSween, which had been returned
to him in normal procedure from the Santa Fe bank. The
check bore the lawyer's signature, although the funds
probably came from Tunstall's own account. The face of
the check read:

LINCOLN, N.M.

No. 300

JULY 31, 1877

First National Bank
of Santa Fe

PAY TO—Wm. Brady, Sheriff and ExOfficio Collector Lincoln Co., N.M.
Fifteen hundred and forty-five 13/100   Dollars
in Territorial (N.M.) Scrip
$1545 13/100 in Territorial Scrip   A.A. McSween

On the back of the check were two signatures:

Wm. Brady
John H. Riley

John H. Riley, a slender, scrappy young Irishman, had several years previously put a $6,000 legacy in the old firm of Murphy & Co. and was now a junior partner to Jimmy Dolan. William Brady was the present sheriff. To both Tunstall and McSween it seemed a clear case of the sheriff turning over county tax money to Riley to be used for the firm's business.

Before leaving Lincoln the young Englishman, with complete disregard of consequences, dispatched the fateful letter regarding the check to the Mesilla *Independent*. It was published on January 26, two days before he arrived in Mesilla and while Dolan was still there. It read:

Office of John H. Tunstall

LINCOLN, LINCOLN CO., N.M.

JANUARY 18, 1878

"THE PRESENT SHERIFF
OF LINCOLN COUNTY
HAS PAID NOTHING
DURING HIS PRESENT TERM OF OFFICE."
GOVERNOR'S MESSAGE FOR 1878

Editor of The Independent:

The above extract is a sad and unanswerable comment on the efficiency of Sheriff Brady, and cannot be charged upon "croakers." Major Brady, as the records of this County show, collected over *Twenty-five Hundred Dollars,* Territorial funds. Of this sum Mr. Alex. A. McSween, Esq., of this place paid him over *Fifteen Hundred Dollars* by cheque on the First National Bank of Santa Fe August 23, 1877. Said cheque was presented for payment by John H. Riley Esq., of the firm of J. J. Dolan & Co., this last amount was paid by the last named gentleman to Underwood and Nash for cattle. Thus passed away over *Fifteen Hundred Dollars* belonging to the Territory of New Mexico. With the exception of thirty-nine dollars, all the Taxes of Lincoln County for 1877 were promptly paid when due.

Let not Lincoln County suffer for the delinquency of one, two or three men.

By the exercise of proper vigilance the tax payer can readily ascertain what has become of what he has paid for the implied protection of the commonwealth. It is not only his privilege but his duty. A delinquent tax payer is bad; a delinquent tax collector is worse.

J. H. T.

It was the spark that set off the powder keg of the Lincoln County War, which would involve the Kid one way or another as long as he lived.

2

The immediate effect of the damaging Tunstall letter was to align the entire Dolan-Santa Fe Ring faction against himself and his colleague McSween, who was recognized as at least a co-author of the communication. McSween at once ran into his full share of trouble. The examination for bail that McSween had requested was held before Judge Bristol. Col. Rynerson, the Prosecuting Attorney and an avowed Ring man and friend of Dolan's, was antagonistic and difficult. Assets totalling $30,000 as security were refused by Rynerson. Finally when writs of attachment were issued against all the property and assets belonging to McSween in Lincoln, the lawyer and his guard, deputy A. P. Barrier, were permitted to leave Dona Ana County.

Early Tuesday, February 5th, the Tunstall-McSween party left Mesilla and headed home. The horses forded the Rio Grande and hit the long grade up the western slopes of the Organ Mountains. It was late afternoon when the riders crossed over the San Agustin Pass and pulled up their horses for a rest.

The little group, still only partly conscious of the dangers awaiting it, slowly followed the trail that led to the great springs and the buildings of Shedd's ranch and stage stop, halfway down the slope to the right. Night was swiftly closing in, and there was a penetrating chill to the winter air. Stars were popping out in the deep purple dome overhead, but even their splendor could not drive away the mood of foreboding.

Suddenly tall, swaggering Jesse Evans, packing a six shooter and a rifle, strode into the camp near the springs. Three of his Banditti, as his gang was now called, were at his heels. These were the killers, the most dangerous men in New Mexico. Evans gruffly demanded if they knew when Jimmy Dolan would be showing up.

So that was it! Dolan had sent for the Pecos gunmen to meet him here at Shedd's, more than a hundred miles to the west. They would thus be able to trap the Tunstall party on its way home from Mesilla and force it into a fight.

Dolan arrived sometime during the night and early the following morning barged into the little group, a carbine on his shoulder and Evans at his side. He taunted the Englishman for his letter to the *Independent*. He called him a coward and vilified him. In every way possible he tried to provoke him into a gun fight. Tunstall, calm and reserved and realizing the odds against him, quietly refused to take the bait. Finally deputy Barrier who had McSween in tow interceded and Dolan left, still damning Tunstall and warning him that the next time he'd get him.

It was Saturday when the Tunstall party reached Lincoln to find the town in an uproar. A Dolan messenger had made a record ride from Mesilla and Sheriff Brady nad already attached all the property legally belonging to McSween. Then, contending that McSween was a partner in both Tunstall's store and his ranch, Brady forcibly took the Tunstall store keys from Bob Widenmann, a trusted friend of the Englishman's, posted his attachment notice on the door and placed five of his armed deputies within the establishment.

The Kid and several other Tunstall men were in Lincoln at the time, but they were helpless to make any move to stop the outrage. When Tunstall arrived he was shocked at the injustice of the attachment of his own property on a writ that concerned only McSween. At once he filed his protest with Sheriff Brady, whose men were now ensconced in the Tunstall store. The best that the Kid could do was to join Widenmann and the quarter-breed Cherokee Fred Waite and stick close to the young

Englishman while he interviewed Brady. All three of the
Tunstall guards carried their rifles in their hands.

Tunstall was able to secure nothing but an exemption
of certain of his horses which were obviously his personal
mounts. He immediately dispatched three of his men to
drive the few head he kept in his corrals behind his Lincoln store on south the ten miles to the safety of Dick
Brewer's Ruidoso ranch, part way on the trail to the Rio
Feliz.

The next day Tunstall ordered the Kid and two others
to move the exempted horses the forty miles from Dick
Brewer's place on southeast to his own Feliz ranch and
throw them in with his cattle and a number of his most
valuable horses. The Kid must have understood fully that
it was a moment of decision that called for the judgment
of a man of iron will and wide experience. Instead, the
orders were to come from this brave but inadequate newcomer.

3

The following day, Tuesday, February 12th, Sheriff Brady
made his next move at the behest of Dolan, who had by
now assumed all real authority. Billy Mathews, Brady's
first deputy-sheriff, with a posse at his heels, galloped off
towards Tunstall's Feliz ranch, the Evans quartet from
the Pecos accompanying him as ex officio members.

When the posse reached the Feliz they found that Tunstall's men, including the Kid and Dick Brewer, the
foreman, had fortified the main house. Deputy-Sheriff
Mathews divided his posse and prepared to assault the
barricaded cabin at the front and rear. Finally a parley
was called.

It was agreed that the posse would pull out while Deputy Mathews rode back to Lincoln for fresh instructions
from Sheriff Brady and the real boss, Jimmy Dolan. That
night Mathews sent Billy Morton, foreman of Dolan's cow
camp, over to the Pecos with the word that if the Seven
Rivers ranchers wanted to keep from being run off their
ranges by the Tunstall-McSween-Chisum combination,
they had better join up with the sheriff's posse and settle
matters once and for all with the upstart Englishman.

The same evening that Morton rode off to enlist the

Pecos ranchers, the Kid with Fred Waite and Bob Widenmann started on the fifty-mile ride northwest to Lincoln to report to Tunstall and McSween. The Englishman decided to ride immediately to Jim Chisum, in charge of the South Springs ranch near Roswell while his older brother John was being held under arrest at Las Vegas, and ask for both advice and help. Billy and his companions, worried and uncertain, returned to the Feliz.

Tunstall's long, exhausting fifty-mile ride to the Pecos brought no favorable results, and he hurried back on west to the Feliz. Once at his ranch he learned that a large force, including the pro-Dolan ranchers from Seven Rivers, were gathering at the friendly Paul's ranch to the south of Tunstall's place.

Things were rapidly shaping up for a big fight. Tunstall argued with his men that surely there must be some way to arrive at a settlement other than by violence. Yet he must have known that a crisis was building up, and that those desperate killers were not the slightest concerned with decency or fairness. Somehow he could not grasp the terrible danger he faced.

He ordered one of his men to ride at once to the posse's hangout at Paul's ranch and inform Deputy-Sheriff Mathews that he, Tunstall, was pulling out with all his men except Old Man Gauss, the cook and caretaker. Mathews could move in the next day, round up the cattle, count them and assign a man as agent; the German Gauss would remain with the sheriff's representative to help hold the herd.

It was a full retreat for the Englishman. Every item included in his $20,000 investment was now covered by the sheriff's completely illegal writ of attachment, save only the few head of horses that had been specifically exempted by Sheriff Brady himself. Yet he decided to leave the Feliz ranch the following morning well before Deputy-Sheriff Mathews and his posse of twenty-five men could arrive. It would circumvent any danger of the two armed groups meeting again. Old Man Gauss alone would remain behind, and he was to cook for the posse and do anything they ordered.

There is evidence that on this night of decision the Kid went to Tunstall and pleaded with him to take to the hills,

abandon his horses and save his own life. But the gallant
and romantic young Englishman refused.

4

It was early morning when Tunstall, with the Kid, Dick
Brewer, his foreman, and Bob Widenmann and John
Middleton, pulled out from the Feliz ranch. Here at the
start one man rode on ahead, with the eight or ten
exempted horses trailing behind, and Tunstall and the
three remaining men following to the rear.

The Tunstall party had been gone from the Feliz ranch
possibly two hours when the sheriff's big posse rode in.
To the questioning of Mathews and Dolan regarding the
whereabouts of Tunstall and the others, Godfrey Gauss,
German-born cook and handyman, frankly answered that
after an early breakfast the boss and his four riders had
started off with the little batch of exempted horses for
Brewer's ranch a few miles below Lincoln.

The leaders lost no time; Deputy Mathews lined up his
men and chose a round dozen to make up a special posse
under Billy Morton, foreman of the Dolan cow camp on
the Pecos. They wouldn't need to hurry. Men driving
loose horses usually took their time.

Somewhere along the trail they'd encounter the Englishman. There would be thirteen against his five, all told,
and most of them knew what to do without being told.

5

It had been a rather long day for Tunstall and the Kid
and the three others riding with him. It was now close to
5:30, and shadows were lengthening along the wooded
mountain trail.

There had been considerable talk at the start that they
might be followed, and that there might even be a fight.
But that was long past. No one was worried any longer.
Tunstall was following alone behind the little batch of
ponies.

The Kid and John Middleton were riding a hundred
yards or so to the rear and over to one side of the trail.
Dick Brewer and Bob Widenmann were off on the other
side of the path and some distance away. There was no

longer any need to ride bunched togethei. The danger
was passed; they were almost home.

Suddenly the Kid and Middleton were conscious that
someone was firing at them. They pulled up their horses
and looked behind them. They could make out a group
of riders topping the brow of a hill to their rear.

It was the Billy Morton party right enough. The Kid
could even recognize some of the men and horses. They
would be settling accounts with poor Tunstall. It wasn't
only horses this mob was after; it was the young Englishman, too.

To try to fight them would be suicide. Tunstall might
not be killed if his own men did not interfere. He might
let the posse have the horses, and talk his way out of getting killed.

The Kid and Middleton socked in the steel and spread
the alarm. Apparently one of them raced up close enough
to Tunstall to shout for him to follow them.

But he stayed on with his horses. It was not in his code
of honor to flee from his enemies. He would face the
music.

The posse rode up at a high lope and surrounded him.
He had already dismounted and immediately tried to
hand his pistol, butt forward, to Billy Morton.

There were angry words and Tom Hill, of the Evans
gang, who was still on his horse behind Tunstall, cursed
him and then shot him in the back of the head. A bullet
from another gun tore through his collar bone as he lay
dead on the ground. A third lead slug ended the life of
the valuable half-thoroughbred he was riding. Contrary
to the general belief there were no rock bruises on Tunstall's face.

The Kid played no hero's part. He knew that if he
and the other three guards tried to fight the posse they
would all be killed.

Four months after the affair, the Kid gave his version of
what happened in an affidavit to a government investigator
from Washington. It was written out by Widenmann but
signed "William H. Bonney," the name the boy was now
using. Terse and stark, it tells in the Kid's own crude words
his memory of the tragedy. The last part reads:

I and Middleton at once rode forward to inform

the balance of the party of the fact, who were some
200 or 300 yards to the left of the trail, when the attacking party cleared the brow of the hill and came
firing at us. I and Widenmann and Middleton and
Brewer rode over a hill towards another which was
covered with large rocks and trees in order to defend
ourselves and make a stand. But the attacking party,
undoubtedly seeing Tunstall, left off pursuing us. We
heard two or three separate shots and the remark was
then made by Middleton that they [the attacking
party] must have killed Tunstall. I made my way to
Lincoln in company with Widenmann, Brewer and
Middleton, stopping on the Ruidoso in order to get
aid to look for the body of Tunstall. Neither I nor
any of the party fired off either a rifle or a pistol, and
neither I nor the parties with me fired a shot.

It was strictly a matter of arithmetic; four men and the
inexperienced Tunstall against Bill Morton and his dozen
gun-fighters. The thirteen were a tight, deadly wedge
driving at a gallop between the scattered elements of the
Tunstall crowd. At best, not more than three of the five
could have taken a defensive position and tried to fight
it out. The odds were ten to one that they all would have
been wiped out in a matter of minutes.

It probably never occurred to the boy or his companions that they had abandoned Tunstall to his fate. In their
eyes they had simply followed the ancient and primary
law of self-preservation.

But the senseless brutality of the cold-blooded murder
of his friend was to exert a profound effect on the boy
throughout all the remaining days of his tragic young
life. Save only the death of his mother, nothing had ever
touched him so deeply and so irreparably.

It was largely to shape his destiny and decide his fate.

It was ten o'clock that night when the Kid and the three
others pulled up at McSween's residence, next to the
Tunstall store. The news of the killing spread rapidly up
and down the single street of the village.

Towards midnight some forty men assembled in the
living room of McSween's home. The lawyer made a short
speech; justice must be done. But there must be no sum-
mary action by unauthorized groups, despite the provoca-
tion of this high-handed murder. Surely there was some
law left in Lincoln County.

Suddenly the front door burst open and Jimmy Riley,
junior partner of the hated Dolan, pushed into the room.
Obviously he was drunk or he would have had more judgment than to present himself to this group of incensed
friends of the man his cohorts had just killed. Riley, like
Dolan and Murphy, was Irish born, and was well-known
as a sharp trader.

A half-dozen men jerked out their pistols and threw
down on him. Riley handed over his loaded six-shooter to
George Washington, a Negro cook and handyman of the
McSween household. He was ordered to empty his pockets of papers. With a silly grin he spread their contents
on the table before him. Apparently he had wandered in
to discover the temper of the gathering and was too drunk

to understand the danger he faced. Nor did he realize how the documents he took from his pockets would implicate him.

McSween, pleading caution and legal action, intervened and showed Riley to the door. Then someone thumbed through the papers he had left on the table. On the last page of a paper-backed notebook was a list of code names of men involved in furnishing stolen beef to the "House" to fill its contracts with the army and the Indian reservation. It showed, as well, the various sums due a number of the Seven Rivers thieves for cattle delivered at $5 a head, less than a third of their true value. And there was a recent letter from Col. Rynerson, the prosecuting attorney, to Riley advising the Dolan faction to "shake that McSween outfit up till it shells out and squares up and then shake it out of Lincoln. . . . I shall help you all I can."

It was all grim business to the little crowd gathered in McSween's home, and to the other small groups scattered over the worried community. There was little sleep that night for anyone. The Kid must have fully realized that the war was on. He had chosen his side.

At dawn John Newcomb, a respected farmer with a small ranch on the Ruidoso, started out with four neighbors who were native New Mexicans, in search of Tunstall's body. They led a gentle pack horse and by backtracking up the trail from the river they reached the spot of the tragedy.

Tunstall's body, partly wrapped in a saddle blanket, was lying close to his dead horse. Both were found some little distance from the path the loose horses had been travelling. Obviously the Englishman had made no real effort to escape.

His revolver was found close by, with two chambers of the six empty. A search was made for empty shells but none were found.

The five men lifted the body and placed it crossways on the pack saddle and tied it down. Tunstall was tall and slender, and his legs and feet dangled from one side of the horse, while his loose arms and hands flopped pathetically on the other side.

Proceeding at a slow pace the men piloted the pack horse down the winding, narrow trail to Newcomb's home on the Ruidoso. A team was hitched to a wagon, hay spread in the bed and the body taken from the horse and placed in it. It was a fair piece on down the Ruidoso to where it emptied into the Hondo, and then sharp left on the road up the North Fork, called the Bonito, to Lincoln. It was growing dark when the little cortege pulled in at McSween's corral.

That same morning Dr. Taylor F. Ealy, with his wife and two small children, arrived at the McSween home on the last lap of their exhausting journey from the East. The Doctor was a medical missionary. When McSween, eager to bring a Protestant doctor and teacher to the little community, had applied for help, the Presbyterian Mission Board in New York had sent out Dr. Ealy. An attractive young woman named Katherine Gates, who was Mrs. Ealy's companion and helper, journeyed with them.

His first task was to assist the Post Surgeon, Dr. D. M. Appel, in a post-mortem. In the report made later to the official Washington investigator, Judge Angel, the surgeon took oath that two wounds were found on the body, one from a bullet that had entered the right side of the back of the head, emerging ovei the left eye; another bullet had plowed through the collarbone. There were no other bruises on the head or body. Finished with the examination, the army surgeon embalmed the body, McSween having promised him a fee of $100. The plan was to transfer the remains later to a metal coffin, which would be sent to England.

Even before the body reached Lincoln the wobbly wheels of justice were put in motion. The Kid and the Cherokee breed, Fred Waite, appeared at Justice "Green" Wilson's office and made sworn statements charging murder against J. J. Dolan, William Morton, and most of the dozen men in the posse which had killed Tunstall. The warrants weie given to Antonio Martinez, the spunky local constable of Lincoln precinct, and he immediately chose the Kid and Fred Waite as his deputies to help serve them.

The Kid and the two otheis were certain that some of the mob which had killed Tunstall were holed up at Dolan's store, and the three men boldly walked up the street and entered the front door. Sheriff Brady, his rifle cradled handily in the crook of his left arm, met the trio and promptly put them under arrest on the charge of disturbing the peace. Brady's men angrily crowded around them, and once again the Kid exercised that fine sixth sense which is so often required for survival. He knew that to fight back now would mean only that all three would be killed.

The three were disarmed and herded in a back room under guard. Later that afternoon Constable Martinez was released but the Kid and Fred Waite were still held, Sheriff Brady making clear his utter contempt for Billy and his companion. As against this unnecessary brutality stood the fact that Brady made no move to arrest the men who had killed Tunstall, although warrants had been formally sworn against them before Justice of Peace Wilson.

For the two following days the Kid and his close friend, the breed Cherokee, Fred Waite, were held incommunicado. They were repeatedly taunted and insulted by their jailors. They could only guess what was happening outside the room in the old Murphy-Dolan store where they were heavily guarded.

The Tunstall funeral was held at three o'clock Friday afternoon, with most of the countryside attending the simple rites. Contrary to published versions the Kid did not attend the services. A small organ that belonged to the absent Mrs. McSween was moved out to the open ground just beyond the Tunstall store. Around it stood the men and women of the community who were deeply aroused over the brutality and lawlessness which had brought on the murder of the kindly and ineffectual young Englishman. Dr. Ealy took charge of the services and his remarks were translated into Spanish, since most of those attending could speak little or no English.

There was much comment over the fact that two of Tunstall's most trusted men, who had been riding with him when he was murdered, were still held under arrest by Sheriff Brady and denied the right to attend the funeral of their friend. Within a few weeks the Kid was to show his terrible resentment over what he must have considered to be the sheriff's personal insult to him.

They buried Tunstall in a pine coffin at a spot outside the east wing of his own store, close to what had been his bedroom. With the services ended the men gathered at a mass meeting in the parlor of McSween's house next door, the lawyer acting as chairman. The first motion made was

that Sheriff Brady be called upon to explain why he still
held the Kid and Fred Waite. However, the question was
automatically answered when Billy and Fred Waite appeared.

But the issue which aroused the most intense indignation was the complete refusal of Sheriff Brady to make any
move against the men known to have been in the crowd
which killed Tunstall, although there were adequate warrants for them bearing Justice Wilson's signature. After
the meeting broke up a little group of men, largely Tunstall's neighbors and employees, remained behind to form
a fighting organization to be known as the Regulators.
Each man pledged to stick with the others until justice
was done. They would do their best to follow McSween's
orders and advice and take no lawless action.

Certainly in the Kid's mind there was no minimizing
the dangerous situation which was swiftly building up.
Dolan and his henchmen in Lincoln, backed by Evans'
Banditti and the unfriendly Seven Rivers-Pecos ranchers,
and with the full support of the Santa Fe Ring, were obviously out to get the men who challenged their suprem-
acy in Lincoln County. They had already liquidated Tunstall. McSween would come next. Then the Kid and the
Regulators would be ticked off one at a time.

McSween was urged to go immediately into hiding, and
on Monday he made his will and put his affairs in order.
On the following Friday he left Lincoln with his faithful
George Washington for the safety of the hills behind the
tiny settlement of San Patricio, a few miles to the south
on the Ruidoso.

The Regulators quietly formulated their own plans.
Dick Brewer almost automatically assumed the role of
leader. His first assistant was Frank McNab, who had long
been one of Chisum's foremen and had been loaned by
Chisum to help out. Doc Scurlock, the Mississippian who
had studied medicine and taught school, probably stood
third in order of command. The Kid was still only one of
the "privates" who now pledged their lives to see that
Tunstall was avenged.

The legality of the Regulators was covered by the appointment Dick Brewer, Tunstall's foreman, held as Special Constable, and the official warrants he received from
Squire Wilson for the arrest of the men involved in the

Tunstall killing. Since Sheriff Brady, a Dolan man down to the butt of his pistol, would make no move to bring justice, the members of this Brewer posse were sworn to see what they could do about it.

It was Saturday, March 2nd, when the men swung up in their saddles and headed eastward for the Pecos country.

5

The Kid was easily the youngest member of Constable Brewer's posse of eleven Regulators, angry and determined to square accounts with the men who had killed their friend.

It was around noon on the second day when they flushed a human covey of five in the rough country below the lower Peñasco. The men were resting in the shade of a lone tree, the split reins of their bridles dangling on the ground, when the Brewer posse suddenly appeared over a rise a hundred yards or so away. In a matter of seconds the wanted men grabbed up their loose reins and vaulted into their saddles.

A mile or two ahead, two of the five escaping men swung off to the west towards some rough hills. They were slightly behind their three mates, and the pair were recognized by the pursuers in the lead as Billy Morton and Frank Baker. Morton, foreman of the Dolan cow camp on the Pecos, was the special deputy who had been in charge of the actual party that had murdered Tunstall. Baker, a part Cherokee, had been one of the same gang. Dick Brewer shouted to his men to let the three others escape and concentrate on these two.

Some of the horses in the posse were beginning to play out, but Brewer and the Kid and two or three others were

closing in when the pair wheeled their ponies sharply to
the right. For a few seconds their mounts presented a
broadside, and there was more shooting. Stumbling and
spent the two horses went down at almost the same moment.

The two men found their feet and by luck reached a
sort of sink hole in the center of a basin once overgrown
with tall cattails. It gave them temporary protection. Apparently one of the pair had pulled out his Winchester
before his horse fell, and he was able now to hold back
the men on horseback.

The siege was a dreary one. Finally, beaten down by
thirst and hunger and with ammunition almost gone, the
two men accepted Brewer's promise of protection. Darkness was coming on and the posse, with their captives,
pointed towards a Chisum line camp a few miles away.
Here they cooked supper and spread their blankets. The
next day the group rode north to Chisum's South Spring
Ranch.

There was still much arguing and violent debate as to
what the posse should do with their prisoners. In a way it
seemed foolish to take them the long ride to Lincoln and
turn them over to Sheriff Brady. He would certainly see
that they escaped from his custody, and then the Tunstall
avengers would have two more active enemies who would
shoot them down at the first chance.

It was towards evening when the Kid and the others,
with their two prisoners, pulled up at the thick-walled,
adobe fortress that was now Chisum's headquarters, five
miles to the south of the trading post of Roswell. When he
had finished the food brought to him, the captured Billy
Morton asked for paper and ink. That night he wrote two
letters; one to a sister in Virginia and a second to a distant cousin, who was a lawyer.

Both the men and their horses were still pretty well
worn out the following day, and Brewer decided to delay
the start for Lincoln until the second morning. His decision rested partly on a rumor that a gang of Brady-Dolan
men were gathering at Lincoln to intercept the Regulators and rescue Morton and Baker.

After breakfast on this second morning the posse and
prisoners started off despite the continued threat of an ambush. They made their first stop at the Roswell store where

Ash Upson, the fabulous old newspaperman, was acting as clerk and postmaster.

Ash certainly had few illusions regarding the probable fate of the prisoners. Brewer generously halted the party long enough to let young Billy Morton register the letter he had written to his Virginia lawyer-cousin that first night at Chisum's ranch.

It was an unforgettable human document, and proves the inner courage and proud resistance of this strong-willed determined man. Towards its close it showed clearly his own presentiment of what would happen to him. It read in part:

SOUTH SPRING RIVER, N.M.
MARCH 8, 1878

H. H. Marshall,
Richmond, Va.
Dear Sir:

. . . We arrived here last night en route to Lincoln. I have heard that we were not to be taken alive to that place. I am not at all afraid of their killing me, but if they should do so, I wish that the matter should be investigated and the parties dealt with according to law. If you do not hear from me in four days after receipt of this, I would like you to make inquiries about the affair. . . .

I will arrive at Lincoln the night of the 10th and will write you immediately if I get through safe. Have been in the employ of Jas. J. Dolan & Co. of Lincoln for eighteen months since the 9th of March '77 and have been getting $60.00 per month. Have about six hundred dollars due me from them and some horses, etc. at their cattle camps.

I hope if it becomes necessary that you will look into this affair, if anything should happen, I refer you to T. B. Catron, U.S. attorney of Santa Fe, N.M. and Col. Rynerson, District Attorney, LaMesilla, N.M. They both know all about the affair and the writ of attachment was issued by Judge Warren Bristol of La Mesilla, N.M. and everything was legal. If I am taken safely to Lincoln, I will have no trouble, but will let you know.

If it should be as I suspect, please communicate

with my brother, Quin Morton, Lewisburg, W.Va.
Hoping that you will attend to this affair if it becomes necessary and excuse me for troubling you if
it does not, I remain

Yours respectfully
W. S. Morton

LINCOLN,
LINCOLN CO., N.M.

There was much muted talk between various members
of the Regulators as they rode towards Lincoln strung out
in little groups of two and three. Ash told them that Governor Axtell had reached Fort Stanton, and had immediately issued a proclamation firing Squire Wilson as
Justice of Peace. It was bad news. There could be no question but that the report of this capture of the two men by
the Brewer posse had reached Lincoln and Fort Stanton.
It was possibly sound reasoning to figure that Sheriff
Brady and Dolan might get their friends to attempt a rescue of prisoners on the theory they would not be turned
over to the sheriff.

The Kid, as far as is known, never gave his own version
of the events which shortly followed. Possibly the most
trustworthy account of what actually happened is found in
a letter sent to the Mesilla *Independent* by Ash Upson on
the following day:

Editor, *Independent*.
Richard Brewer and a constable's posse with legal
process arrested Wm. S. Morton and Frank Baker on
the banks of the Pecos after an 8 mile chase. The
prisoners are charged with the killing of J. H. Tunstall.
The posse arrived at Chisum's ranch on Friday, 8th
inst. It left for Roswell where Morton registered a
letter about 10 o'clock on Saturday morning. Morton at the post office expressed fears that he would be
lynched and declared his willingness to stand trial.
About half after ten the party left with their prisoners ostensibly for Lincoln. About 5 o'clock P.M.
Martin Chaves reported here that the party had left
the road to their left and gone toward Black Water
holes. This Sunday morning Frank McNab, one of

the arresting party, returned. His statement of events
after leaving here are in substance as follows:

"When we had ridden some 20 miles and had
reached a point about 5 or 6 miles from Black Water,
Morton was riding side by side with one of the posse,
when he suddenly snatched McClosky's pistol from
his scabbard and shot him dead.

"Although mounted on a slow horse, he put him
to his best speed, closely followed by Frank Baker.
They were speedily overtaken and killed."

McNab said as he had no further business in that
direction he returned. Whatever face or color future
developments may put upon the face of the affair,
there is no doubt but that McClosky, Morton and
Baker are dead.

2

That Saturday night the Kid with Dick Brewer and the
other Regulators hid out in the hills below Lincoln, and
late the following evening Dick slipped into town. He
sought out McSween and the two had a long talk behind
closed doors and shuttered windows.

The lawyer recounted that when word had been
brought to him of the arrival of Governor Axtell at Fort
Stanton, he boldly returned to Lincoln in the hope of
having an opportunity to explain to the Governor his side
of the feud. But the Governor refused to see either Mc-
Sween or Bob Widenmann, the murdered Tunstall's close
friend, during the scant three-hour visit he paid to Lincoln.

As a result of his one-sided investigations, Governor Axtell issued a hurried proclamation in which he relieved
"Green" Wilson of his authority as a Justice of the Peace.
This meant that Dick Brewer's commission as a special
constable under Wilson was no longer valid, and that
from now on the posse of Regulators was merely a Vigi-
lante Committee without so much as a semblance of legality.

"Dick," McSween is reported to have said, "you'd better
take to the hills."

Dawn was breaking when Brewer rode his horse down

the silent dirt street and then turned off into the rough country to join up with the Kid and the now outlawed posse. Later that morning McSween left with his Negro servant and the deputy sheriff from Las Vegas, who still refused to turn over the lawyer to Sheriff Brady. McSween planned to camp out in the canyons of the Pecos near John Chisum's ranch until court opened.

During the next few weeks Sheriff Brady with a clattering little detachment of Negro troopers of the 9th Cavalry at his back, played a desperate game of hide-and-go-seek with Brewer and the Kid and the other Regulators in the hills between the Bonito and the Ruidoso. Suddenly the grapevine telegraph reported to the McSween men that army orders had been received at Fort Stanton stating that Governor Axtell's request for the use of troops by the county authorities had been approved by the President. From now on a county sheriff could ask a post commander for troops to assist him and the request must be granted.

It was a matter of the greatest importance to the Kid's side. Certainly it would make Sheriff Brady even more arrogant and overbearing. Not only had he made no effort to arrest the men who had killed Tunstall but he had virtually placed the culprits under his own protection and a number of them were actually serving as his deputies.

It was all deeply disheartening to the Regulators. To them it must have seemed that all the machinery of law and government was now combined against them and their cause. In their eyes the chief symbol of injustice and tyranny was the square-shouldered figure of the fifty-six-year-old Major Brady, now backed by the might and prestige of the United States Army. The Kid personally still demanded revenge for the way the sheriff had treated him and Fred Waite when he had kept them from attending Tunstall's funeral.

For the time being the Regulators split up, the Kid and probably five or six others seeking safety in one direction, while the rest hid out in another. Their hate and resentment centered more and more on Sheriff Brady. They rehashed the report that he owed $1,500 to Dolan, and was completely under his thumb.

Matters seemed hopeless and futile to the Kid and his immediate *compadres* as they rode the dangerous trails at night. Brady had not only become their principal enemy: he was now their tormentor and their scourge.

But they were not entirely bereft of friends, or without at least the help of a few influential individuals who understood the terrible situation in Lincoln County. One of these was an important attorney of Cimarron, living in the old Maxwell Grant of Northern New Mexico; his name was Frank Springer, and he was a bitter political foe of Governor Axtell.

At this exact period, when the Kid's party seemed to be at its lowest ebb, Springer wrote a letter to the Honorable Rush Clark, a member of Congress. It is of special value as a piece of unbiased evidence as to the true state of affairs:

> There is no doubt in my mind from a mass of private information I have received that the whole power of the Territorial government, strengthened by the active aid of the U. S. military forces, has been either ignorantly or intentionally used to protect and assist a small combination of corrupt men, speculating in military and Indian contracts—against the best men in the county. That the men thus protected and aided by the government had in their employ members of a band of desperadoes, cattle thieves, highwaymen and murderers who have infested that region for a long time to the terror of good citizens, and that J. H. Tunstall, an estimable man, connected with a wealthy family in England, was murdered by these very outlaws who were serving on the sheriff's posse attempting to seize Tunstall's private property for another man's debts.
>
> There is no doubt that the U.S. troops have been employed in a most illegal manner. No effort has been made by the Territorial Governor to arrest the murderers of Tunstall, but the Governor by the President's authority called upon the troops practically to protect them from arrest.
>
> The people seem to be driven to desperation by these acts and scenes of violence that have been enacted. I have no interest in the matter and no acquaintance with the principal actors, but I would like to see an end to wholesale crime in the Terri-

tory and would like to see the powers of the U.S. government employed to punish and not to aid in protecting criminals. I believe the people there have done some wrong, but they have been crazed to see the murderers of Tunstall running at liberty under the protection of the authorities. I have sent you newspapers with reports of all the late doings there, and most of it I believe to be reliable. The Republican party and a Republican administration owes it to itself to see that such abuses are not perpetuated under its name.

It might have been of some consequence to the morale of the Kid and the other Tunstall avengers had they known that there were a few such men as Frank Springer who were secretly aiding their side.

While the Kid and his *compadres* were still hiding out in the hills below Lincoln there was considerable excitement around the Chisum ranch headquarters near the Pecos, fifty miles or so to the eastward, during these late March days. A mysterious Judge Leverson, looking for a tract of land for Mormon colonists from England, arrived and rode over the country with Jim Chisum. Soon afterwards the alert and indefatigable Susan McSween appeared en route home to Lincoln from her visit in Kansas. Then John Chisum himself drove up in a hired rig from Las Vegas, having finally won his release from arrest at the hands of Catron & Thornton.

Suddenly on March 28th Sheriff Brady, accompanied by Captain Smith and a detachment of soldiers from Ft. Stanton, jingled up and dismounted at the South Spring Ranch. The Sheriff explained that he was seeking jurors for the term of court opening April 1st at Lincoln, and he had availed himself of his new authority to have soldiers detailed to accompany him on his duty.

That day a conference concerning the absent McSween's attendance at the court was held at the ranch between Chisum, Mrs. McSween, Sheriff Brady and Captain Smith, with the visitor Leverson taking an active part. Captain Smith pledged that he would give military protection to

McSween at Fort Stanton until the term of court opened. And Sheriff Brady agreed that he would not serve the warrant he held for McSween, and that a detail of soldiers should accompany the lawyer to the army post and thus guarantee protection en route.

Sheriff Brady and the soldier detachment, however, did not wait for the McSween-Leverson party but pushed through from the Pecos as swiftly as possible. Brady insisted that he must be in Lincoln by Sunday night, for the spring term of court was to open on the first Monday of April. However, he had miscalculated the time, for when he consulted his clerk of court at Lincoln on Monday morning he discovered that it was not until the following Monday, April 8th, that the session began.

It was between nine and ten A.M. when he and his deputy, George Hindman, started down the middle of the street to change the notices on the small adobe courthouse, which was further along on the street and east of the Mc-Sween home. Some distance behind the two men followed three more of the Sheriff's party, Billy Mathews, Jack Long and George Peppin. All were fully armed and they had taken the middle of the road perhaps because there were no sidewalks. Hindman was a tall, hard man with a crippled hand and arm which had been badly mauled by a bear. Mathews had for some time been connected with the Murphy & Dolan firm; Long and Peppin were both regular deputies.

Sometime during the previous night Billy and a small group of Regulators quietly eased into Lincoln, concealing their horses in the adobe stable behind the McSween house. Their leader Dick Brewer was not with them nor was McSween on hand to advise them.

There seems to be some basis for the theory that the Kid and his gang heard the rumor that Brady was figuring on intercepting the McSween party on its way from Chisum's into town this coming morning of April 1st. This might explain in part the frightful action that soon took place. A simpler explanation is that the Kid and his friends were at the end of their string; either they must move quickly and decisively to eliminate Brady, or he and his posse and the soldiers he now could command would liquidate McSween and Chisum and then one at a time kill off all those who were now fighting on their side.

It must have been with some such desperate thoughts in their minds that Billy and the five men with him slipped out of the McSween house that Monday morning. They took positions behind the plank gate just to the east of the rear end of the Tunstall store. It led to the corral on behind. This wooden gate was hung in line with the back or north end of the building.

Men lounging behind this plank gate could not be seen by anyone coming down the dirt road from the right or west until they had actually passed the store. It was long accepted that there existed a high adobe wall at this spot where the plank gate actually hung and that this adobe wall offered a secure rampart for anyone behind it. This is incorrect, for both Dr. Ealy, the medical missionary, and others familiar with the settings made positive statements that there was no adobe wall but only an ordinary swinging gate on hinges, with a wooden fence running at right angles to the rear.

Brady and Hindman had no suspicion of lurking danger as they walked from the Wortley Hotel at an ordinary pace down the middle of the street. Each man carried a Winchester as well as a six-shooter. Mathews followed a short distance behind them. And some paces to the rear were Long and Peppin.

Without warning the six men behind the plank gate suddenly opened fire. Brady and Hindman crumpled up in the dust, their bodies riddled with lead slugs. At the first shot Mathews turned and broke for the protection of the nearest house back to the west and across the road.

The Kid and Fred Waite hurriedly climbed over the gate and raced to the dying Brady and Hindman with the idea of securing their rifles. There is some evidence that the Kid did not have a late-model Winchester at this time and that the new rifles of the officers offered too great a temptation for him and Waite to pass up.

As they stooped over to pick up the rifles lying alongside the mortally wounded men, Deputy Mathews fired from the safety of the house across the road and to the west, inflicting a flesh wound in the side of the Kid and slightly injuring Waite. The two boys managed to make their way back to the corral and join their companions. In the general fright and confusion they quickly mounted their horses, slipped out of the corral and headed south

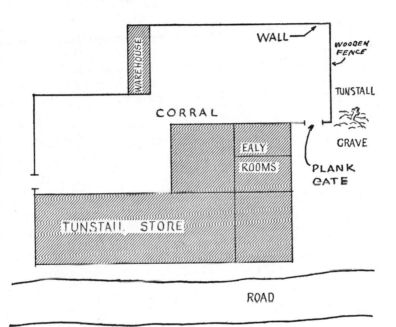

WALL

WOODEN FENCE

TUNSTALL

GRAVE

WAREHOUSE

CORRAL

EALY ROOMS

PLANK GATE

TUNSTALL STORE

ROAD

into the hills toward San Patricio, eight or ten miles away.

News of the terrible situation in Lincoln County had already penetrated to the White House. President Rutherford B. Hayes was now to be further informed by a long personal letter from the rather important Judge Leverson, written shortly after the tragedy, which he had missed by a matter of two or three hours. His excited report showed his marked approval of the McSween side and apparently exonerated the Kid and his companions. It read in part:

> I have not yet been able to get a trustworthy account of the affray; what I have been informed, but still not from any of the actors in the tragedy, is this; that in violation of the pledges made by himself and by Captain Smith, who failed in leaving any escort (a corporal's guard would have been sufficient) for McSween at Lincoln, Brady had started out with Hindman, his deputy Peppin, and 2 other men to go down the creek and meet McSween (really there can be no doubt to murder him) and who he knew in reliance on Captain Smith's plighted word was on his road to the fort, but had to pass through Lincoln to reach it. Brady and his party were met by 7 citizens, some of them, I am assured on excellent authority, being among the best citizens of the county; how the firing commenced I have been unable as yet to learn, but Brady and Hindman were killed and two of the citizens were wounded.

2

Some time the following day the Kid and the five men with him who had killed Brady and Hindman contacted Dick Brewer and the other Regulators over in the Ruidoso country. Dick and the older men of the Regulators felt that the Kid and the others had used extremely bad judgment. As a matter of fact, the Tunstall avengers were now in a far more precarious position than ever before. They had by this rash act burned all their bridges behind them.

Their numbers were now strengthened by a rather singular recruit. He had made his way by horseback into the dangerous area from his home in Uvalde, Texas. By some twist of fortune he apparently ran into the Kid in one of the tiny native *plazas* on the Ruidoso, probably at San Patricio. The little community was almost exclusively Spanish-speaking and friendly to the Tunstall-McSween side. The Kid, in particular, always seemed completely at home among these humble, earthy people.

The newcomer was a tall, lanky boy, with large hands and feet, and was of a gentle and kindly disposition. He was almost the exact age of the Kid, and the two at once took a liking to one another. The newcomer explained that his name was Tom O'Folliard, and as time went on and he grew closer to the Kid he told bits of his background: his father was from a good family in Ireland but he had fallen into some sort of serious trouble there and fled to America, ending up at Uvalde, in south-central Texas. Here he married the eldest daughter of David Cook, one of Uvalde's prominent citizens. But he seemed obsessed by the shadow of some vague fear, and finally he took his bride to Monclova, State of Coahuila, in northern Mexico.

Shortly before the Civil War broke out a virulent smallpox epidemic swept through that part of Mexico and the romantic Irishman and his young wife were among those who succumbed. Their baby boy survived and was cared for by a Mexican family. When word of the tragedy reached Uvalde an uncle, John Cook, journeyed to Monclova and brought back the baby. The uncle and his sister, Margaret Jane, took care of the little orphan until the auntie married and then the boy was sent to live with his grandmother, Mrs. David Cook. Uncle John Cook later was killed when a horse fell with him. Another uncle, Thalis Cook, a deeply religious man, now assumed responsibility for the child's upbringing.

Uncle Thalis was a Texas Ranger, despite the fact that he was an epileptic. Knowing the danger he faced when riding alone in this vast, waterless land of West Texas, he trained his horse to stand by when he was forced to slip out of his saddle and lie helpless in a paroxysm. His dog, too, was taught to watch by his side until he regained consciousness. Thus the three worked together against the dread malady.

But even such fine contacts and such brave backgrounds as belonged to the boy could not keep down the wanderlust and the call of wild adventure. So the day came when he said goodbye and rode off. The tales of the terrible feud in Lincoln County seemed to draw him like a magnet, and he finally reached this bright little valley of the Ruidoso a few miles below Lincoln during the very crisis of the vendetta.

The Texas boy and the Kid became friends at their first meeting. And, following the Brady affair, when Billy returned to his companions he took with him a new recruit for the Regulators.

On the morning of April 4th, three days after the shooting of the sheriff, Dick Brewer led the Kid and the rest of his men out on what might be termed a scouting expedition. They were looking for no one in particular, but high in their list of wanted men was a hard case named "Buckshot" Roberts, a one-time Texas Ranger and army deserter who had been with the posse that had murdered Tunstall and consequently would be most welcome grist to the Regulators' mill. Matters were not helped when the report came to them that the Dolan faction had promised a bounty of $100 for every McSween man killed.

The Kid and the Regulators cut across a portion of the Mescalero Apache Reservation in the western part of Lincoln County and pulled up at a long, adobe building that was occupied by a fifty-year-old "Yankee" named Doc Blazer. The house stood on a shoulder of land that rose well above the little valley of the South Fork of the Rio Tularosa. At the foot of the steep rise was a sawmill, with the race that furnished power for the water wheel; the race ran from a dam up above. Blazer owned a few acres where his buildings sat and the Apache Indian Agent Godfrey rented a room in the house as his office. Oddly enough, the ownership of this little strip of land was later to be a matter of considerable importance to the Kid.

Blazer, born in Washington, Pennsylvania, on August 20th, 1829, had migrated to Illinois and then to Mt. Pleasant, Iowa. He was a practicing dentist when he enlisted in the Union Army, but soon was badly hurt when a horse fell with him. He developed tuberculosis and was discharged from the service. His next stop was San Antonio, Texas, and soon he was freighting out of Ft. Davis for El Paso.

The war had been over less than two years when Doc Blazer came to the Tularosa canyon and traded his wagon

train for the water-driven sawmill. Situated on the main
trail from Lincoln and Ft. Stanton on southwestward to
Mesilla and the Rio Grande country, the Blazer house was
a regular stopping place and way station where travellers
could get a meal or be put up for the night. Doc Blazer, a
man who strictly minded his own business and had taken
no active side in the feud, cordially welcomed the Regulators on this day of April 4th. Dinner would be ready in
a half hour or so. Meanwhile the men sat on their heels
against the wall. It was better than 7,000 feet altitude here
in the heavily wooded Apache reservation, and even at
noontime there was a chill in the air.

Soon a man on a mule was seen to ride down to the far
bank of the swift little stream, cross over and make his way
up the shoulder of the hill towards the house. Frank Coe,
who had been one of the Kid's first friends when he arrived from the Pecos some four months previously, recognized the rider as "Buckshot" Roberts. Frank called to
Dick Brewer and the men lolling on the far side of the
house, explaining who the visitor was and adding that he'd
been friendly with the old reprobate and that he might get
him to surrender without having to kill him.

Roberts was a small, tough individual who besides being
an army deserter had a criminal record. He was, nevertheless, a proud and brave man, and when he pulled up his
mule and dismounted he jerked his rifle from its boot un
der his left stirrup leather. He had not until that moment
seen the saddled horses cropping the sparse grass back of
the house.

Frank Coe met him by an open doorway and with a wry
grin chided him for riding head-on into such a situation.
The rest of Brewer's men were on the far side of the house
and out of sight.

The two men sat down on the doorstep and talked over
matters. Coe explained that if Roberts surrendered peacefully he might not be killed, but he sure would be rubbed
out quick enough if he tried to fight back. The gnarled
old warrior argued that he'd heard what had happened to
Morton and Baker when they had surrendered to the Regulators and he wanted none of that brand of treatment.

Minutes passed and the men on the far side of the adobe
building grew restless. Why fool with this man who had
helped kill Tunstall? Finally Dick Brewer, the leader, said

that while Roberts might prove a tough customer to handle, if some of the men wanted to help get him he'd lead the way. The Kid, Charlie Bowdre, John Middleton, George Coe and one or two others, along with the lanky Tom O'Folliard, rose to their feet. Several of the men eased their six-shooters out of their holsters. They moved in a crowd around the corner of the building.

Charlie Bowdre, his gun in his hand, barked out for Roberts to surrender.

"Not me, Mary Anne!" the tough old warrior shouted back.

The two men fired at almost the same moment, Roberts pulling the trigger of his Winchester as he held it slanted across his body; his left arm had been so badly hurt years before that he was unable to lift his rifle to his shoulder. The bullet from his Winchester careened off the heavy buckle of Bowdre's gun belt and ripped into George Coe's hand, tearing off his trigger finger and shattering several small bones.

The heavy forty-five lead slug from Charlie Bowdre's pistol buried itself in Roberts' stomach, the fatal gut-shot of the frontier that meant sure and agonizing death within a dozen hours. The stricken man pumped a second shell into his rifle and sent the bullet through the left lung of young Frank Middleton. Then firing wildly the mortally wounded Roberts drove off his half-dozen attackers.

Holding his left hand across his fatal wound, he staggered through the doorway of the bedroom used by Doc Blazer. His roving eyes located a heavy buffalo gun leaning against the doorjamb, a belt of 50 calibre cartridges hanging by its buckle over the muzzle of the barrel. A single window stood open next the door, with a bed alongside. He managed to double up the mattress and lying on it rested the barrel of his Winchester on the window sill. He had the buffalo gun by his side.

The Regulators, now safely around the corner of the house, were aghast at the deadly strike of the old rattlesnake. Dick Brewer, angry at the setback and realizing that anyone who came within gunshot would be killed, concluded the only safe way was to find a spot somewhere in the valley below where he could draw a quick bead on the old gladiator and kill him. Ordinarily, the thirty-year-old Brewer was a man of calm and sound judgment, but he was now upset and wanted revenge. He was not certain how badly Roberts was wounded, and he wanted to finish him off at once and have it done with.

He told the Kid and his other men to let him handle the situation: he would slip down the high bank to the saw-mill, and locate a place from which he could fire. Several minutes later the men heard a single shot from below. It was followed immediately by an answering shot from the room where Roberts had found refuge. Obviously Dick had missed.

There was a lull in the firing. Then, after a pause, there was the roar of a heavy calibre gun from Roberts' bed-room. There was no answering shot.

The men looked at one another with wonder and un-certainty. Then they heard Roberts shouting something that sounded like, "I killed the sonofabitch! I killed him."

There was a long wait, and they could hear Roberts cursing. He was daring them to come on and fight it out.

Finally two or three of the men made a long detour around the house that carried them down the hill and to the rear of the sawmill. Peeking through the cracks in the warped boards on the sides of the half-open shed, they could see Dick Brewer lying in the sun, a heavy log in front of him. The top of his head had been blown off.

The two men slipped out from their hiding place and crept back up to the hill and reported the terrible news to their companions. They had lost their leader.

They could still hear the old warrior who had killed Dick moaning and cursing in the room on the other side of the house. They knew now that he was dying, and while they wanted to kill him, they could not help but respect him for the utterly brave man that he was. He had out-gamed them all. He had shown what iron nerves and stamina could do.

Death had been looking out of his eyes as he marked the spot where Dick raised his head over the log in the valley below to fire his first shot, which had torn off a corner of the window sill in the bedroom. Roberts drew a bead along the sights of the heavy buffalo gun and waited. It had required all his strength and will power to lift the rifle to the window sill.

When he saw the top of Brewer's head slowly rising, he squeezed the trigger. The human target was fully 125 yards away. It would have been good shooting for an expert marksman under the most ideal circumstances.

John Middleton, a young man from Kansas still in his early twenties, was propped against the side of the house. The rifle bullet had completely passed through the upper part of his left lung. If he was to live he would have to be moved at once to some friendly house and given complete rest. George Coe was suffering intensely from his shattered hand. He, too, would need special care.

They could probably kill the old tiger by sneaking up along the outside wall and shooting quickly. But Roberts deserved the little victory that was his. He alone had virtually whipped a dozen men. Neither the Kid nor any of the others wanted to bother with him.

They helped Middleton and Coe mount their horses, and with a man riding on either side of Middleton they took off at a walk, well out of sight of the dying Roberts.

Doc Blazer promised he would take care of Dick Brewer's body. A mile or two away lay the Apache Agency buildings, and from there a telegraph line ran to the Fort, some fifteen miles distant. He'd send word to the post for the army surgeon to come over as quickly as he could. He'd do his best for Roberts.

And he'd get his old carpenter to knock together two coffins: one for Dick and one for "Buckshot." He'd bury them side by side in a plot on the hill behind the house.

7

The Kid was perfectly satisfied with Frank McNab as the new leader of the Regulators. It was a tacit selection: he was the eldest and most experienced man remaining in the little group of a dozen fighters and he was simply accepted as captain. For two or three years he had been one of John Chisum's foremen.

The April term of Court, with its important session of the Grand Jury, opened April 8th, the second Monday in the month. Certainly it was a good time for the Kid and his gang to stay well away from Lincoln. As a matter of fact, the killing of Sheriff Brady and his deputy left affairs in a complete state of turmoil. Peppin, holding a warrant as a deputy, attempted to take over the sheriff's duties.

McSween, his brother-in-law Shield and one or two other completely innocent people had been arrested and taken to Ft. Stanton at noon on April 1st following the killing of Brady. The lawyer was still formally in the custody of the deputy Barrier from Las Vegas, and even though his old enemy Brady was dead McSween felt that he himself might be killed.

Suddenly a brand new element was injected into the picture by the arrival of Lt. Colonel Nathan A. M. Dudley as the new Post Commander at Ft. Stanton. There was general rejoicing on the part of the McSweenites over the relief of Brevet Colonel Purrington, despite the fact that he would remain on at Stanton as a troop commander.

Some six months before this date Dudley had been court-martialled at Fort Union, in northern New Mexico, on the charge of forcibly compelling a civilian to marry the daughter of a noncombatant officer of the post in what was known at the time as a "shotgun marriage." His own heavy drinking had been brought out in the testimony.

On January 26th of this present year of 1878 the papers in Santa Fe printed an account from the New York *Sun* stating that the Colonel was found guilty and the Army Court had ordered his dismissal from the service. However, due to his long years and fine war record, higher army authority suspended the verdict and he was let off with a severe reprimand.

So it was that on April 5th, the day after the tragedy at Blazer's Mill, Lieutenant Colonel Dudley suddenly appeared at Ft. Stanton as the new post commander. He was an imposing figure with a mop of graying hair, flashing eyes and the heavy cavalry mustaches of the period. In a few weeks he would be 53, a hard, heavy-drinking and thoroughly experienced soldier. Originally from Lexington, Massachusetts, he had been an officer in the Regular Army for twenty-three years, and for the past eleven years he had been Lt. Colonel of the 9th (Negro) Cavalry. During this period he had seen much Indian fighting and service in the Southwest.

But of more importance to the people of Lincoln than his imposing army record, was the fact that at his court-martial at Ft. Union he had been defended by Tom Catron, senior partner of the law firm of Catron & Thornton, and the recognized head of the Santa Fe Ring. But despite Dudley's close association with Tom Catron and his reputation as a meddler, McSween and his associates welcomed the officer's arrival at Ft. Stanton. So bitter was the feeling against the former Post Commander, Brevet Colonel Purrington, that at a mass meeting of citizens held at Lincoln at the close of the April term of court an unusual resolution was passed by acclamation which showed the new temper of the community towards the army as the result of the change in command. The resolution was to the following effect:

That the thanks of the people of Lincoln County are due and hereby tendered to Lt. Col. Dudley, U. S. Army, commanding Fort Stanton, N.M. for his conduct as an officer and a gentleman. That we do and will consider the day he took command at Fort Stanton an important era in the history of our country. That we assure him of our appreciation of the intelligent, cautious and earnest manner in which he has applied himself in ferreting out the cause of our trouble. This—his nonpartisan conduct and frankness towards the people on one hand and these men on the other, is a guarantee that he *alone* is the commanding officer at Fort Stanton. Therefore we tender him our heartfelt thanks in recognition of our appreciation of a man who discharges his duty faithfully.

Unfortunately the happy honeymoon between Dudley and McSween's partisans was to last only a short time. Temperamentally, and in background and association, the old Regular officer was exactly the opposite of the lawyer and his impulsive and energetic wife, the black-eyed, vivacious Susan McSween. Both sides were sincere and acting according to their lights. But it was inevitable that they should soon clash violently and irrevocably.

2

The Kid and his *compadres,* hiding out along the Ruidoso and the Feliz, were kept well-informed by McSween agents of the changing affairs in Lincoln. A native New Mexican would casually ride out of Lincoln and shortly appear at the camp of the Regulators.

There was some adverse comment by the Kid's gang over the news that the first action of the new Ft. Stanton commander was to send a little detachment of troopers posthaste to the Tularosa country to escort Judge Bristol, Prosecuting Attorney Rynerson, the Clerk of the Court, and Col. Fountain and one or two other attorneys en route to Lincoln for the opening of court on April 8th. It was rumored that Dudley acted on the advice of Major Murphy, now grievously ill in an upstairs room of his big store ("the House"). Murphy insisted that the Regulators planned to waylay the Judge's party.

A more gratifying report came to the Kid's crowd when the secret courier brought the news that the County Commissioners under Juan Patron had met in Lincoln on April 10th and appointed John H. Copeland as Sheriff in place of the dead Brady. The older Regulators knew Copeland as a friendly but inadequate man who would try his best to be fair to them.

Then the news came that the coroner's inquest held over the body of "Buckshot" Roberts at Blazer's Mill resulted in a finding by the jury that the deceased came to his death from gunshot wounds at the hands of Richard Brewer and ten other men. The last name on the list was "W. H. Antrim, alias 'The Kid'." Often now the boy, under one or another of his aliases, was appearing in the various Territorial weeklies which were running regular columns entitled *Lincoln County Items.*

On April 24th the court and grand jury finished their work in Lincoln and were dismissed by Judge Warren Bristol. He appeared to be a just and impartial man, except in one respect: he seemed to have a compelling prejudice against everything that had to do with the McSween side. His charge to the grand jury developed into a bitter personal attack against McSween, and he virtually accused the lawyer of appropriating a part of the $10,000 Fritz insurance money. In asking the grand jury to consider the case Bristol showed that the New York attorney who made the initial collection received $2,800 for his fee which, added to a reasonable 10% fee for McSween, or $1,000, left $6,200 for the lawful heirs. No mention, however, was made of McSween's heavy expenses in New York. Bristol's remarks made clear his opinion of McSween:

> It was McSween's duty to hand this over to the administrator at once, but he has never done it. . . . McSween had no right to retain it for a day longer than was necessary to turn it over to the administrator . . .
>
> Now the trouble with McSween seems to be an attempt on his part to usurp the functions of administrator, of Judge, court, jury, witness and (probably) heirs to the Fritz estate. We have seen what it

had led to. . . . En route to St. Louis McSween gave $100 each to Mrs. Scholand and Charles Fritz, and this is all he did give them out of the $10,000.

But despite the rather vicious attack by the Judge the grand jury entirely exonerated McSween on the charge of embezzlement. There was, however, one particular sour note in the accounts of the grand jury and court sessions that were carried to the Kid and his fellow Regulators. It concerned a conversation between Colonel Rynerson, the District Prosecuting Attorney, and Jimmy Dolan which occurred shortly before the court adjourned. It was overheard by Atanacio Martinez, a constable friendly to the McSween side. It was passed on to McSween, and finally relayed below to his gun-fighters.

Colonel Rynerson, a determined and often unscrupulous man, was reported as saying to Dolan: "Don't give up, Jimmy! Stick to that McSween crowd. I will aid you all I can and will send you twenty men. Stick to the fight and give it to those rascals. This is the only way to win."

The one really disturbing part of the conversation was the single sentence in which Rynerson promised to send twenty men. The Kid was probably sure that they would be John Kinney's loosely-handed but completely desperate gang of outlaws which operated up and down the Rio Grande into Old Mexico and on west to the mining camps. They were killers and most of them had indictments for murder hanging over their heads. Due to this stern fact they had no alternative but to obey Prosecuting Attorney Rynerson's orders to serve as gun-fighters under Dolan unless they were willing to be arrested for murder and face certain conviction in Mesilla.

But the menace of the intrusion of the Kinney gang still lay in the future. Here at the moment things were looking up for the Regulators. There was a new Sheriff now who certainly would not be too unfriendly, and McSween had proven that his side still had the support of most of the community. The same messenger who brought them this new threat of a mob from the Rio Grande, handed them a copy of the Santa Fe *New Mexican* that carried an interesting advertisement:

A Card to the Public: The condition of affairs now existing in this county is such as to make it unsafe for the undersigned to further continue business as they have heretofore done. They take this occasion to assure their friends and the public that the suspension will be only temporary, and that they will resume when peace and quiet shall take the place of lawlessness, and order shall be restored in the county. Asking for continued confidence, and hoping for a renewal of business relations, we remain,

Very respectfully,
Jas. J. Dolan & Co.

LINCOLN, N.M. APRIL 17th, 1878

Tom Catron in Santa Fe had lost no time in moving in to protect his interests. He quietly arranged to take up the chattel mortgage which Dolan and Riley had given him for his endorsement of their notes held at the First National Bank of Santa Fe. And on May 1st he announced that his energetic young brother-in-law, Edgar Walz, from Blue Earth County, Minnesota, would be put in charge of all the interests in Lincoln County now belonging to him.

As part of the general liquidation, Dolan moved the ailing Major Murphy to Santa Fe, where he died of cancer at St. Vincent's Hospital on October 29, 1878. He was a scant 47, but he had drunk a vast amount of his own whiskey and lived hard.

3

Towards the end of April affairs quieted down so that the Kid and the McSween fighters more or less came out of hiding and began to show themselves in little groups of two or three men. Frank McNab, the new captain of the Regulators, met Frank Coe and Frank's brother-in-law, Ab Sanders, in Lincoln about 3 o'clock on the afternoon of April 30th and the three men jogged on down the Bonito. Suddenly the little party ran into an ambush of Seven Rivers men at Fritz's Spring Ranch, eight miles on east of Lincoln.

McNab was killed in the first volley. The two others tried to escape but their horses were shot from under them and Ab Sanders was badly wounded in the foot and the hip. Frank Coe, his six-shooter empty, was surrounded

and finally surrendered to an old friend who was now
with the Pecos crowd.

The following day, May 1st, there was considerable
shooting in the streets of Lincoln between the McSween
men, with the Kid more or less taking orders from Doc
Scurlock, the former Mississippi dental student who was
now the oldest and most experienced member of the
Regulators. But the skirmish was little more than a dress
rehearsal for a later affair that was to be the real showdown.

The Kid and the little crowd of McSween gun-fighters
soon rode on east towards the Pecos. On May 14th they
invaded the former Dolan cow camp, which now belonged
to Tom Catron. The raid, which ended in a short fight,
netted them twenty-seven head of horses. They set afoot
the Dolan-Catron ranch hands.

No man in the entire Territory quite equalled Tom
Catron's unique position and prestige. Certainly he was
a curious sort of pioneer lawyer whose vast ambitions and
hard measures were tempered by innumerable charities
and generous actions. He had been a boy-captain of Confederate artillery in Missouri, but when he came into
New Mexico via the Santa Fe trail with his equally re-
markable and talented schoolmate from the University of
Missouri, Stephen Benton Elkins, he at once decided that
to prosper here he must turn Republican. Elkins, a former Union officer, had had considerable experience in
Territorial politics and was able to help him over the
initial hurdles.

From the start Catron proved to be an outstandingly
rugged individualist on a hard frontier where men who
succeeded must stand squarely on their own feet. His genuine talent for making and helping friends was matched
by his pure genius for making enemies. On the whole, the
good of this strange character outweighed the bad side. As
far as his relationship with the Kid was concerned, Catron
apparently was to remain the boy's persistent and merciless enemy, surpassed in this respect only by Col. Rynerson and Jimmy Dolan.

[The extremely able Southwestern historian, William A.
Keleher, tells a memorable little story that brings out the
true humanness yet hidden shyness of Catron: Along about
1890 Catron, certainly the leading attorney and most pow-

erful figure in the Territory of New Mexico, happened to be in the town of Socorro, a hundred and forty miles down the Rio Grande from Santa Fe. By chance he heard that the wife of a struggling young lawyer there, just starting practice, was very ill. Catron had never met the harassed young man, but he lumbered into his office and introduced himself. Without further ado he rather apologetically laid a roll of bills on the desk, remarking in his gruff manner that he'd heard he was having a little hard luck and that this might tide him over. The young man could pay him back someday when things started to break his way . . . In due time, the young lawyer prospered and paid back the $600. Eventually he became a Justice of the Territorial Supreme Court. Catron, at this time, was fighting desperately and with no holds barred in the defense of some client, and having had offended the highest court, he was forced to face a trial of disbarment. He was acquitted by a vote of two to three. The one-time Socorro lawyer was later asked by a close friend, who knew how Catron had helped him as a young man, how he had voted. The Judge's answer might have been slightly cryptic but it was clear enough: "What would you have done had you been me?"]

Catron in Santa Fe did not hear of the raid on his Pecos cow camp until some ten days after the event occurred. He immediately wrote a letter to the Territorial Governor demanding that soldiers be sent from Ft. Stanton to guard the interests of himself and the other anti-McSween Pecos ranchers.

The harassed Governor agreed to Catron's demands and immediately wrote a request to Brevet Major General Edward Hatch, commander of the Department of New Mexico with headquarters at Santa Fe. The Governor's request was far from unreasonable and in part read:

> To prevent further bloodshed and to enable Mr. Catron to secure the cattle and have them driven to some safer locality, I have respectfully to request that you will order a sufficient number of troops to remain on the Rio Pecos in the vicinity of Roswell, Lincoln County, to keep the peace, and also that you will direct the officer in charge of troops to disarm all bands of armed men which he finds in the county of

Lincoln, whether claiming to act as sheriff's posse or otherwise.

Two weeks later Colonel Dudley ordered the personally unpopular Captain Purrington to mount his Company H, of the 15th Infantry, and proceed to the Pecos.

The Kid, Doc Scurlock and the rest of the unofficial Regulators knew nothing of the moves being made in Santa Fe to oppose them. In those late May days of 1878 they felt fairly satisfied with the way affairs were looking up for their side. Sheriff Copeland was friendly and would make no energetic move against them. Certainly, on the surface at least it seemed that Colonel Dudley was holding his soldiers in tight rein.

Then on May 28th the Governor made a move that struck them with the force of a thunderbolt:

PROCLAMATION BY THE GOVERNOR

For the information of all citizens of Lincoln County, I do hereby make this public proclamation;

First: John H. Copeland, Esq. appointed a sheriff by the county commissioners, having failed for more than 30 days to file his bond as collector of taxes, is hereby removed from the office of sheriff, and I have appointed George W. Peppin, Esq. sheriff of Lincoln County. This had been in compliance with the laws passed at the 22nd session of the legislature assembly relating to sheriffs.

Second: I commend all men and bodies of men now under arms to disarm and return to their homes and their usual pursuits, and so long as the present sheriff has authority to call upon U. S. troops for assistance, not to act as a sheriff's posse.

Third: And in conclusion, I urge all good citizens to submit to the law, remembering that violence begets violence, and that those who take up the sword shall perish by the sword.

S. B. Axtell,
Governor of New Mexico

In George Peppin the Kid and the Regulators now had to face a sheriff who not only was a deadly personal enemy but a man who was a complete tool of the old Murphy-

Dolan interests. Their easy days were over. Once again they had to be on their guard night and day.

Fortunately the Jesse Evans Banditti, who had been so effective in the middle February days, were only memories. Tom Hill had been killed by a half-breed Indian when he and Evans had attempted to rob a floating sheep camp, and Evans with a shattered wrist was now in jail at Mesilla waiting trial.

But there were plenty of hard enemies left, and over on the Rio Grande and here to the east where the Black River emptied into the Pecos there were ample reservoirs of gun-fighters for hire by the anti-McSween faction.

8

One piece of good news for Billy and his *compadres* softened the blow of Peppin's appointment as sheriff.

On the same day that Governor Axtell removed Copeland and put in Peppin, there arrived in Santa Fe a special agent of the Department of Justice and the Department of the Interior. He was a distinguished lawyer of New York City named Frank Warren Angel. He carried extraordinary powers in support of his mission to investigate the death of Tunstall. He was also to report on the charge that the Governor and the Territorial officials had been negligent in their failure to bring to the bar of justice the men who had killed the young Englishman.

The Tunstall family was demanding indemnity for the murder, and the British Minister in Washington, Sir Henry Thornton, requested a full report of the outrage. Angel had begun his investigation in Santa Fe, and soon he arrived in Lincoln to continue his work on the spot.

Behind the new investigator stood the entire power and dignity of the United States Government. It was the first time that the scheming New Mexican politicians, with their powerful Santa Fe Ring, had been called upon to face a completely impartial and fearless examination.

No longer would Billy and the little band of devoted Regulators fighting their lonely battles in the dangerous stretches of Lincoln County need feel quite so deserted and handicapped. There were now forces at hand which could not be pushed aside or intimidated by the overbearing Ring and its hired fighters. Even the Governor and the military were under question and were the subjects of investigation by this courageous fact-finder from the national capital.

Judge Angel's suspicions were almost immediately aroused by the official cold shoulder given him by the Territorial Government in Santa Fe, from the Governor on down through the various levels in its organization. His task was primarily to discover why the killers of the Englishman had not been apprehended, and from the start he encountered a hostile attitude towards himself. His keen mind quickly analyzed the conflict evolving around the business and political control of the vast, isolated and backward area of Lincoln County.

Cruising along the sluggish, brick-colored Pecos, riding back in the canyons and narrow valleys that cut westward, there was always the possibility of the Kid and the rest of the Regulators picking up a little fight with the Seven Rivers men or the Rio Grande toughs who rode with them. Men in the two opposing camps now stuck fairly close to their own gangs, since it was dangerous to be trapped alone or with only two or three companions.

Peppin had qualified as sheriff and consequently was in a position to call on Colonel Dudley for help whenever he wished. He felt that the time had now come for him to make a master stroke. McSween was hiding in his house in Lincoln, and it was known that Billy with Doc Scurlock and the others had left the Pecos and been seen in the county-seat town.

At Peppin's request for a detachment of troopers, Col. Dudley, the Post Commander, sent Lieutenant Goodwin and twenty-seven men. The combined posse and soldier detachment quietly surrounded Lincoln town, but the birds had flown. One week later a sheriff's posse suddenly ran smack into McSween riding with former Sheriff Copeland, Doc Scurlock, Billy and six or eight more Regulators. The groups were less than two hundred yards apart when they sighted each other, and in the quick exchange of shots the horse ridden by Long of the sheriff's posse was shot out from under him.

The following day was Friday, June 28th, and after spending the night in the neighborhood of San Patricio, on the Ruidoso, the Kid and the McSween crowd decided to move eastward to the safety of the Pecos and the Chisum headquarters. They had just made the decision when they were faced with the reality of the very threat they feared: Captain Carroll with thirty-five men suddenly clattered into San Patricio, where Sheriff Peppin's posse was assembled. The combined party was at the point of moving out against the Regulators when a soldier messenger, riding at top speed, pulled up in front of Captain Carroll, dismounted and saluted sharply. He handed the Captain a message from Colonel Dudley at Ft. Stanton.

The message carried the information that a telegram had just arrived from General Hatch at Santa Fe announcing that a new War Department order prohibited the further use of troops as a sheriff's posse. Captain Carroll was to return to the post with his detachment.

So it was that McSween with the Kid and a handful of men virtually acting as a bodyguard, rode unmolested on eastward to the Chisum stronghold on South Spring River. Two days later a friendly rider came in with the news that on June 18th the U.S. Congress, in passing an amendment to the Army Bill, had slipped in the clause that soldiers were no longer to be used in civilian disturbances. In a matter of minutes after Colonel Dudley received the confirming telegram he wrote out the message recalling Captain Carroll, and sent it posthaste by a trooper to San Patricio. It was a lucky break for the Kid and his little crowd.

On July 3rd Billy and his *compadres,* scouting in the canyons back of Seven Rivers, had a long-range brush with a small bunch of Pecos men. It was bloodless and the Kid led the way back to Chisum's fortress home. The following day there was a second shooting match between a group of Seven Rivers fighters and the Regulators who were posted on the flat dirt roof of Chisum's adobe house at South Spring. The score was nothing to nothing.

The eighteen-year-old Sally Chisum and her two younger brothers thoroughly enjoyed the 4th of July celebration. Their Uncle John was away, probably partaking of the safety of Santa Fe. The shrewd old cowman, now fifty-six, usually found it profitable to pull out from the Pecos when the going got heavy. He had not been in Lincoln since he had driven into town with Judge Leverson, on the morning that Sheriff Brady and his deputy were killed.

In an odd sort of way Chisum and McSween were cut from the same piece of cloth; neither would carry a gun, thus giving them the very real advantage of the frontier code which held that an unarmed man must never be a gun target. But while McSween followed the practice largely because of his religious beliefs, crafty old John, his twinkling blue eyes betraying his own guile, simply figured it was the best way to keep from getting shot.

From the early March day when Billy had ridden into the Chisum headquarters as the youngest member of the Regulators—with the doomed Morton and Baker in tow— Sally Chisum had unquestionably been interested in the unusual lad. And now four months later, Sally was again to spend some time with him. It was a lonely life she led, with no female intimates save the old Negro cook whom Uncle John had long ago brought from Texas.

The slight figure of the homeless, motherless boy, cast in his desperate role, must have appealed to this romantic girl with the compassionate heart—just as it touched the native New Mexican women in the tiny villages along the Ruidoso and the Bonito. To them all he was *muy simpatico*. Much of the hidden meaning of this simple phrase is lost in translating it as "very sympathetic." It was the finest thing that could be said about an individual, and carried with it true affection and tenderness.

2

Things were rapidly moving towards a climax. The Regulators, with McSween riding in their center, openly pointed north up the Pecos in an endeavor to deceive their enemies. Toward evening they turned sharply to the left and rode deep into the night. It was along towards dark on Sunday, two or three days later, when, unbeknownst to the townspeople, they quietly forded the Bonito behind the Tunstall store in Lincoln and dismounted at the corral.

McSween had reached the end of his strength and patience. His wife, worried and uncertain, had remained quietly at home during the past four weeks. Her sister, Mrs. Shield, with her lawyer husband and children, occupied one wing of the large McSween house. Next door to the east, the missionary doctor, Rev. Ealy, and his family lived in what had once been Tunstall's own quarters.

"I'm not leaving any more," McSween announced with utter finality, while he and the riders waited for their coffee. He was done with the bitter days and nights of hiding out. He would suffer no more the humiliation of this role of a hunted man.

The Seven Rivers contingent from the Pecos was now centered somewhere in the vicinity of San Patricio, ten miles across the rough hills to the south of Lincoln. For several days the Kinney gang depredated here in innocent San Patricio, reducing the tiny settlement to a state of abject terror. But the Kid and his crowd of unauthorized Regulators could do nothing to relieve the intolerable situation.

Certainly the legitimate little ranchers from the Pecos country who had thrown in their lot with the bitter Dolan interests had nothing to do with these latest outrages. They were stern and determined men and they bore no semblance to the senseless killers from the Rio Grande under Kinney's command. They sincerely believed they were fighting for their rights and their property against the greed and domination of Old Man Chisum and the ambitions of McSween. These small ranchers had fought Indians and resisted the deadly plagues of droughts, sweeping blue blizzards, loneliness, thirst and hunger, and the score and one other hazards of the hard Pecos country. They were far from hired killers and heartless men. They, too, believed in the righteousness of their cause. The Kid had once eaten their bread and accepted their hospitality and, although he was now against them, he certainly had no personal quarrel with them.

Young Bob Beckwith, only a little over a year older than Billy, was a typical example of these Pecos ranchers. On Wednesday, July 11th, the tall, attractive Bob took time out to write a letter to a younger sister back home in Seven Rivers. Her name was Josie, and by some strange set of circumstances the touching note he sent her is still preserved:

My dear sister:

Today we will start to look after them. We do not know where about in the country they are but suppose they are at Ruidoso or the Feliz. Our party or sheriff's posse number about 35 men. The Mob are too cowardly to come to us and fight—we will have to look for them like Indians. The Mob was routed on the 3rd and the sheriff pursued them down to the Pecos. We would have captured them but they returned to the plaza and 12 of us only had to contend against them at South Spring River. We held them there the 4th all day and they did not dare to come out and fight us—they shot a few shots at us from the house and did not touch any of us. Had the men from here come to our assistance we would probably have got some of them but they did not come until we sent for them, and when they came McSween's mob had escaped.

Now, Dear Sister, do not fret yourself about us, it does no good—and tell Mother and Camilia and Ellen not to either. God will be with us, and these murderers will not touch a hair on our heads. Dear Sister we are having a rough time of it but ere long we will be about ready to go home again.

Soon it was Sunday night July 14th, and McSween and his fighting men were gathering in the lawyer's fortress house. Messengers were quietly spreading the word to all the followers to report.

It would be a fight to the finish this time. For once there would be no military force rushed in from Ft. Stanton, eight miles away, to interfere and throw its weight on the Dolan side.

This would be *It*. And the Kid and the rest of McSween's bodyguard gladly accepted the challenge.

9

It was after midnight when Martin Chavis rode in with
his neighbors from his fine little ranch on the Hondo near
Picacho. There were some thirty men in the cavalcade,
and they had come for business. Most of them were native
New Mexicans, and they looked up to Don Martin as their
leader.

Shortly after the tall young Tom O'Folliard enlisted under Billy's banner for life, the two had dropped in at Martin's valley ranch. They were leading a pack horse loaded
with odds and ends of camp equipment. Horse thieves
had recently stripped Martin bare of everything but a
single animal, and he was trying desperately to plow with
it. Billy dismounted, and he and Tom shifted the gear
from their pack horse to their own saddles, and then they
turned the spare animal over to Martin.

Later when the boys again rode in, Chavis tried to give
the pony back to Billy. The Kid grinned and with a shake
of his head remarked that Martin didn't need to return
the horse. But the rancher insisted Billy take him back.
[Years later Martin Chavis said to Miguel Otero, one-time
Governor of the Territory: "Billy was one of the kindest
and best boys I ever knew. He was not bloodthirsty, he
was forced into killing in defense of his own life. . . . In

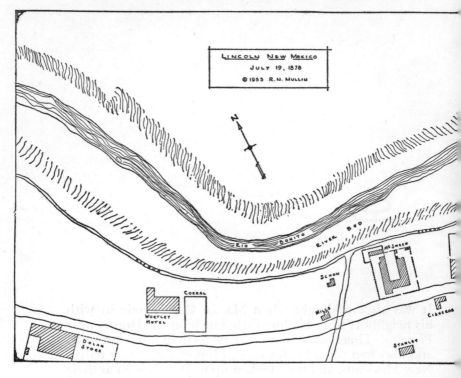

LINCOLN NEW MEXICO
JULY 19, 1878
© 1953 R. N. MULLIN

all his career he never killed a native citizen of New Mexico, which was one of the reasons we were all so fond of him."]

And now just as dawn was breaking Chavis and Billy met in the McSween corral. They embraced as old friends and expressed their happiness at being together. They were both brave men and true fighters. Together they walked into the house where McSween, Doc Scurlock, and several others were discussing the situation.

About all they were sure of at the moment was that the Peppin-Dolan faction had planted five or six men in the round, thick-walled, stone tower east of the Tunstall store, and that the main force was some distance to the south in the neighborhood of San Patricio. Apparently the sheriff expected to encounter the McSweenites there.

This older eastern part of the single-street town of Lincoln was largely made up of anti-Dolan residents. On to the west, upstream, and a good quarter mile away, was the

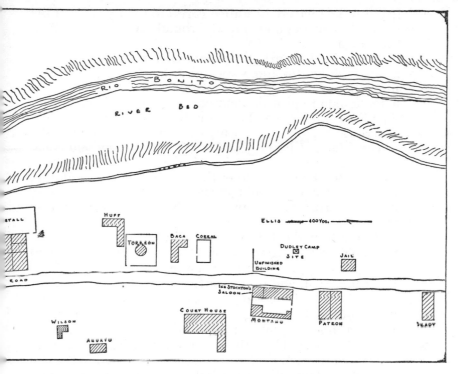

former Murphy-Dolan store, now under the charge of
young Edgar Walz, Tom Catron's brother-in-law. Across
the street from this store and a little to the east stood the
Wortley Hotel, long used as a sort of boarding house and
bar for men connected with the various Murphy-Dolan interests. It was Sheriff Peppin's hangout, and undoubtedly
it would now serve as his headquarters.

It was to be expected that before long "Dad" Peppin
would be galloping into town with his own posse, strengthened by the ranchers and hard fighters from Seven Rivers.
Eventually he was certain to have the Rio Grande killers
under John Kinney.

It didn't take long for the men in the McSween home to
formulate their plans. They assigned most of the volunteers under Martin Chavis and Doc Scurlock to the heavily built Montano building, to the east and across the road.
Some 300 yards further on they planted men in the Ben
Ellis store building. All the horses of the Regulators were

led into the high adobe-walled corral to the rear. This Ellis establishment was on below the round tower, held by Peppin's men.

George Coe, Henry Brown and Dick Smith were sent to a small adobe storeroom and bunk house a few yards behind the west end of the Tunstall store. This left about a dozen men to protect McSween in his fortress-like home: The Kid, Jim French, Tom O'Folliard, Jim Davis, Harvey Morris, a boy of twenty who was reading law under McSween, Martin Chavez, Jose Chavez y Chavez and Florencio Chavez and some five or six other native New Mexicans. Safely settled in their four thick-walled adobe buildings the McSween side could muster between forty and fifty men, well armed and supplied with plenty of ammunition and food.

By the time the July sun had climbed up over the low, flat roofs everything was in order for a full siege; buckets of water were placed in each house, shutters closed, loopholes prepared, and every provision made for a desperate fight. There had been some talk of Mrs. McSween and her sister and family leaving their house and taking with them Dr. Ealy, his wife and two little girls, Pearl, aged four, and the four-month-old Ruth, and the attractive twenty-year-old young woman, Katherine Gates, now settled in the east wing of the Tunstall store. But the women refused to budge.

Along towards noon Deputy Sheriff John Long approached the front of the McSween house and shouted that he held warrants for McSween, the Kid, and several others, and he called upon them to surrender to the law. There were angry and derisive answers from inside the house, and Long turned and walked away. He had made his gesture and escaped unharmed.

2

The Kid and the other fighters in McSween's own group soon decided that Sheriff Peppin's men in the ancient round torreon were too great a threat and must be forced out. The riflemen posted there were getting their water and supplies from Captain Baca's house that lay close by. Both the tower and the Baca dwelling belonged to McSween, and he at once dispatched a note to the heavy-whiskered New Mexican. McSween did not particularly relish the orders he wrote out:

LINCOLN, N.M.
JULY 15, 1876

Captain Saturnino Baca,
Sir:

I want you to vacate the property now occupied at once. Unless you leave the house within three days proceedings will be instituted against you without further notice.

You have consented to so improper use of the property by murders for the purpose of taking my life, and I can no longer consent to your occupancy thereof.

Respectfully,
A. A. McSween

The harassed and frightened Captain Baca, who up to the present had held a middle course in the vendetta, sent off a note to Colonel Dudley at Fort Stanton, eight miles to the southwest. He explained that a few days previously his wife had presented him with a baby and that she could not safely be moved. He pleaded that as an old soldier he deserved special protection for his wife and nine children. Col. Dudley at once sent Dr. Appel, the post surgeon, to investigate. The doctor talked over matters with McSween, who agreed that the family could remain on for the present if Baca did not give further aid to the Peppin men in the tower.

Late that Monday afternoon the Seven Rivers contingent rode into town, and the firing began. There were no casualties save for a horse and a mule. The Pecos men established themselves at the Wortley Hotel, a good 200 yards to the west.

By Tuesday the McSween men, posted on the flat, dirt roof of the Montano building, controlled the single street of the village and pretty well dominated the situation. Sheriff Peppin countered by sending sharpshooters to the hills south of the *placita,* and a bloodless, long-range shooting match took place. Towards evening Jimmy Dolan convinced the sheriff that he should send a messenger to Colonel Dudley. The appeal read:

LINCOLN, N.M.
JULY 16, 1876

Genl. N. A. M. Dudley,
Comdg. Fort Stanton, N.M.
General:

I have the honor to respectfully state that mostly all the men for whom I have United States warrants are in town, and are being protected by A. A. Mc-Sween and a large party of his followers. They are in the houses of A. A. McSween, Ellis Sons, J. B. Patron and Jose Montano. They are resisting, and it is impossible for me to serve the warrants. If it is in your power to loan me one of your howitzers, I am of the opinion the parties for whom I have said warrants would surrender without a shot being fired. Should it be in your power to do this, in favor of the law, you would confer a great favor on the majority of the people of this county, who are being persecuted by a lawless mob.

Geo. W. Peppin,
Sheriff, Acting Deputy
U. S. Marshal.

Lt. Col. Dudley, who held the rank of Brevet Brigadier General of Volunteers and thus rated the courtesy title of "General," apparently was scrupulous in his decisions. He refused the request, but in his answering note made it clear that he would have willingly furnished the help if it had been possible to do so under his stringent War Department orders not to interfere nor to use his troopers as a *posse comitatus*. He dispatched a mounted soldier with his reply.

A single rifle shot was fired in the general direction of the courier riding down the middle of the dusty street, shimmering under the hot July sun. It is logical to assume that it may have been done deliberately by a Dolanite, but the incident was immediately blamed on the McSween side and was so reported by the soldier.

It was too good a chance to pass up, and when Private Berry Robinson, Co. H, 15th Infantry, rode back to the fort after delivering his note to the sheriff, he carried a second message from Peppin:

General:

I have the honor to acknowledge the receipt of your very kind favor to date; am very sorry I can't get assistance I asked for, but I will do the best I can. The McSween party fired on your soldier when coming into town. My men on seeing him tried their best to cover him, but of no use. The soldier will explain the circumstances to you.

I take this opportunity of thanking you for your kindness in name of all my posse.

Wednesday broke clear and hot. Firing had ceased between the men on the flat roof of the Montano building and the two Peppin sharpshooters hiding behind the rocks on the hillside to the south. The sun was blazing down through a cloudless white sky, and no breath of air relieved the terrific summer heat. The pair of possemen on the hillside, deciding that there was little need to remain longer under the pitiless sun, boldly but unwisely started for the Wortley Hotel, Charlie Crawford in the lead.

At that very moment Fernando Herrera raised his head over the roof parapet of the Montano house and took a quick look. Instantly he brought up his buffalo gun for the long shot. The heavy slug tore through Charlie Crawford's hips. Charlie's sidekick, Lucio Montoyo, took it down hill on a high lope, dodging in and out among the giant boulders until he reached the safety of a small arroyo. All that morning Crawford lay hatless and helpless, under the cruel midsummer sun. There were no Peppin volunteers to try for his rescue.

Along about noon Captain Blair and a young lieutenant, accompanied by Dr. Appel, rode into town with a detachment of cavalry, to conduct a semi-official investigation of the charge that Private Robinson had been shot at while performing his duties. It was a slender reed for Colonel Dudley to lean upon, but it offered some little possibility of finding an excuse to bend his strict War Department orders to his liking. Captain Blair called McSween to his front door for an explanation, and the lawyer insisted none of his men had fired at the courier. But the officer favored the testimony of the Peppin men that the shot had come from one of the four barricaded houses occupied by the McSweens.

The Private Robinson investigation, however, was pushed aside when the officers heard of the pitiful position of Charlie Crawford, lying mortally wounded halfway up the hillside. Here was an errand of mercy worthy of a post surgeon and a cavalry officer of the United States Army. Boldly they walked up the hillside to the critically wounded man. Dr. Appel gave him first aid but the loss of blood and the shock and the deadly exposure to the sun had left little hope. The two men began the difficult descent, packing Crawford between them. They were soon met by several troopers, and the wounded man was carried to The House, and an orderly was sent posthaste to the fort for the ambulance. The unfortunate Charlie died two nights later in the fort hospital.

Late on Wednesday afternoon, shortly after Army Surgeon Appel had taken the wounded Crawford to Ft. Stanton, young Ben Ellis was struck in the neck by a stray bullet while feeding the Regulators' horses in his corral. As soon as it grew dark and just before the moon came up, two of the McSween men from the Ellis home quietly waded up the Bonito, crawled over the corrals at the back of the Tunstall store, and approached the Ealy living quarters. Dr. Ealy readily agreed to accompany them back in order to minister to young Ellis, but they were fired on from the torreon and forced to abandon the attempt.

Early the following morning Dr. Ealy, carrying his medical case and accompanied by his wife and two children, walked straight down the center of the street to the tower. No shot came from the Peppin men there. On down past the Montano house, with its large detachment of McSween men, the plucky quartet marched. Still no shot. And now the strange little procession turned in at the barricaded store and dwelling of the Ellis family. The good doctor tended the sick man and was invited to remain but declined. Then the little army without banners or drums valiantly retraced its steps to the Tunstall store.

Later, the desultory firing was resumed, and Thursday morning passed at a snail's pace. With Dudley and his troopers restrained by army orders from openly interfering, it was clear to Peppin and his posse that, unaided by the military, they could never dislodge the McSween men from their heavy defense positions that were covered with cross fields of fire.

In desperation Jimmy Dolan rode over to the fort. Apparently, on the Monday when most of the householders had pulled out, several neutral women had refused to leave Lincoln, but on this Thursday those who had not left dispatched a note to Dudley asking for protection. It might well be that it was this request, possibly instigated by the sheriff, rather than Dolan's argument that turned the trick of bringing in the soldiers.

That night, when Dolan returned from Ft. Stanton to the Wortley Hotel with a hopeful report, Andy Boyle, one-time British officer and ne'er-do-well, sneaked down to the tower and passed the word to the men to hold on, since tomorrow their luck would change. Deputy Jack Long accompanied Boyle back to the hotel. Long wanted to be sure he missed nothing.

No hint of any change in the general situation had come to the Kid and the McSween followers, but there seemed little doubt in their minds that morning would bring a victory for their side. The Peppin-Dolan people had not so much as dented their defenses. The attackers would soon have to acknowledge they had once again failed.

The moon was bright this night and the guards on the roofs and by the portholes had never seen the eastern sky more colorful than it was when dawn broke and Friday the 19th swept in.

3

Brisk firing began around seven o'clock in the morning. Billy and the ten men in the McSween house took keen pleasure in sniping at any of the Peppin-Dolan crowd they sighted outside the thick walls of the Wortley Hotel up the street or in the round tower to the east.

Despite the fact that, while most of the McSween men were settled in the Montano and Ellis dwellings below, there was no question but that the Kid and the other fighters in the lawyer's house continued to be the main target of the sheriff's posse, McSween was the man who was most wanted. As long as he lived the war would go on. With Tunstall killed and with John Chisum run off from his Pecos holdings, the lawyer was the one remaining figure big enough to supply the ammunition and other necessities to a fairly large group of followers.

Capture the thick-walled McSween stronghold, Peppin and Dolan commanded, or destroy it by fire or cannon or by any other method; force McSween and the others to surrender, or kill them if they tried to escape. But never forget that McSween was the man most wanted.

Inside the McSween house there was considerable rejoicing. Billy and the others had crossed up the sheriff's posse. The Regulators installed here and their companions entrenched in the houses down the road covered the single street and the approaches to the lawyer's adobe fortress. They were winning. Hold out a little longer and the sheriff's gang would have to pull out.

So hopeful of victory was McSween himself that early that Friday morning he wrote a short note to Ash Upson in Roswell. Recently Ash had opened a sort of perambulating school for the few ranch children in the neighborhood—and he wanted his pay. Ash had managed to carry water on both shoulders through the desperate six months of the war. He was an amiable near-genius, a scraggly, slender, broken-nosed man in his middle fifties, who made it his business never to drink except when he was alone or with somebody. The letter read:

ALEX A. MC SWEEN
DAVID P. SHIELD

LAW OFFICE
of
McSween and Shield
Lincoln County Bank Building
LINCOLN, NEW MEXICO
JULY 19, 1878

Dear Ash—

Please send me $3.00 in stamps. I am here O.K. I suppose you hear queer versions. Right will triumph.

Just as soon as the Commissioners can come together your school business will be attended to.

Yours,
A. A. McSween

Stamp the letters *un*stamped now.

The note was never mailed. And by some queer twist

of fate it survived the tragedies of that desperate night and is still preserved.

4

Shortly before eleven o'clock that Friday morning a lookout on the roof of the McSween house shouted down that there was a cloud of dust rising in the west where the road from Fort Stanton entered the upper end of the town. The man's relayed bulletins soon left little doubt as to the new and deadly turn of events.

The dust settled for a spell on the brow of the hill, a short distance west of the old Dolan store. Through his glasses the lookout could see men dismount, while others piled out of several wagons in the rear. Then a column was formed. They were soldiers, right enough.

Several officers were out in front with a small detachment of cavalry. Horses were hitched to two or three objects that looked like small cannon or possibly Gatling guns. Behind them came a file of foot soldiers and two or three wagons. The column was moving out. It was passing the old Murphy store now. Soon it halted in front of the Wortley Hotel, and Col. Dudley on his bay horse was leaning over and talking with Sheriff Peppin.

Now they were coming down the road at a walk. No one was in sight save this column of soldiers. They were almost in front of the McSween house. You could count them now; thirty-five soldiers, with Colonel Dudley and Captains Purrington and Blair, and Surgeon Appel and three or four lieutenants. And there were two small mountain howitzers and one Gatling gun mounted on gun carriages.

McSween and Billy and the others in the house tensely watched through their portholes. The column silently marched on down the street, half enveloped in the dust kicked up by the horses and the foot soldiers and issue wagons trailing behind.

Some of the men within the house cursed in desperation. The Kid did his best to minimize the new danger. Firing ceased, and only the jingling of the troopers' rifles and their accoutrements, and the creaking of the wagons, broke the silence.

Then the lookout shouted down that the detachment

had halted in the open space just beyond the Montano store. Soon Colonel Dudley's headquarters tent with several smaller ones were pitched in the vacant lot. The officer approached the Montano building and now Martin Chaves, one of the McSween leaders, could be seen leaving the house and walking up to Colonel Dudley's tent.

Soon Surgeon Appel headed for the Ellis store below and then returned to Dudley's headquarters with Isaac Ellis. And now Sheriff Peppin came riding down the road from the west, past the McSween house, with three troopers as an escort.

McSween and the tight-lipped men with him in his beleaguered house could only guess what had happened; Colonel Dudley, halting his column in front of Wortley's Hotel, had called for the Sheriff and formally announced that he had not come to help him but only to protect the women and children in the town who had asked for assistance. A little later Dudley had bluntly informed Martin Chavis of the Regulators that, should any of the soldiers be fired on, he would turn his howitzers on the house from which came the shots; and that if there were any women or children in the Montano building they must leave at once.

Nor could the Kid and the others now trapped in the McSween house know that when Surgeon Appel came with Isaac Ellis to the tent they were joined by Sheriff Peppin, and that to them Colonel Dudley had repeated his ultimatum: at the first shots from any house he would bring his cannon into action. This went for both sides, he had insisted.

McSween's men were also in the dark as to what had transpired in Dudley's subsequent interview with Squire Wilson: that Colonel Dudley told him the three officers comprising the informal Board of Investigation the previous day had found the McSween side guilty of firing on Private Robinson, when this mounted messenger rode into town on official business.

Dudley demanded that the Justice of Peace immediately issue a warrant for the arrest of McSween as the responsible party. Wilson shook his head. The matter was a federal affair, and he had no authority to make out such a warrant.

Dudley's face reddened with anger. By God! if Wilson

didn't immediately sign a warrant he would put him in irons! Wilson held out for a spell, but he finally gave in and filled out the paper. It was handed to Sheriff Peppin, who turned it over to Marion Turner for service.

There was more movement out front of the McSween house. The sheriff with his guard of three troopers trotted back westward up the street. And now Marion Turner came straight to the McSween house with five armed men of the sheriff's posse.

For the McSween men to fire on them would obviously bring on some terrible but uncertain reprisal from the soldiers. The deputies marched up close to one of the closed shutters at the front and shouted that they held a warrant for McSween's arrest.

"Hell! We got warrants for some of you men!" a voice inside the house answered.

"Why don't you come out and serve 'em?" Turner asked.

Dire warnings were given that the military had cannon and would blow the house to bits if any soldier was fired on. Then Turner and his five from Seven Rivers turned on their heels and walked away.

There were stray soldiers up and down the street by this time. It meant that the McSween men would have to hold their fire. They'd be licked now. It was asking a man to fight with one arm tied behind his back. The Kid's work was cut out for him from then on. Some of the men were beginning to grumble openly.

5

The suspense had already begun to tell on McSween. While the six-man posse was still on the outside of the house, the lawyer hurriedly began a note to Dudley. Minnie Shield, the courageous little twelve-year-old niece of Mrs. McSween, volunteered for the ticklish job of delivering it to the soldier's camp. It was inconceivable that any man would deliberately open fire on a child. The note read:

Gen. Dudley, U.S.A.

Would you have the kindness to let me know why soldiers surround my house. Before blowing up my property, I would like to know the reason. The con-

stable is here and has warrants for the arrest of Sheriff
Peppin and posse for murder and larceny.

> Respectfully,
> A. A. McSween.

The wisp of a girl walked straight out of the front door,
on down past the tower and the Montano house, to the
camp. A soldier led her to the Colonel's tent and she delivered her letter. The Colonel gently asked if she would
take back an answer and she replied that of course she
would. The Adjutant wrote out the communication under the Colonel's dictation:

> I am directed by the Commanding Officer to inform
> you that no soldiers have surrounded your house, and
> that he desires to hold no correspondence with you.
> If you desire to blow up your house, the Command-
> ing Officer does not object, provided that it does not
> injure U.S. soldiers.

In the meantime other important events had been tran-
spiring. Martin Chavez, returning from his short conference with Colonel Dudley, had explained to the score of
men with him the ultimatum he had been given. Their
usefulness was now ended. They could no longer protect
the front and east ends of the McSween and Tunstall positions, because at best they would have to fire over the
heads of the soldiers, who were walking back and forth
between them and their friends.

The only thing to do was to slip out of the back door
of the Montano house, sneak over to the Ellis lot, get
their companions there, saddle up their horses in the corral to the rear, and ride off. They might be of some service
as a free-moving force on the outskirts of the town.

The Chavez group were immediately joined by Doc
Scurlock, Bowdre, and Middleton, and shortly the whole
crowd mounted and trotted out of the east corral gate.
They cut across the Bonito and found a trail that led them
into a narrow canyon north of the Bonito. They could
work their way on west to a point behind the McSween
house, where they might render some aid to their trapped
companions.

The group had little more than pulled out from the
Ellis corrals when the tall, pleasant Bob Beckwith, the

nineteen-year-old son of old Hugh Beckwith of Seven Rivers, appeared with one or two men in the little store in
the front part of the Ellis building. He demanded a can of
coal oil. Ellis had nothing to do but fill a gallon can from
his barrel of coal oil and turn it over to young Beckwith.

Possibly two and a half hours had now passed since
Dudley's column had marched down the street to the lot
below the tower. All McSween men in the important
Montano and Ellis buildings were now gone. Suddenly
the lawyer's house seemed to be practically surrounded
on all sides by Peppin's gang.

In the lull that had followed the realization of the terrible consequence if a stray bullet from the McSween
house should hit a soldier or a noncombatant, the sheriff's
men had been able to occupy the Steve Stanley home and
the other adobe buildings to the west. Armed possemen
could be seen at the northwest corner of McSween's back
lot and behind the adobe stable. A wave of excitement
broke over the men in the McSween house when a soldier
or two were spotted moving among the sheriff's men now
settled around the house.

The lawyer was taut, his nerves all but gone. Billy coolly
moved from one lookout point to another. He was cheery
and undaunted. Now and again he whistled some little
tune. Without even knowing it he had become the leader.

The presence of Dudley's troopers placed a terrific
handicap on the men inside the house. They had no illusions as to what would happen if a soldier was hit or could
even claim that he had been fired on. But the defenders
dared not stop all firing.

For the moment they were busy watching from the
front and west wing of the big house. The Shields' kitchen
at the back end of the east wing was apparently left un-
guarded for a short period. John Long and a partial mute
known as "Dummy" suddenly crossed the empty lot to the
rear and, pushing open the door, threw in some paper and
shavings and dumped the contents of the coal oil can on
the wooden floor. "Dummy" had just struck a match when
firing opened on the trespassers from the McSween guards
posted in the storeroom and bunk house behind the Tunstall store, possibly thirty paces to the east.

Buck Powell stepped out from the protection of the
adobe wall and walked to the open gateway in the rear in

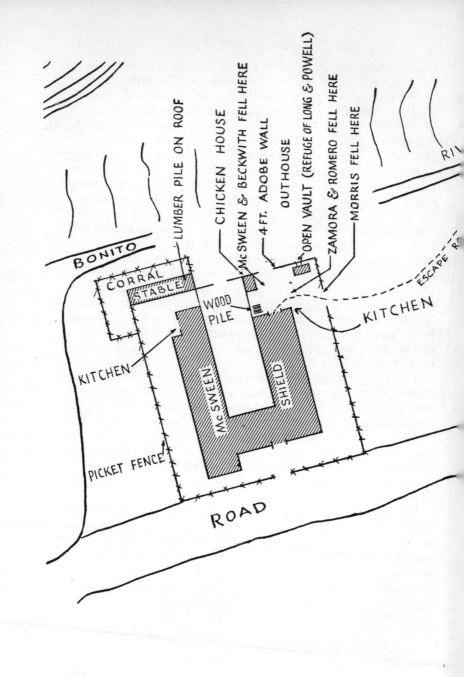

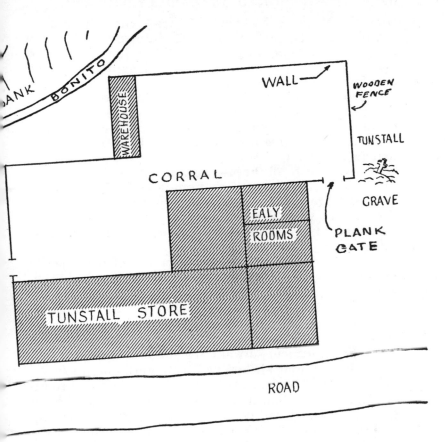

order to cover John Long and "Dummy." That moment
bullets zinged by Powell, cutting him off from the wall.
Close by stood the McSween "two-holer," its pit an open
trench leading to the irrigation ditch 25 or 30 feet away.
All three Dolanites were now under fire from the men
looking out through a high ventilator in the storeroom at
the rear of the Tunstall store.

The three broke for safety. "Dummy," who had difficulty in talking and had no more brains than the law al-
lows, ran ahead and managed to reach the cover of the
adobe wall which bordered the rear of the McSween back
yard. Long and the tough Buck Powell, under heavy fire
and cut off from the protection of the back wall, zigzagged
to their right and jumped into the open sewer that led off

from the McSween backhouse. It was a vile and unpleasant place but far preferable to the alternative of lying in
the yard under a boiling July sun with a shot through the
guts. The two deputies remained in their unhappy port
of safety until darkness rescued them.

When little Minnie Shield came flying into the living
room of the east wing with the news that the kitchen was
on fire, her mother grabbed a reserve bucket of water and
succeeded in putting out the flames. The three men hidden in the Tunstall storeroom had done the firing and
were able to control the area around this rear door. They
gleefully saw to it that Jack Long and Buck Powell remained marooned in their privy sewer. The attempt to
fire the east wing of the house had failed, and only poor
shooting had kept all three of the men involved from being
killed.

Leading off from the northwest corner of the opposite
or west wing, was a second small kitchen that had originally been intended only for summer use. With the arrival of the Shield family, Mrs. McSween had given up her
own living quarters in the east wing and converted this
small hot-weather kitchen for her regular use.

In the excitement surrounding the first attempt to use
fire, this northwest kitchen had temporarily been left un-
guarded. Andy Boyle, ex-British soldier and general roustabout, carrying a bunch of shavings and several dry boards
he had ripped off the roof of the nearby stable, slipped up
and quickly placed his tinder on the wooden steps of the
entrance and against the rear door. He carefully touched
a match to the shavings, and when he saw they were well
afire he pulled out at a run for the safety of the high wall
behind him.

A brisk wind was blowing from the west. By the time
the men in the McSween house smelled the smoke the
kitchen door and planks underneath were ablaze. Billy
and the others kicked open the door and tried to put out
the flame, but it only created a draft for the fire. It was
this strong west wind that did the dirty work. But even
with this help, it was a deadly slow process for the fire to
creep across the wooden floors and along the round cedar
vigas of the ceilings, and then burn through the door of
each succeeding room of this west wing. Thick choking

smoke now and again pushed on ahead of the slow fire.

Only the miracle of a sudden shift of the wind might have helped. The men inside were caught in an ever narrowing trap—and they knew it.

The Kid grinned a little more than usual. He wasn't whipped yet. He was gay and encouraging. Come on, Mr. McSween, don't take it so hard! They'd still find a way out. Maybe the wind would shift.

Quien sabe? Who knows? Who knew anything but to keep on fighting. And you died but once!

6

It was close to four o'clock when Mrs. McSween, fearful of the heavy firing, crawled on her hands and knees to the front door, opened it cautiously, then rising boldly walked to the street and straight to the army camp. She pushed her way by the guard and entered Colonel Dudley's tent, interrupting the drink he was having with John Kinney, the leader of the Rio Grande mob. The interview was stormy and it came to nothing. Mrs. McSween berated the pompous officer for permitting the sheriff's ruffians to burn down her house and possibly kill her husband. Dudley suggested that for all he knew McSween might have set fire to the house himself, as the lawyer had threatened to blow it up in his note.

He had never sent any such note, she shrilled. Show it to me! Give me that note! How dare you refuse me?

She was beside herself in anger and fear. Hate of this officer, who had betrayed her husband's almost certain victory and now refused to help him escape death, fairly consumed her. She was like a mad woman as she screamed her denouncements. Then, exhausted and defeated, she swung out of the tent and walked back to the doomed house.

She had no more than reached its temporary safety when the Chavis-Scurlock riders appeared at the mouth of the canyon across the river to the north and began firing at the Peppin men in the upper part of the town, to the west of the soldier camp. The sheriff spread out his possemen in a skirmish line and moved on foot towards the mounted group, opening fire at 600 yards.

The McSweenite riders saw that their rescue attempt was futile, and they rode off. Even if they whipped the posse they would still have to fight the soldiers and their deadly cannon.

10

Gloom and fear was almost as thick as the smoke that filled the few rooms still remaining in the McSween house. There were murmurs of surrender.

Why stick in this death trap until you were burned to death or killed trying to escape? Why not give up?

The Mexicans spoke their pieces in their native tongue. Billy answered them in Spanish; he was soft-spoken and did not curse them; he was their *amigo*; they could trust him; he'd get them out alive. Just be *muy valiente! Muy fuerte, amigos!* Be very strong and very brave, pals! Trust him to lead them out. Wait until it was dark. Then they could slip out for the river.

They slowly backed from the big living room, facing the street. There were only three rooms left in the east wing. The dull-red, slowly-moving fire was creeping towards them like a deadly snake. But twilight would be coming soon. Then it would grow dark. That would be the time to try for an escape into the welcoming night.

The men grimly took up their positions behind the deep window ledges and the portholes. The four children of the Shield family were almost underfoot, with the mother holding her nursing baby and quietly directing her flock. Some weeks before this her lawyer husband, conscious of the violence of the feud, had left for Las Vegas to open a law office and find a home for his family.

All this wild day Mrs. Shield had remained with her sister, Mrs. McSween, refusing to leave the house despite the terrible danger she was taking with her children's lives. She had carefully settled them against the thick adobe walls and kept them well below the level of the bottom of the window sills and safe from any possibility of rifle shots.

Mrs. McSween stayed close to her husband, save only for the humiliating visit she had made to Colonel Dudley's tent. McSween had utterly exhausted himself and seemed on the verge of collapse.

Billy looked down at the courageous and strong-willed Susan McSween, and bowed slightly. His remarks are authenticated: "I expect, Ma'am, you better leave soon. A dress ain't very good to make a run in."

He gestured towards the Shield family as he spoke. But there was sturdy discipline and character in these Pennsylvanians. They would not desert their relative, Mrs. McSween. They would wait for her to make the move.

Some thirty yards to the east of the burning McSween home stood the Tunstall building, and in the far or east end Dr. Ealy, his wife and two children and the young Katherine Gates, had settled themselves during the long siege. They were of the missionary breed. No blood lines tied them to this hard, bitter woman next door, but they, too, were stern and unbending. They had refused to accept asylum when they marched together down the street to give aid to the stricken Ben Ellis. They had proudly returned to their dangerous post. Dr. Ealy felt deeply the justice of the McSween cause, but he saw now that it was not fair to these women and children for them to chance being killed for the sake of pride. It was high time to leave.

He turned to his desk and wrote out a brief note to Colonel Dudley, asking that his family and their few possessions be rescued by the military. Katherine Gates, the attractive young companion and helper, volunteered to deliver the message.

Colonel Dudley was courteous but formal. He would comply with the request. He at once ordered Captain Blair, Lieutenant Goodwin, and three soldiers to take a wagon to the Tunstall building and remove the family and their personal possessions.

Bright colors were beginning to show in the western sky when the wagon drew up. All firing ceased while the two officers and their men went swiftly about the business of the rescue. They were almost finished when Mrs. Mc-Sween stepped out the door of her own burning home and crossed to the gate in the board fence which separated the two lots. She addressed Captain Blair, and there was no longer abuse and violence in her tone. Could the Shield family and herself have protection?

"Yes, madam," Captain Blair answered stiffly. "If you will all come over here and join the Ealy group."

Mrs. Shield gathered up an armful or two of clothing, and a few pieces of furniture. The soldiers carried them to the wagon; they then helped the Shield children join the missionary brood from the Tunstall building, shepherded by the pretty Katherine Gates.

It was a terrible moment for the McSweens. They both knew how little chance there was that they would ever again see each other alive. They kissed goodbye. Holding herself erect, the woman stepped out the door of the doomed house. She walked towards the little group waiting for her in front of the Tunstall store. For a moment a billow of smoke from the burning *vigas* and pine floors of her home seemed to drop like a curtain between the heartbroken woman and all that she treasured in the world. Then the west wind blew it on by. But Susan McSween did not look back as, with head up, she marched down the street to the front of the Tunstall house.

2

By the time darkness came the dozen men inside the Mc-Sween house had been driven to the kitchen, the last remaining room of the east wing. There was nowhere else to go now. No longer was there time to waste.

A sense of futility and utter helplessness gripped McSween during this last hour. He had spent most of the period slumped in a corner, a broken and resourceless man, with all sense of leadership and pride gone.

The pure excitement and high adventure of the coming moment of decision sustained most of the others. But they were grim and there was no talk in them.

Not so with Billy. He seemed actually to relish the dangerous prospect that lay ahead. He danced a little jig and slapped the men on their backs and called them by their names. It would soon be dark enough to make the big break. Cheer up!

Each man must freshly load his pistol; put shells in all six chambers; fill up the magazines of the rifles; see that there were no empty loops in the leather cartridge belts.

Billy would give the signal: when he kicked open the door the men were to dash out single file; no jamming up at the door. There was a gate in the fence to the right, and another through the wall at the back towards the river. The gate to the right was best. The point was to help get McSween out alive.

Billy took a peek through a slit in the broken window shutters. The moon had not yet come up, but the slow-burning fire gave a dull glow to the whiffs of smoke driven by the wind into the patio in the rear. The southern stars hung like tiny lanterns in the dark-blue dome overhead. Now was the time, before the moon could betray them.

Billy was positive he had glimpsed soldiers in the uncertain light. Now and again he caught sight of a black shirt and army hat, as some tongue of bright flame from the burning building licked out into the darkness. He was sure he had seen at least three soldiers in the lot between the McSween and Tunstall buildings.

Tall, brave Tom O'Folliard said he'd go first. Jim French stood directly behind him. Young Harvey Morris stepped into the next place; Harvey, deep in his law reading, was only twenty and this was not his quarrel, yet he had elected to stay to the finish. Jim Davis was next in line.

Billy continued with his final orders: he would go out directly ahead of McSween, and the rest should follow as fast as they could get through the door. The first little group would try their best to keep down the fire of the men stationed behind the rear wall. They would break trail for McSween; he must give them a few moments' start in order to drive off the riflemen. Then he must follow close behind.

Billy helped the exhausted lawyer to his feet and tried to push a six-shooter into his hand. "Let's go out fighting," he urged. But the poor man could only shake his head and speak of God looking after him. It was a Colt that the Kid looked to for his own salvation.

Carefully Billy opened the door a scant inch. His men were lined up on one side, guns ready. A puff of smoke drifted from the lower west corner and for a moment blacked out the area ahead.

Billy flung open the back door and shouted, "Now, NOW!"

Like flashing shadows the men darted through the moving smoke and made for the gate to the right. They fired at the top of the wall as they ran. Then they slowed up the pace and deliberately emptied their guns. But they could not keep down the fire of the men crouching behind the wall barricade and rising only to shoot without aiming.

Young Harvey went down first, almost at the mouth of the east gate. Tom O'Folliard stooped to pick him up but changed his mind: he would only be killed himself. Jim French and Joe Chaves and the Kid broke out. There was firing from two sides as they made for the gate. They had done their best to open a path for McSween and the rest. They ran now like frightened deer towards the little river on to the left, each man for himself.

Lead was pouring into the east gate from two sides. McSween and the three natives with him hesitated, and then darted back. They could not face the hail of lead. Crouching low, they found shelter behind the wood pile in the southwest corner of the yard beside the kitchen door. It was a narrow back yard, 18 by 32 feet; the back of the kitchen made the south side, a four-foot adobe wall the west and north sides, and a wooden fence separated the yard from the Tunstall property on the east.

In the north wall of the yard, opposite the kitchen door, was a second gate. On to the east stood the outhouse, whose vault had proven so salutary for Buck Powell and John Long.

In the opposite, or northwest corner, near the rear gate, was a small chicken house. Two of the McSween party now ran through the smoke and gathering darkness to this final refuge.

The shooting slackened off. Six or seven yards away Bob Beckwith, Andy Boyle, Johnny Jones, Marion Turner, Joe Nash and "Dummy" guarded this north gate. They could not see their prey through the smoke and darkness, but they knew they had the remaining men trapped.

For a moment there was a lull in the firing. Then they could hear the voice of McSween asking if there was someone there who could receive his surrender.

"Yes," answered young Bob Beckwith, stepping out from the protection of the high adobe wall. "I can take your surrender."

Johnny Jones, a neighbor boy about his own age, joined him, along with Joe Nash and "Dummy." It was still too dark to make out anything but the outline of a man a short distance off.

A pistol shot barked out from the darkness. There was a dull grunt, and then the firing became general. Bob Beckwith, standing in the open gateway, went down with slugs through his head and wrist. Obviously he had been unaware of the McSween men concealed in the chicken house, hardly an arm's length away.

Five bullets tore the life out of McSween, and he fell half on top of Beckwith's body. Near him lay Vincente Romero and Francisco Samora, riddled with bullets. Close by Ygenio Salazar sprawled out, hit by two rifle shots.

There was a long moment of caution, followed by shouts and yells of victory. The sheriff's men poured into the patio. They bent over the dead men to identify them.

Over by the gate lay Harvey Morris. Next to the dead McSween were the three natives. They found their own Bob Beckwith near the adobe wall alongside the lawyer's body.

Later that night old Andy Boyle, poking with the muzzle of his rifle among the dead men, was not quite sure about Salazar. But why waste another shell on him?

The main thing was that McSween was as dead as a doornail. That was revenge enough. He was the man they had been after.

Break out the rotgut and let's have a celebration! Dolan's trip to Fort Stanton had done the trick. Lt. Colonel Dudley ought to be made a full major general. Open up another bottle!

Too bad that damn Kid Antrim didn't get his. God! he was hard to kill! But he'd be next. They wouldn't quit until they got him.

Look at that old moon coming up! Bet it was that lousy

Kid who figured out when to make the break from the house, while it was the blackest.

Five days it had taken to do the job. But it was worth it. Too bad old John Chisum hadn't been caught here with McSween. But he wouldn't bother 'em any more for a while. He'd been scared off.

3

A coroner's jury was called the first thing Saturday morning, for everything had to be legal and proper. It was a six-man jury composed completely of native New Mexicans, who were easy for Peppin to handle. The jury found that McSween, Harvey Morris, and two New Mexicans had come to their death by rifle shots from the hands of the sheriff's posse, while resisting arrest. Robert Beckwith had met his death by rifle bullets from the aforesaid quartet while he was trying to discharge his duty as a deputy sheriff.

Young Beckwith's body was taken to Fort Sumner and buried in the post's cemetery. The bodies of Francisco Samora and Vincente Romero were duly turned over to their families and hauled away.

Mrs. McSween, stern and dry-eyed in her grief, dispatched word to Sheriff Peppin for him not to dare touch her husband's body. She could not bring herself to look at him. The two Negro employees of the lawyer were sent to wrap his body in a blanket, and bury it in a simple pine box next the grave of Tunstall, a few yards to the east of the store.

There had been three native New Mexicans lying near McSween's body when the last of the sheriff's posse had pulled out from the smoldering building to their wild celebration at Wortley's Hotel. By morning when the men drifted back to look over the dead, there was one body missing. It was that of Ygenio Salazar.

Towards noon a woman quietly approached Dr. Appel, the army surgeon at Col. Dudley's camp. Would he come with her to examine a wounded man? He picked up his medicine case and followed. She led him to a little *adobe* house at the eastern end of town. Salazar was lying on the bed with two bullet wounds.

Dr. Appel dressed his wounds and told him that he

would live to tell his strange tale. For half a century he did just that: he had been crouching near McSween when the latter called out to surrender. Some of Salazar's own side had apparently started the firing. He felt the blow of a heavy .45 slug and was knocked unconscious and left for dead.

It was hours before he opened his eyes. The moon was high in the sky. Carefully he tried to move his hands and legs. In a little while he regained full consciousness and rejoiced that he was still living.

It took him a long time to crawl away from the dead men, slip through the north gate and down to the Bonito. He took a big drink of water and started working his way on hands and knees east to the house of his sister-in-law. Having heard that he had been killed, she was half frightened out of her wits when, just as dawn came, he called to her through the closed door and told her who he was. She took him in and late in the morning went for the army surgeon.

When Dr. Appel returned and reported to Colonel Dudley, the officer sent him back to get a sworn deposition from the wounded man. It took a second attempt before the man-who-couldn't-be-killed signed his mark on a paper that suited the worried Colonel. It might prove invaluable if Dudley had to face a court-martial as a result of his part in the bloody events of the previous day.

Late Friday night and Saturday morning men looted the Tunstall store. John Kinney and his Rio Grande killers fitted themselves out in new suits. Two or three of the more greedy New Mexicans carried away goods by the wagon load. The store records were torn and scattered and a new mowing machine Tunstall had ordered as a part of his program to improve agricultural practice in the valley was senselessly smashed to bits.

Sam Corbett, who had been in charge of the store, came in from where he had been hiding out during the fighting and tried unsuccessfully to board up the doors and windows. When he appealed to Sheriff Peppin to stop the looting, the sheriff merely shrugged his shoulders. It wasn't any of Peppin's business. However, for the clerk to have drawn a gun on the looters would have meant certain death to him.

4

The whole day of Bloody Friday had been a terrible experience for the men who had survived the ordeal of the burning house and the dash for life. Even Billy, hard as he was in spirit and body, must have felt all but the will-to-live drain out of him as he ran blindly down the rocky bank of the Bonito, finally falling exhausted on the rough ground on the right bank of the river.

He heard someone call out his name in a low voice. It was Tom O'Folliard. Jim French and one or two others were with Tom. Billy stood up and in the half darkness walked on down to where they lay. Maybe they better move further on, he whispered to them. Once they got well below the town they could turn right, cut across the road and follow the twisting trail that led south over the hills to the valley of the Ruidoso.

He was dead tired but he managed to pull himself together. He must get these boys of his away from this dangerous spot and to a place where they could hide and get some sleep.

Sleep! That's what they needed. They'd been fighting and riding and doing with a few hours' rest for days, even before they'd ridden into Lincoln. It seemed like months ago. And then had come these five awful days and nights at the McSween house when a man was lucky if he got as much as an hour or two of sleep at a stretch.

But sleep could wait. They had to keep moving now. They were still in the zone of danger. They had to keep going.

Billy walked on ahead. He was sure their three *compadres* planted in the little storeroom behind the Tunstall store had slipped out for the river when it began to grow dark. And the same would be true of Doc Scurlock and Fred Waite and Charlie Bowdre at the Ellis house. It was a safe bet that they had ridden off with Martin Chavis and his gang.

Billy and Tom and the others who had stuck with Mc-Sween had gotten the dirty end of the deal, but that was all right. They could still hear the bursts of reckless firing and then the yells of the sheriff's men, while they were hiding along the river.

Poor McSween! He'd ducked back just before he'd reached the gate. That meant sure enough that he'd been killed.

The moon was well up now. If they had waited another forty minutes it would have been so bright in the patio that none of them would have ever gotten out alive. It was something to be born lucky.

If they could just keep going another two hours they could split up and hide out in one or another of the little adobe houses along the Ruidoso. The native New Mexicans would take them in.

They were fagged out, at the end of their rope. They pulled off the trail to one side for a little rest. They had to have it.

Billy let them sleep for maybe an hour. He dozed off himself a time or two, but he had to keep awake, with his ears tuned to the possible sound of hoofbeats. You couldn't tell about that gang of bastards over at Lincoln: they'd be drunken crazy by this time. They might try to trail them down.

The moon was straight up in the bright blue sky when he spoke to his men. Though he still lacked four months of being nineteen, that's what they were now—*his* men.

He hadn't had to be elected captain at the time of crisis. He had simply taken over from the moment the soldiers marched into Lincoln and he knew the jig was up.

PART TWO

The Young Captain

11

Two mornings later the little bunch of survivors met in the hills back of the native ranch house where Billy and Tom O'Folliard had hidden out and slept the clock around.

Doc Scurlock was at the get-together, and so were Fred Waite and Charlie Bowdre and John Middleton, almost recovered from the bullet wound in his chest he had got in the fight at the Blazer Mill. There was bad news to report: Kinney's gang had been on east below where the two mountain streams formed the Hondo. The mob had ridden over to Tinnie and Picacho, probably thinking that what was left of the one-time Regulators would rendezvous at the Coes'.

Nothing was said about a leader, but everyone knew now that Billy was it. Doc Scurlock was six or eight years older and educated, but the war was over as far as he was concerned. He had his own little ranch and a New Mexican wife to worry about. The same went for Charlie Bowdre, who hailed from Texas and had a native wife and a two-room adobe on to the southeast in a bend in the Peñasco.

Most of them were ready to settle back and quit. Unfortunately that decision was not theirs to make. John Kinney's murderous crew and a few hard cases in "Dad" Peppin's old posse wouldn't let them quit.

The real conflict, called by the newspapers "The Lincoln County War," was over. But not so far as these boys, who had thrown in with John Tunstall and McSween and old John Chisum, were concerned. They were still in it up to their necks. They were now on the defensive. They were the ones being hunted. They had been on the right side, but unfortunately the right side was the side that had lost.

Let the Kid figure it out. He thought they ought to play mighty scarce for the next few days. Don't try to pick a fight. Run away from one if they had to. Get some horses, and then maybe head on east for the Pecos. Old John Chisum had skinned out, but his two brothers, Jim and Pitser, were there, still running the much smaller Chisum place, as well as what was left of the big Hunter & Evans outfit. Why not try it over there, at least until things quieted down here in the mountains? Men had to eat whether they were on the dodge or not.

It was now Sunday, August 5th. Nineteen days had dragged by since the Bloody Friday of the big killing. Most nights the men made dry camp wherever it looked safe, but now and again they would spread their blankets close to some little spring or seep of water. Once or twice Billy or one of the other men shot a deer and that night they'd feed good.

It was a loosely knit gang that rode with Billy. Men would casually ride in for two or three days, and then quite as casually slough off. Several native New Mexicans joined up. They liked Billy not only because he could talk their native tongue perfectly but because he was always thoughtful and kind to them. That was different from the way most Anglos and almost all *Tejanos* acted. "Beelie" was always taking the *Mexicano* side when there was any dispute.

2

The Kid hadn't forgotten his vow to get even with the gang that had killed the man he had worshipped more than any human being he had ever known, save only his mother. And in a rather odd way he still felt that it was his responsibility to look after what was left of the 400 head of cattle Tunstall had on the Rio Feliz when he was killed. Billy heard now that a part of the herd had been driven west and were being held at Frank Wheeler's ranch over in the Organ Mountains, on the other side of the White Sands. The trail leading there crossed through the Apache Reservation. Billy felt that it might be worth the try.

Agent Fred C. Godfrey and his clerk, young Morris J. Bernstein, were in the issue room of the agency giving out supplies, when a squaw by the door shouted, *"Tejanos!"* There was terror in her voice. The Texans were here—the feared and hated Texans.

Bernstein grabbed his rifle and ran to his horse that stood near the door "tied to the ground" cowboy fashion, the open reins dangling from the bridle. He was a salty, medium-sized young man in his middle twenties, and two years previously had been sent down as bookkeeper to the Murphy-Dolan store in Lincoln by the big wholesale firm of Speigelberg Bros. in Santa Fe. He had ended up as chief clerk at the Apache Reservation. He seemed to enjoy danger, for early in 1877 he had ridden with Frank Coe, Doc Scurlock, and Frank Freeman in a desperate attempt to trail a bunch of Mexican horse thieves to the Puerto de Luna country on the Pecos.

On this August day a year later he showed far more guts than judgment when he spurred his horse over the brow of the hill and disappeared into the timber of the far slope. Two or three young Apache bucks apparently rode with him.

Agent Godfrey, a rather unfortunate and misplaced man who was derisively called "the Presbyterian fraud," had taken over the Apache Reservation two years previously. He shouted to an Indian boy to make tracks for Blazer's Mill, a mile or two west, and bring the three soldiers stationed there. The boy was barely out of sight when the clerk's riderless horse galloped back to the issue house. The sound of firing had stopped. Godfrey excitedly asked one of the agency Indians to investigate; the Apache carefully made his way through the tall pines to the far side of the hill. In a few minutes he reported back that Bernstein was dead, with several bullet holes through him. The Indian was certain that he had seen men from the Ruidoso who had long been involved in fighting the soldiers and the Murphys. They were heading back east and it looked as if they were driving some loose ponies in front of them.

Godfrey had the Indian take him to Bernstein's body. He was sure that it was the work of that fellow they called Billy the Kid, probably with George Coe and some of those other Anglos who dubbed themselves Regulators. When Godfrey had got himself a little organized he dispatched a runner to Fort Stanton with an official message to be sent to the Indian Bureau in Washington. There was a new telegraph line that ran from Santa Fe down to Mesilla and on east through the agency to Fort Stanton. He still was a little excited when he wrote out his report:

SOUTH FORK, VIA MESILLA
AUG. 5, 1878

Morris J. Bernstein my clerk today was brutally murdered by McSween outlaws near the issue room. Myself and Indians were also fired upon but escaped unhurt. Attacking party supposed to number forty. Business of this office will be somewhat delayed in consequence.

The Apache messenger carried such additional information to Colonel Dudley as the frightened agent had been able to gather. With Godfrey's telegram went one from Dudley to his superior officer, General Hatch. The report was handed out at Santa Fe, and the various men and groups interested saw that it was given plenty of circulation: newspaper correspondents in the New Mexican capital wired the news to their city papers; Sheriff Peppin reported it in an affidavit. Colonel Dudley enlarged on it in his official report. Governor Axtell telegraphed his version to Secretary of the Interior and to the President, in support of his request for troops. Always it was the McSween adherents who had committed the outrage.

That week's issue of the Mesilla *Independent* gave a little different version. The piece was reprinted in the Cimarron *News & Press*:

> It is positively asserted that Bernstein was killed by a Mexican who was with a party bound from San Patricio to Tularosa to assist in recovering a lot of stolen stock in the possession of Frank Wheeler and others at San Nicholas. When the Mexicans reached the water alongside of the road above the Agency, they stopped to water their horses. Bernstein saw them and probably supposing them to be a party of the Regulators, attacked them with a party of Indians; he rode upon one Mexican and fired two shots at him; the man took shelter behind a tree. Bernstein still advancing rode close to the tree and fired again at the man who returned the fire and killed Bernstein.
>
> The Mexican says he acted strictly in self-defense and will at any time deliver himself up for trial. His name is Atanacio Martinez.

Before Dolan and Sheriff Peppin became supreme, Martinez had served as a constable in Lincoln and had been definitely pro-McSween. It was he who went to the Dolan store with Billy and Fred Waite with warrants for the Tunstall murderers and was arrested and held by Sheriff Brady along with the other two.

Martinez was never indicted for the Bernstein killing, but federal warrants were immediately issued against Billy, George Coe, Fred Waite, and Henry Brown. Later the government quashed all the indictments save that against the Kid.

It was to be that way from now on. Billy was to be held personally responsible for fully half the crimes committed in the county.

3

The day following the tragedy at the agency, Colonel Dudley ordered Lieutenant Goodwin and a detachment of troops to pursue Billy and his party. It was a federal matter and Dudley moved on his own authority. But he was wasting his men and horses.

Word was brought to Billy as soon as the troopers trotted out of the Fort. The news settled all indecision on the part of the Regulators. It was time to pull stakes.

Frank and George Coe, and an older cousin Al who had remained peacefully minding his own business on his Peñasco ranch during the feud, made immediate plans to leave for the new San Juan County up in the northwestern part of the Territory. Within two or three years they would be back on their rich little ranches on the Ruidoso. [Almost a half century later Frank Coe, a competent and successful citizen, wrote out for an El Paso paper his estimate of the boy with whom he had ridden stirrup to stirrup. It is as authentic a picture of the Kid during these days of the Lincoln County War as will ever be found:

> Billy the Kid took sides with the people of the country, to fight for our property and our lives. He stood with us to the end, brave and reliable. He never pushed in his advice or opinions, but he had a wonderful presence of mind; the tighter the place the more he showed his cool nerve and quick brain. He was a fine horseman, quick and always in the lead, at the same time he was kind to his horses and could save them and have them ready and fresh when he needed to make a dash.
>
> I hope I have made it clear that at the beginning he was not the blood-thirsty, hard desperado that history has made him out to be. That he ever killed as many men as he is given credit for, or ever killed for money, is absurd. He never seemed to care for money, except to buy cartridges with; then he would much prefer to gamble for them straight. Cartridges were scarce, and he always used about ten times as many as anyone else. He would practice shooting at every thing he saw and from every conceivable angle, on and off his horse. He never drank. He would go to the bar with anyone, but I never saw him drink a drop, and he never used tobacco in any form. Always in a good humor and ready to do a kind act to some one.
>
> Billy never talked much of the past; he was always looking into the future. He often spoke of his mother.]

Most of the older fighters were pulling out now. There can be little doubt but that they urged Billy to go along with them. Stay and a man would get killed. Leave the dangerous country for a while and then come back when the shooting was over.

Even Juan Patron, leading New Mexican of Lincoln and speaker of the Assembly in Santa Fe, finally left and located in Puerto de Luna, forty miles or so on north of Fort Sumner on the Pecos. [Within a year or two the brave Don Juan was shot to death as he sat by a lighted lamp in a house in the little village perched on the high ground above the twisting Pecos. The town bore the beautiful name of *Puerto de Luna,* Gateway of the Moon.]

Billy and his *compadres* figured they'd be safe up around Fort Sumner on the upper Pecos. It was in San Miguel County and thus outside the borders of Lincoln County. A murderous new gang called Selman's Scouts was forming on the lower Pecos below Seven Rivers. John Selman was a hard Texan who had drifted in from the buffalo country. And John Kinney and his Rio Grande toughs were still riding high, wide, and handsome in the mountain valleys and native *plazas* that bordered Lincoln and San Patricio. Maybe it was wrong to be leaving poor Lincoln County to these *bandidos.*

But Billy knew they'd all get killed if they stuck around. A man had to be practical in this tough world. So he gathered his little gang together and pulled out for the Pecos. There was Tom O'Folliard who always rode up ahead with him; and Fred Waite, the quarter blood Cherokee whom Billy thought a lot of; and Henry Brown and John Middleton. Doc Scurlock and Charlie Bowdre had decided they wouldn't leave their women here on the Ruidoso: they would keep well under cover, and maybe they'd move over to Fort Sumner after a while.

That made five of the old guard who still stuck together. They took along a pack horse to carry grub and their blankets. It was August now and, while the days were scorching, the nights were cool and pleasant.

Cautiously they rode up to the old Smith & Wilburn store at Roswell which had been run by Marion Turner and John Jones. The men watered their horses in the cold, clear North Fork of the great springs that broke out of a cutbank three or four miles to the west. Ash Upson met them at the store door. The town site and store had just acquired a new owner named Captain J. C. Lea, Ash explained. Lea was originally from Missouri, and he was supposed to have ridden with Quantrill's men during the Civil War: this was said at that time about most Missourians far away from home. He was close-mouthed and highly intelligent, and he knew exactly what he was after. At the moment he was out looking over a little batch of cattle.

But the really big news was that the Chisums had at least temporarily pulled out of South Spring, lock, stock, and barrel. They'd left two weeks ago, taking with them Old John's own private herd of 2,500 bred-up cattle. They were headed for the Canadian River country, over in what was called the Panhandle of Texas. It lay above the Staked Plains, and a hundred miles of waterless desert country separated it from Fort Sumner on the Pecos.

Kindly old Ash was talkative. Sure, he told the Kid, the whole Chisum outfit had cleared out: Old John's two brothers, Pitser and Jim, and Jim's two boys, and Miss Sally, the whole durned kit an' boodle. Right now they ought to be resting up at the old Chisum headquarters at Bosque Grande, thirty miles or so on up the Pecos.

Billy and his four followers made camp that night a few miles out of town. The sun was just beginning to boil down on them that next morning when they turned right and forded the Pecos at Lloyd's Crossing. There had been an unusual amount of rain, and the reddish, alkaline water was almost swimming-deep even here at the ford.

They'd get to the Bosque Grande around twilight; it was too hot to push horses. Billy would be glad to see Sally Chisum again. She was just about the first Anglo girl he'd known since he was grown who had been kind to him.

Maybe this move to Fort Sumner would open a new life for him. He'd done his best for John Tunstall, and for McSween, too. Uncle John Chisum owed plenty to him and the other boys. Maybe they'd get something out of him—and maybe not. He recalled a story Doc Scurlock told him about Old John: Doc was riding line above and back west from the Pecos with a young fellow named Newt Huggins. They'd each cover about ten miles, Hug-

gins riding east and Doc to the west. They'd meet each
noon at a little stone hut next to a spring.

One day when Doc rode in he found his mate stretched
out dead and scalped. Apaches or Comanches, Doc
couldn't be sure which. Doc dragged the body inside the
hut and pulled the door shut so the wolves couldn't get
at it, then he hit it back to the river and on downstream
to the ranch headquarters at Bosque Grande. He told
Uncle John about the tragedy and asked for his pay. He'd
had enough. Old John told him to forget it and go on
back to his line camp.

When Doc left that night he gathered up six head of
Chisum horses and lit out for Fort Sumner almost sixty
miles north. He figured the ponies would be worth about
what was coming to him in pay. Old John sent a couple
of his bullies to trail him, retrieve the horses, and have
Doc arrested. But when they caught up with Doc at Sumner and he told his side of the story, they turned their
ponies around and headed on back to the Bosque Grande.
All the poor Huggins boy who was killed and scalped got
out of it was to have the spring named after him.

John Tunstall would never have acted like that: he'd
have paid Doc and sent him to another camp. It was true
that the Tunstall estate still owed Billy and the others
wages for several months. Poor John couldn't help that.
Besides, nobody cared.

But rich Chisum was another matter. He owed the Regulators money, too. He had a bankful salted away up north
from the sale of his cattle.

It was time he settled up. A man couldn't live forever
on jawbone.

4

The cook was about to shout "Come and get it!" when
Billy and his four men jogged up to the old log headquarters at Bosque Grande.

Jim Chisum, the widower who was father of Sally and
her two brothers, told the boys they were just in time for
supper. A half dozen other men were squatting on their
heels near the front door or lounging against the ancient
hitching rack. The posts were peppered with holes the

boys had made in long-ago days when they had practiced with their six-shooters.

The log buildings were set in a grove of giant cottonwoods, from which the place took its name of *Bosque Grande*—Big Woods. The Rio Pecos lay west down the slope maybe a quarter mile away. There was a small spring back of the main house, but closer up was a dug well.

Uncle John had bought the place in 1867 from Jim Patterson, the first American with sufficient guts and fortitude to fight the Indians and white thieves and stick it out against loneliness and unrelenting attacks of a cruel Nature. Patterson had also built the big adobe fortress house on down the Pecos at South Spring, which he sold to Chisum in 1874.

This middle part of the great north and south range, which had once been the key to the Chisum empire of grass, had been transferred to the Hunter & Evans interests when Old John had pretty well gone out of the longhorn business three years before this. It is probable that this early August day of 1878 was the first time Billy had ridden in to the old headquarters here at Bosque Grande. Chisum had moved to his new headquarters at South Spring in 1875, and Billy had been at the big house there several times. Sally Chisum had always had a little special interest in the slender boy with the quick smile and the attractive personality. If this isolated frontier of eastern New Mexico was lonesome for a young fellow, it was ten times more bleak for a romantic girl.

Shortly before Christmas of 1877, someone gave the eighteen-year-old ranch girl a small, morocco-bound notebook. It might well have been brought in with the special order John Tunstall purchased for the Chisum family on his buying trip to St. Louis, and delivered to the South Spring ranch two months before he was killed. How the little red book survived the trying period of the "war" and the subsequent moves and years no one can ever know. But it did survive, and the several items that briefly cover this Odyssey of the Chisum family and herds to the Canadian River country and then back to South Spring, are of some value in fixing exact dates and proper sequence. In the misspelled words and fading pencilled script are touching glimpses into the lonely heart of a frontier girl.

The items are put down exactly as they appear in the uneven chronicle:

> July 31: We came to Bosque Grande on 31st.
> August 13: Regulators came to Bosque Grande. Indian tobacco sack presented to me on the 13th of August by William Bonny.

It was Billy's first gift to her. Eight days before he gave it to Sally he had been nearby when the courageous Bernstein was killed at the Mescalero Apache reservation. He might have picked up the white buckskin pouch, decorated with its bright-colored porcupine quills, on the wooded hillside where the little battle took place, or he might have won it in a poker game played on a blanket beside a campfire; or he might have bought it from some Apache buck for a handful of contraband cartridges.

The next item in the diary read:

> August 14th: We stayed at Bosque Grande 15 days— then started to Fort Sumner on Friday. It taken us Friday and Saturday and part of Sunday. Made acquaintance of Mrs. Ballard on the 21st of Aug. Had a very nice time while we stayed there. Left there on Wednesday 11 Sept. 78.

Then as a sort of afterthought she pencilled in a new item dated while they were still at Fort Sumner.

> August 22nd: Two candi hearts given me by Willie Bonney on the 22nd of August.

Only oldsters can remember these "candi hearts" of the long-ago days. They were several inches across and of gay pinks and whites and blues, and to lone riders of the high desert mesas they were the last word in sentimental gifts.

It seems reasonable that Billy and his quartet of side-kicks probably helped out the Chisum men on the three- or four-day drive up the Pecos to Fort Sumner country and the Round Grove of ancient cottonwoods nearby called *Bosque Redondo*. Fort Sumner had been a famous place since it was built by the Union forces in December, 1862. It marked the gateway to the lower Pecos, its narrow canyons and bad lands breaking into the broad river valley below. Since Charlie Goodnight and Oliver Loving first had started their Texas herds upstream in 1865, this point of Fort Sumner and the *Bosque Redondo* was the great cattle mart of this far-western trail. Literally tens of thousands of longhorns were sold here to buyers who drove them north to the fattening grasslands of Kansas, Colorado, Nebraska, Wyoming, Montana, the Dakotas, and Alberta.

Other tens of thousands were bought by the government to feed the 8,000 Navajos and New Mexico Apaches who had been gathered like sheep and driven to this unhappy reservation. Fully half of them died of loneliness and hunger and heartbreak. They had been captured and corraled here by the famous Kit Carson, then Colonel and Brevet Brigadier General of New Mexican Volunteers, under the orders of the determined General James H. Carleton, leader of the famous California Column and commanding general of the District of New Mexico.

Old Kit lay dying of cancer of the throat at Fort Lyons in Colorado in 1868 when he heard the happy news that Sherman, commanding general of the Army, had journeyed to Fort Sumner to make arrangements for the few Navajo survivals to start back on the Long Walk to their own poor lands and barren mountains they loved so much.

For more than thirty years Kit was the boon companion of old Lucien Maxwell, who in 1874 was to buy this abandoned Fort Sumner, here at the great circular cottonwood grove at the bend of the Pecos. They had been mountain men together, in 1852 driving a band of 5,000 sheep over the old Spanish Trail to the gold camps of California. And they had lived close together on Renado Creek in the lush valleys and sweet hills of the Maxwell grant below Cimarron, New Mexico.

It was from the purchase and resale of the Maxwell Grant that the Elkins-Catron combination of Santa Fe had made their first great fortune. Old Lucien B. Maxwell figured the Spanish-Mexican grant, given to his wife's father and uncles, embraced an area totalling somewhere between 36,000 and 100,000 acres; under an official government survey of the tract manipulated by the new owners, the property miraculously expanded to a million and a half acres, worth several times the purchase money.

The gullible and inexperienced Lucien was paid $600,-

ooo in cash for his beautiful and priceless empire. Most of
the money quickly melted away in his open, trusting
hands. He moved to Santa Fe and dropped a tidy fortune
for the honor of signing his name as President of the First
National Bank. Next he woke up holding $250,000 in
worthless railroad stock which his advisors had unloaded
on him. Then came his purchase of the abandoned Fort
Sumner, with three long sets of officers' quarters and an
almost endless array of barracks, stables, warehouses,
stores, and whatnots. In 1874 he moved his family, his
peons, Navajo slaves, his cattle and sheep, and his hang-
ers-on to this lonely Pecos outpost. But his heart ached
for his bright green hills and clear streams, and for all the
rich and varied beauty of his beloved Cimarron country
on north.

Lucien moved his only son, Pedro, and his daughters
and grandchildren into a fifteen-room structure facing the
parade ground. He tried his best to reconstruct the baro-
nial days when he had been King of the Renado and the
Cimarron, but it wasn't in the cards. Instead, within a
year and a half he was buried in the one-time post cemetery; down to the present no permanent monument has
ever been erected to mark the grave of this truly great
frontiersman.

His son, Pedro, crowding thirty at his father's death,
tried to carry on the sprawling ranch, but it was his matri-
arch mother, the once-pretty Dona Luz Baudcin Maxwell,
who was the real head of the family. Some years before
his death Don Lucien had confided to the equally unique
trailblazer, Col. Charlie Goodnight, his secret opinion of
this son Pedro: "I never yet seen one of them half-breeds
that was worth the powder to blow his brains out."

5

Billy and his companions left the Chisum herd over by
the *Bosque Redondo* on the Pecos and rode on down the
hard, flinty trail heading into the old army reservation.
He knew that soon the Chisum outfit would be moving
northeast, across the long, waterless drive towards the
Canadian River country of the Texas Panhandle.

For two years Texas buffalo hunters with their skinners
and wagonmen had been preying on the remnants of the

great herds once numbering over ten million animals, that had meant food and life itself to the disinherited Plains Indians. Texas, Colorado, New Mexican, and Kansas cattle took over the one-time buffalo-grass lands that were now almost the last of the remaining free open ranges. Only a few thousand scraggly, wandering buffalo were left in tiny herds, living out their final days hiding in distant little valleys. Troopers at a dozen frontier forts held the red men to their reservations, while greasy, long-haired, unwashed white men, crawling with lice, quarrelling, murdering, snarling, finished the dirty work— and the happy way of life for the Great Plains Indians was ended forever.

Fort Sumner on the Pecos was more than a hundred miles to the west of the lush grass of the Canadian River country. Now and again one or two of the tail end of the disgruntled buffalo hunters, or some hard-riding outlaw with a good start on a Texas sheriff, would show up at the little community. Then the adobe joints run by the bearded and picturesque Beaver Smith and the younger Bob Hargraves would enjoy a temporary spurt in business. The newcomer might speak to amiable Pete Maxwell about settling down for a spell in a room or two in one of the abandoned adobe barracks. And Fort Sumner would gain a new resident, sometimes permanent but mostly temporary.

This is exactly what had happened some six months previous to this warm August afternoon of 1878 when Billy and his faithful men wrapped their bridle reins around the hitch rack in front of Beaver Smith's combination bar, gambling hall, and eating house. Billy did not drink at this time but he surely tossed a silver dollar on the high bar and motioned for whiskey for the boys.

The man who served him was a tall, lean, wiry man, with long legs and arms and strong hands, and a scrawny neck that sported a prominent Adam's apple. He was hollow-cheeked with wide, deep-set, brown eyes, a thin handle-bar mustache, and a mop of black hair. His shoulders were broad and stooped, and despite his six foot four inches and his skinny legs, he gave the impression of being hard as nails.

He was a good listener and soon he found out that the five boys had come in with the Chisum herd although they didn't belong to the outfit. It probably did not take him long, either, to figure out the identity of the customers when he heard four of them address the smallest and youngest of the group alternately as Kid and Billy. Pretty soon the bartender told the boys that his name was Pat—Pat Garrett to be exact.

It was some time later when Billy and his mates got the full story. Garrett had been born in Chambers County, Alabama, on June 5th, 1850—this made him almost ten years older than Billy. When Pat was six his father moved his family to Claiborne Parish, Lousiana, where he and his slaves farmed 3,000 acres of land. Colonel Garrett died shortly after the Civil War ended, and Pat drifted over to Lancaster, Dallas County, Texas.

He worked on a farm for a couple of years, then rode down to a big ranch in Uvalde County, west of San Antonio, where he learned to be a first-class cowboy. Finally he joined up with an older man named Skelton Glenn, who was organizing a party of buffalo hunters bound for the West Texas country. When the winter hunt was over Pat returned to southern Texas, but the following fall he joined up again with Glenn, along with a young Irish fellow from New Orleans named John Briscoe. The outfit moved up to Fort Griffin for supplies and then drove on west to the buffalo ranges. It was late in 1877, and buffalo robes were the best when the killing was made in the winter months.

The crew did well until the firing pin of Glenn's needle gun broke and Glenn hurried off to Reynolds City for repairs, leaving Pat, Briscoe, and two skinners named Burns and O'Bierne in camp. When he got back a day later he found that tragedy had struck the little camp. Pat had left immediately to hunt up Glenn but missed him. Burns related the terrible details to his boss.

Many years later Mr. Glenn methodically wrote out the details as he had first heard them, and his own simple words tell the story in all its stark reality:

It was before breakfast and Briscoe had taken a piece of soap and gone down to a pool of water to wash a soiled linen handkerchief. He came back to the camp and was standing before the fire holding the handkerchief rather close to it to dry it. Feeling that he had not done a very successful job he remarked to nobody in particular that "it is no use to try to wash in that damn water." Pat volunteered the reply: "Any one but a damn Irishman would have more sense than to try to wash anything in that water." That evidently riled Briscoe, for he retorted warmly, "Yes, you damn Americans think you are damn smart and know a damn sight."

Pat took that for rank impudence, and striking at Briscoe with his fists knocked him over backwards. Briscoe, however, caught himself and kept from falling. As he recovered his balance he struck back at Pat with his fists, but missed him. Then the boy, almost crazed with anger by this time, started over to pick up an axe which was used for splitting wood. Just as Briscoe picked it up, Pat jumped over to the wagon and grabbed up a short-shell .45 which had been left there to be readily available for skunks. No sooner had he snatched up the gun than he fired, wounding Briscoe so that he died about twenty minutes later.

Burns and Pat picked the poor boy up and carried him to one of the beds. As they laid him down, Briscoe said, "Boys, I am getting cold. Please put some more cover on me." After complying with this request, Pat and Burns walked over to the fire and stood there realizing that there was nothing they could do for the poor fellow. Briscoe called Pat, saying, "Pat, come over here, please." Pat with tears in his eyes went over to the bed and asked, "What do you want, John?" Briscoe replied, "I am dying, Pat. Won't you forgive me?" "Yes," said Pat, and then walked back to the fire crying. Then Briscoe exclaimed, "Oh, it's hard for a fellow to die away out here by himself," and then in a few seconds he was dead.

Not long after Glenn got back to the camp Garrett showed up. He had not eaten for eighteen hours, and he was shaken with remorse. Glenn advised him to make a beeline for Fort Griffin, find a Justice of Peace and tell his story. Pat did that and his plea of self-defense was accepted and no charges were brought against him. Two days later he was back at the buffalo camp.

Shortly after that the outfit moved over to the neighborhood of the *Casas Amarillas,* a series of caves called The Yellow Houses. But the hunting was so poor that Glenn and Garrett and a man by the name of Nick Ross decided to ride west in the hope of finding a large herd. They started the middle of February and it was almost two weeks later when, exhausted and half starved, they hit the tiny settlement of Taiban, New Mexico.

That next afternoon they rode the eighteen miles west to Fort Sumner. Glenn and Ross started back east in a few days, but Garrett decided to stay on. He'd been here at Sumner almost six months, helping shape-up and road-brand Texas trail herds moving on up the Pecos, and doing any odd job he could find. At this moment in August, 1878, when Billy and his little gang rode in, Pat was helping out old Beaver Smith in the daytime and playing a little poker in the evenings.

It is a curious fact that often a very tall man and one noticeably shorter are mutually attracted to one another. And often an older man seems to fancy taking a much younger one under his wing. Certainly this was the case with Pat Garrett and Billy. In addition these two had a very great interest in common: they were both inveterate gamblers, the Kid fancying himself as a monte dealer while Pat stuck pretty much to straight draw poker.

Each was a complete individualist in his own right. Each had walked hand in hand with death. Neither was given to too much talk or wild bragging. The tall man was inclined to be moody and, at times, downright cantankerous and even truculent. There seemed to be a shadow across his eyes: maybe he could still hear things, too, that he'd like to forget: like that poor boy whispering, "I am dying, Pat. Won't you forgive me?"

Billy didn't have any such trouble. He was gay and buoyant. He didn't see any ghosts when he looked into camp fires at night; nor did he hear banshee whimperings when the winds blew strong.

Days drifted by and there was fun here at Fort Sumner. Billy and Pat and the boys had already gone to one Mexican dance that they called a *bailie,* and there were more to come. But right now the Kid and his gang were figuring on hitting it down the old government wagon road that led southwest across the high mesas to Capitan Gap and Lincoln. They fixed it up with Pete Maxwell for homes for both Doc Scurlock and Charlie Bowdre and their wives when they should arrive here from Lincoln. Pete Maxwell knew Doc well and favorably from the days when Doc had worked for John Chisum. There was a job waiting for him now.

Bowdre would have no trouble finding work, either. The Kid and Tom O'Folliard and Fred Waite, and John Middleton and Henry Brown weren't looking for work. They had something else in mind.

12

In Lincoln town Billy and his little crowd found the Widow McSween living in the house which formerly had been occupied by Captain Baca and his nine children.

Her smoldering hatred against Colonel Dudley dominated every waking moment of her days. She could talk of little except the actions of the officer and Jimmy Dolan, who were backed up by Catron in Santa Fe and Colonel Rynerson in Mesilla.

Affairs on both the Bonito and the Ruidoso were in a curious situation. The few McSween men who remained in the valleys were more or less headed up by Doc Scurlock and Charlie Bowdre, who were now about to pull out. Sheriff Peppin apparently had been badly shaken by the turn of events on the night of July 19th when the Big Killing had occurred, and he was taking little or no part in subsequent happenings. He was letting things drift along while he sought the sanctuary of the Apache Agency and Fort Stanton.

Colonel Dudley in his weekly reports stressed the fact that utter lawlessness still persisted, and that a new and desperate gang was taking over the district around Seven Rivers on the Pecos. The bitter and relentless tongue and pen of the Widow McSween constantly lashed out at Dudley. She seemed to be bent on his destruction. Dudley was plagued, as well, by the personal animosity existing between himself and General Hatch, who commanded the army in the Territory of New Mexico, with headquarters at Santa Fe.

Altogether Lincoln County seemed once again to be building itself up for some dangerous explosion. The very fact that two of the last of the important Regulators were now moving away and that Billy's stay was only temporary seemed oddly enough to invite a new kind of lawlessness on the part of lately arrived desperadoes.

Around September 1st of this year of 1878 Billy helped load up the two wagons of Doc Scurlock and Charlie Bowdre. Each family possessed only a few *lares y penates,* but they owned extra horses. So it was that the little caravan kicked up quite a bit of dust as it moved slowly out through the Capitan Gap north of Fort Stanton and then across the high, lonely, windswept mesas and rolling desert country northeast to Fort Sumner.

A week or ten days later a band of horses belonging to Charlie Fritz and his sister, Mrs. Scholand, suddenly disappeared from their Spring Ranch on the Bonito, eight miles below Lincoln, where Frank McNab had been killed on the last day of April. It was the natural thing now to blame the Kid or one of his men for the theft. Tom O'Folliard seemed a handy suspect. At the coming spring term of court at Lincoln the tall, lean Tom was indicted and duly tried for the crime, but he was acquitted.

Probably he was present with Billy during the meetings when the Widow McSween spewed out her wrath against Charlie Fritz and his sister for their actions in prosecuting McSween for his nonpayment of the Fritz insurance money; the immediate result, of course, had been the attachment of Tunstall's store and ranch, and from this had stemmed the young Englishman's murder and the terrible Lincoln County War.

Billy was back at Fort Sumner on September 14th when the announcement was made in Washington that President Hayes had appointed the former Major General Lew Wallace, of Crawfordsville, Indiana, to relieve S. B. Axtell as Governor of the Territory of New Mexico. It must have been most unpleasant news to the members of the Santa Fe Ring and to Colonel Dudley and his drinking companions at Fort Stanton.

They could rightly blame the meddler Judge Angel for a major share in this disturbing action. The official Washington investigator had been at Santa Fe when the news came of the Big Killing of July 19th. Mrs. McSween and others had seen to it that sworn depositions concerning the part Colonel Dudley had played in the affair were rushed to Angel. The official investigator left shortly for Washington, and the removal of Axtell and the appointment of Lew Wallace as Governor were the first results of his recommendations. The opening paragraphs of Angel's report, dated Oct. 7, 1878, gave a broad picture of general conditions:

> The history of Lincoln County has been one of bloodshed from the day of its organization. These troubles have existed for years with occasional outbreaks, each one being more severe than the others. L. G. Murphy & Co. had the monopoly of all business in the county; they controlled Government contracts and used their power to oppress and grind out all they could from the farmers and force those who were opposed to leave the country. This resulted in the formation of two parties, one led by Murphy & Co., and the other by McSween (now dead). Both have done many things contrary to law; both have violated the law. McSween, I firmly believe, acted conscientiously—Murphy & Co. for private gain and revenge. . . .

> The leaders of these parties have created a storm that they cannot control, and it has reached such proportions that the whole Territory cannot put it down. Lands go uncultivated, ranches are abandoned, merchants have closed their stores, citizens have left the houses they have occupied for years, business has ceased, and lawlessness and murder are the order of the day.

But now everything would be changed. The distinguished Lew Wallace would work the miracle.

2

Within a day or two after the Wallace appointment, the Widow McSween had her team of trotters hitched to her Hayes buggy and started off with a driver on the long overland trip to Las Vegas. She felt that her actual life was in danger if she stayed on longer in Lincoln. Murderous gangs still roamed the vast, lawless county. Her sister and children had pulled out for Las Vegas the day following the Big Fight, but Susan McSween was made of sterner stuff.

She now turned for help to a one-armed fighting attorney in Las Vegas by the name of Huston J. Chapman. She had met him at Vegas when her husband and John Chisum were arrested there in December, 1877.

All in all, September, 1878, was to be a fateful month for the widow and also for Billy, as well as for the scattered population of war-torn Lincoln County. On the 27th a crowd of ruffians, calling themselves Rustlers or Selman's Scouts, rode up to Hudgens' saloon, a short distance off the limits of Fort Stanton. This saloon had formerly been dubbed "The Brewery," and at one time had belonged to the Murphy & Dolan firm and was operated by the old German Gauss.

The Rustlers were led by a hard character named John Selman. [Seventeen years later Selman, then El Paso marshal, shot the famous gun-fighter John Wesley Hardin through the back of the head in the Acme saloon in El Paso. A few months later Selman himself was to feel the death bite of a lead slug from the pistol of Deputy U. S. Marshal George Scarborough.] At this particular period of his life, in the summer of 1878, Selman may have used the alias of John Gunter or Gunter. Only recently he had barely escaped hanging at the hands of a vigilance committee at Fort Griffith, Texas, by galloping south to the lawless Pecos and Black River country.

Leading a group of his desperadoes to Hudgens' bar and soldier hangout, John Selman tried to induce the proprietor to slip over to the army post and secure a supply of ammunition. When Hudgens refused, four of the Scouts galloped over to the post trader's store and purchased the cartridges. Colonel Dudley, however, got wind of the business, arrested the four men, and ordered the sutler to take back the shells and return the money to the quartet.

Angry at their failure, the men returned to Hudgens' bar, generally wrecked and looted the place, and grossly insulted the proprietor's wife and sister. The Rustlers proceeded to Lincoln, where they attempted to hold up Ellis & Sons' store but found the place barricaded and ready for them. They next rode on east to the junction of the Bonito and the Ruidoso and looted the A. M. Glenny store of $800 worth of goods.

The following day they rode back towards San Patricio, breaking into houses and insulting and terrorizing the settlers, native and Anglo alike. On their return towards Seven Rivers and the Pecos that afternoon the gang, with their bellies filled with frontier rotgut, trotted into a hay flat belonging to Chavez y Sanchez, a highly respected and inoffensive citizen. The men demanded horses of the two young sons of Chavez y Sanchez and, when the boys answered that the visitors would have to see their father first, they were shot down in cold blood. A third boy named Gregorio Sanchez was likewise killed, along with a fourth lad who was half-witted.

This latest outrage was more than the citizens of the community, accustomed as they were to violence, could bear. They needed Billy and the old Regulators, but even without them they were determined to strike back. Theirs was the courage and the righteous wrath of men driven beyond the limits of their patience. Sam Corbett, former clerk of the Tunstall store and ordinarily a mild young man, wrote of their valorous determination to John Tunstall's father in England:

> Some of the citizens, I and Mr. Ellis together with them, got after them, and ran them two days and nights nearly to Seven Rivers, but could not get close enough to kill any of them. We captured all the loose horses they were driving back and all their blankets and provisions.
>
> We are going to start again for Seven Rivers on Friday with all the citizens that can raise a gun, and try to stop their murdering and thieving. I am satisfied that they will make a desperate fight, and I ex-

pect will outnumber us; but we have concluded that
it is better to die fighting for our rights all in a pile
than to be murdered one at a time in our homes. I
am satisfied that some of us will never get back to
Lincoln.

Apparently the expedition of revenge never quite
achieved its fine promise and noble purpose. They lacked
a leader, but those who might have qualified had been
either killed off or driven out of the country. How frightful was the state of affairs is proven in a report filed by a
Dr. Lyons, the new army surgeon at Fort Stanton, who
had been requested to answer the urgent appeal for help;
it represents the fresh impressions of a newcomer and altogether it is a blunt and terrible indictment:

> Made journey to Martin Sanchez ranch 60 mile from
> the Fort on the Hondo. A fast messenger had
> brought news of the mortal wounding of Sanchez'
> son. At junction of the Ruidoso and Bonito, another
> messenger brought news of the young man's death.
> Went with Fritz (Charlie) to Chavez home—found
> the family in pitiable condition—father and mother
> almost crazed with grief and terror-stricken.
>   General feeling in the country is that everyone
> will have to abandon property. No longer a feud be-
> tween Dolan and McSween, but now depredations
> and murders by a band of miscreants who have been
> attracted thither from all parts of the country by
> knowledge of the inability of authorities, civil or
> military, to afford protection. Feeling between the
> survivors in the original disturbances is still bitter;
> and feeling is strong against the military for inactiv-
> ity when the U.S. keeps a military force almost with-
> in gunshot of the scenes of disturbance. Travel is
> dangerous. All strangers challenged by whatever
> party met until their relations or intentions are
> given.

An item in the Las Vegas *Gazette* fully confirmed the
sensational report of the good doctor. It concerned the
desperate plight of the Mormon settlers near Roswell
whom John Chisum had tried so hard to help get placed
in the days before the "war" started:

Six wagon loads of emigrants from North and South Rivers in Lincoln County passed through Tuesday going north. They were driven out by the lawless element of that section. They had tried hard to take no part in the contest and preferred to leave rather than take either side. About 20 horses had been taken from them. A deputy sheriff rode up with a pistol and demanded that they take up arms and go with them and fight. This they refused to do and loaded up and left the country. They left their lands, houses, standing crops, gardens, and everything pertaining to comfortable homes.

3

On to the northeast, up beyond Fort Sumner, Sally Chisum wrote in her little red notebook a new item that is of some importance in fixing the exact dates of Billy's movements:

Regulators came up with us at Red River Springs on 25 Sept. 1878.

The days at Fort Sumner, following Billy's last Lincoln visit, were comfortably busy for himself and his men. By one means or another they had gotten together a fair-sized batch of horses, possibly some forty head. Some of them might well have been the Fritz horses from the Rio Bonito country. And there were unquestionably animals from the herds of the picturesque Polish rancher Grzelachowski, who ran a store and stopping place on the west side of the *plaza* of Puerto de Luna, forty miles above Fort Sumner. He operated several small spreads, but his main ranch was at Alamo Gordo.

Some years before this, Grzelachowski had come out to the Territory as a priest, but the wild western life had offered too many temptations for transgression, and he had been unfrocked. He was a powerful, energetic man with a great flowing beard and flashing black eyes, and a booming voice that commanded fluent Spanish. He raised several sets of children, and before he was struck down he accumulated large herds of cattle, bands of sheep, and ranches, and money. He will appear again in this chronicle.

Back before he left Sumner for his visit to Lincoln, Billy had figured out where he proposed to dispose of the horses once he had secured them. For untold centuries there had been a buffalo crossing on the Canadian River, a hundred miles or so east of the Texas line. On this spot had grown an enterprising little supply depot for the great ranches that had only recently been established in the Panhandle. It was called Tascosa although its proper name was Atascosa, which in Spanish means "boggy." There would be fun here, racing and trading horses, dealing monte, and attending the Mexican *bailies*.

So in these bright September days of 1878 Billy and his four men ate the dust of the little batch of horses which they had acquired mostly by their long ropes. Plains Indians looked upon horse stealing as an honorable although somewhat dangerous game which was part of a young buck's training. Billy's point of view was probably not much different.

He was the complete product of an environment that often failed to draw fine moral lines. And he was sustained by the definite sense that a once-worthy cause gave him the right to plague his enemies every way he could. The same environment, however, had taught him the wisdom of always being fortified by bills of sale. At least such documents lent some slight color to his arguments that his horses had been acquired legally.

Doc Scurlock decided to stick with his job as a top cowhand with Pete Maxwell at Fort Sumner. Charlie Bowdre elected to risk adventure with Billy, but at the last moment he changed his mind and sold out his interests in the little band of horses. Charlie decided to stay on at Sumner and work for either Pete Maxwell or a rancher named Yerby. So it was that only the original four—Fred Waite, Tom O'Folliard, John Middleton, and Henry Brown—who had followed Billy from Lincoln to Fort Sumner in middle August, now rode with him towards Tascosa.

They had barely crossed into the Texas Panhandle when a matter of large importance to Billy and his future took place in Santa Fe. A new figure was now to enter the orbit of his life and in deadly significance he would rank with John Tunstall, Jimmy Dolan, and Pat Garrett. He would be the fourth of the quartet, half of whom were

friends and half enemies, who marked and influenced the
boy's fate.

The pink and rose colors of the swiftly falling twilight
were turning to lavendars and deep purples when General
Lew Wallace pulled up at the old Central Hotel, facing
the two-hundred-year-old plaza in the territorial capital.
It was the last day of September and he had ridden 130
miles by buckboard from the railhead at Trinidad, Colorado. The newly appointed Governor of New Mexico was
51 years old. His carefully trimmed beard was now tinted
reddish brown from the dust kicked up by his tired team
as it slowly made its way through the Apache Pass and on
up the rough, steep grade to Santa Fe, almost a mile and
a half above sea level. He had the unfinished manuscript
of a novel, already entitled "Ben Hur," in one of his
valises. His somewhat controversial war days had been followed by an adventurous but unproductive period in Old
Mexico. After a long sojourn at home in Crawfordsville,
Indiana, he longed for new worlds to conquer.

The new appointee had been well briefed in Washington by the special agent, Judge Angel, and by the German-born hero, Major General Karl Schurz, then
Secretary of the Interior. They apprised him of the intolerable situation existing throughout the Territory of New
Mexico, particularly in Lincoln County. But it is doubted
that even his romantic mind could have envisioned the
singular train of events that were soon to unfold.

Two hundred miles to the eastward the young leader
of the remnants of the Regulators rode the drags of his
little band of horses, absorbed in the trying ordeal of
crossing the waterless desert. Billy had heard that a new
Governor was coming, but he probably considered that of
little concern to him; far less, in fact, than the immediate
question of how far he would still have to go before he
struck the first water.

But in this surmise he was surely wrong.

4

It was a beautiful country they came to, after the long dry
drive. The grass had turned brown but the young cottonwoods and willows were still green along the tiny creeks
that had been kept alive by the unusually late summer

rains. Billy had never gazed upon so fair and rich a land. It seemed endless, and it filled his eyes with wonder and a strange joy. It was an incomparable land.

The party was only ten miles from Tascosa when they met a young fellow driving a buckboard, which had all the appearance of being a mail wagon. Billy and the others raised their hands in friendly greetings. The driver answered the salutes and pulled up his team. He was from Minnesota and his name was Dr. Henry E. Hoyt. He was a recent graduate in medicine enjoying a final fling at romantic adventure before his profession claimed him.

He had drifted on to the Pecos from Trinidad, Colorado, and had fallen in with John Chisum. Old Uncle John had heard of an outbreak of smallpox over in the Canadian River country around the new cow town of Tascosa, and he advised the adventurous medico to go there. He fixed him up with a quarter of beef and a keg of water and set him off with a song in his heart.

The young doctor loitered on the trail to hunt buffalo and antelope, and to stare wide-eyed at the unforgettable scene of a herd of wild horses standing on a rimrock in early morning. In the afternoons an autumn haze gave a tone and texture to the vast emptiness which made it as lovely and elusive as the shimmering mirages hanging by magic threads on the distant horizon. A never-never land seemed here and now.

The news of Dr. Hoyt's coming reached Tascosa long before his arrival and a messenger on a swift pony was dispatched to bring him in at top speed: the daughter of the powerful Casimiro Romero, patron of the native section, lay in serious condition. Hoyt had no drugs or medical supplies, and while he found the girl's health improving, the terrible itching of the smallpox pustules was driving her half mad. Knowing that gunpowder contained sulphur, saltpeter and charcoal, he obtained a few pounds from Howard & McMaster's store and made a paste which instantly relieved the young lady. His welcome was now secure.

But since it was adventure and not medical practice that had drawn young Hoyt to the southwest, he turned to the open cattle ranges and the round-up wagons. By the time he met up with Billy and his mates the doctor had advanced from a line rider and promising cowboy to the post of temporary mailman, running the buckboard between Fort Bascom and Tascosa.

The two young men exchanged greetings but not names, and Billy made some quiet inquiries about Tascosa and the nearby ranches and the general lay of the land. He explained that the little band of horses off there a way belonged to him and his friends. They hoped to sell or trade them in Tascosa. Soon young Hoyt drove on with the mail, telling Billy he'd see him later in the afternoon in the little town a few miles on ahead.

The two-year-old settlement was built up from the Canadian River around a *plaza* that was roughly a hundred yards square. All the buildings were single story and constructed of adobes. On the north side of the square was Howard & McMasters' store; on the east the house of Pedro Romero, nephew of old Don Casimiro Romero; on the south the blacksmith shop of Henry Kimball and his helper "Bronco Jack," who at the moment was suffering from a bullet wound in his leg. On the west side of the *plaza* stood the Rinehart store and a small saloon kept by Jack Ryan. Off a short distance was a second *plaza*, with a few houses and various buildings occupied by native New Mexicans.

Billy left his bunch of horses and one of his riders in a grassy elbow of the Canadian, and the four others rode on up to Howard & McMasters' store. It wasn't long before the news spread around that Billy the Kid and some of his Lincoln County fighters had arrived with a bunch of saddle stock.

The next day there was a meeting of ranch foremen in one of the stores, and Billy and his boys were called in. "Outlaw Bill" Moore from the LXs and Charlie McCarty from Major Littlefield's LITs did the talking. They told Billy they recognized him and wanted to know what his game was.

Billy's straightforward answer has been reliably reported: "Gentlemen, we're from New Mexico. We heard there were some ranches down here that were short of horses and we brought some down here to see if we could supply you."

"If that's so, Billy," McCarty replied, "it's all right. But don't try to turn any tricks down here."

Billy assured the gathering that they had no intention

of trying any tricks, and then all adjourned to have a drink. According to Dr. Hoyt's personal reminiscences, written up some years later, Billy definitely did not drink but he gladly paid when his turn came around. And during the weeks the visitors were in the community there was no serious complaint against them.

One of the top riders with the LITs was a young Texan named Phelps White, a nephew of Major Littlefield and later one of the very great cattlemen of New Mexico. Years afterwards, when White was an old man living in Roswell, he described these days to J. Evetts Haley, the distinguished historian of the Panhandle. White had never forgotten Billy and what he told of him can be classed as authentic:

> He had hardly arrived when he matched a race with old man Rinehart's horse, Spider. Spider was a race horse, and we knew it. We didn't mean to beat him so badly at first, but when we found out that it was Billy the Kid, we thought we'd better beat him good so there would be no squabble. They agreed on a short race and we were not to have starter judges. Fred Waite, a Kid man, and I were judges at the finish. So the Kid and McCarty went down just to see that they got off all right. Everybody could see at the finish that the Kid's horse was badly beat, but Fred Waite claimed a foul, and said his horse came out six or eight feet ahead.
>
> "If Spider didn't beat him fifty feet," I said, "then he didn't beat him fifty inches." The Kid came loping up about this time, and we explained the matter to him, Fred contending for the foul, now saying their horse was beat only a few feet. But the Kid settled the matter peremptorily by commanding:
> "Give it up, Fred. We're beat."

Billy became close friends with young Dr. Hoyt. They attended the *bailies* together and took part in shooting matches and various frontier sports. Billy opened a monte game a few times, but it was primarily a Mexican game and he had few customers. Hoyt recalled one special dance that was held at the home of Pedro Romero: it seemed that there was an unwritten law that boys attending the dances must leave their guns at either Howard & McMasters' or Rinehart's. This night Billy and young Hoyt strolled across the plaza to Rinehart's store for a soft drink, and when they were ready to start back Hoyt offered to race Billy to the house. The doctor led Billy all the way and, as the pair got up close, Hoyt slowed up, but Billy miscalculated the doorstep and shot through the opening and sprawled on his face in the center of the dance floor. Instantly four men with drawn guns surrounded him. They were the Kid's faithful, who had concealed their forbidden pistols in boot tops and under coats. It was an unfortunate move because their failure to obey the no-guns rule debarred them from future dances at this particular home.

5

By late October Dr. Hoyt had a chance to accompany the new mail contractor to Las Vegas, New Mexico. He had taken a great shine to the Kid, and as a keepsake he gave him a lady's gold watch with a long, braided-hair chain. He had won it in a poker game, and it was the only valuable thing he possessed. Billy kept it for some time and, in the daguerreotype that long has been claimed as the single true picture of the young outlaw, the chain can be identified.

On the day Hoyt left Tascosa the Kid rode in leading his favorite race horse, a spirited chestnut sorrel named Dandy Dock. The Doctor had often ridden the animal and greatly admired him. He was a handsome mount and showed a very definite Arab strain. It was Billy's going-away present to his friend. He stepped into Howard & McMaster's store and wrote out a bill of sale, exactly as if it had been a cash transaction. It was formally witnessed by the two merchants. Many years later the slip of paper was sent by Dr. Hoyt to the Panhandle-Plains Historical Society Museum in Canyon, Texas, where it now remains on proud display.

TASCOSA, TEXAS
THURSDAY OCT. 24, 1878
Know all persons by these presents that I do hereby sell and deliver to Henry F. Hoyt one sorrel horse branded BB on left hip and other indistinct Branded

on Shoulders for Sum of Seventyfive $dollars in hand received

W. H. Bonney

Witness Jas J. McMasters
Geo. J. Howard

With it lives on a touching little story that may or may not be true: when Charlie Siringo showed a copy of the bill of sale with the description of the horse to James Brady, the son of Sheriff Brady who had been killed in Lincoln that fateful April 1st of 1878, the son cried out, "That's the horse my father rode into Lincoln the morning he was killed. It was given to him by Major Murphy."

Along with young Dr. Hoyt's present of the gold watch and long, braided-hair chain to Billy, there was included some earnest advice for him and his four companions. It was the half-plea, half-argument that they must not return to New Mexico and deadly Lincoln County and the certain fate that awaited them there. They should either go back to their several homes or possibly pull out for Mexico and the fabulous adventures they would find on below. Start all over again! Why walk into death when life could be so free and sweet?

But there was no hurry to make the final decision. The lovely fall days drifted by, and eventually the last of Billy's little band of horses was disposed of and the money spent.

So it was time to move. Would it be north, or south, or east, or on back west to the old days, the old feuds, the old dangers and intrigues?

John Middleton, the oldest of the five, who still carried the bullet wound in his chest, figured he'd strike north for his old camping grounds in western Kansas. Henry Brown decided he'd ride with him as far as Dodge City and then visit his home at Rolla, Phelps County, Missouri.

It took Fred Waite quite a little time to make up his mind. He truly loved Billy. He saw great qualities of loyalty and leadership in this lad with the magnetic personality and the cool courage. He shared Billy's affection for the memory of John Tunstall. Fred hated to leave, but he knew it was the wise thing to do. He pleaded with Billy to come with him to his home in Pauls' Valley in the Cherokee Indian Nation in lower Indian Territory. His people were well fixed and they would welcome Billy.

But Billy only shook his head. No one was waiting for him to come home. He didn't have any home to go to, anywhere. For him the word meant only a bit of level ground by a water hole or along a tiny stream under the stars, with a blanket for a bed and a saddle for a pillow— or possibly a shakedown in the adobe hut of some kindly native, happy to share his pot of *frijoles y tortillas* with a smiling boy who was even poorer than himself.

No, he would not leave, save to go back west to the Pecos. That left only one of his followers still undecided— the tall lad from Uvalde, Texas; the boy whose romantic father had fled from the memories of some sin he had committed in Ireland; the boy whose mother had followed his strangely tormented father to Mexico and died there with him; the boy whose uncle was a proud Texas ranger; the boy who had attached himself to Billy almost as a faithful dog follows a master; the boy who, as Frank Coe was to testify, would hold Billy's horse half the night while he courted some *señorita*. No, Tom O'Folliard wasn't leaving either—he was staying with Billy from now on; from now on to eternity.

So it was that when the three men who wanted no more of Lincoln County mounted and headed north into the teeth of the cool winds blowing down from Kansas, the two others, Billy and Tom, turned their ponies westward; westward to the Pecos and Fort Sumner, to Lincoln County and the Capitans; to the little rivers that flowed eastward through the rich, narrow valleys—the rivers with the beautiful names—Bonito, Ruidoso, Hondo, Peñasco, Feliz, Seven Rivers.

Two left out of the five who had so gaily ridden away from the sullen Pecos for the lovely grasslands of the Canadian. That meant that with Doc Scurlock and Charlie Bowdre at Sumner, there would at best be a grand total of four—four faithfuls of all the brave crew who had ridden and dared and fought together in the old days and remained true to the memory and the cause of John Tunstall.

And they had once numbered a score and more.

13

Things had changed little around Fort Sumner when the Kid and Tom O'Folliard returned to the old wind-swept army reservation in late November of 1878. They found both Doc Scurlock and Charlie Bowdre still working for Pete Maxwell and fairly well established.

Pat Garrett had branched out into a small trader, buying and selling little batches of cattle and picking up an odd dollar or two wherever he could. He had pretty well decided to settle down here on the Pecos and grow up with the country. His Spanish was improving and he enjoyed attending the native *bailies* which were held once or twice a week as the Christmas season approached.

Billy and Tom hitched up with Pat and a pleasant fellow of about twenty-five named Barney Mason. The four made somewhat of a splash when they appeared together at a *fandango*. Pat and Billy took a fair amount of good-natured ribbing over their differences in size. The few Anglos often referred to the pair as Big and Little Casino. Most of the time the native New Mexicans called the slender boy "Beelie," but some of them used his nickname which they pronounced "Keed."

A number of events which directly concerned Lincoln County had occurred during Billy's absence of two

months. He found some of them chronicled in old copies
of the newspapers, while Scurlock and Bowdre filled in
with the current gossip. It is likely he was supplied with
additional information by the one-armed lawyer Chapman when he stopped over at Sumner on the long buggy
trip from Lincoln to Las Vegas.

Immediately upon the new Governor's arrival in Santa
Fe he was proffered every sort of advice by every sort of
informant. Jimmy Dolan hurried down from Lincoln to
present his side of the feud. And Lawyer Chapman lost
no time in airing the McSween version.

On October 10th Colonel Dudley sent Governor Wallace a letter from Fort Stanton with a report of general
conditions in the harassed county. In this note the army
officer tried his best to conceal his displeasure and suspicion over the appointment of the new Governor.

Wallace at once telegraphed his superior in Washington, Karl Schurz, Secretary of the Interior, telling him
how matters looked at the moment. Obviously the term
"murderous bands" did not refer to the Kid or the handful
of old Regulators who remarried:

> I received by mail last night a petition signed by the
> Probate Judge, two county commissioners, four jus-
> tices of peace in Lincoln County, representing the
> county infested by bands of non-residents who rob
> and kill at pleasure; that inforcement of the law is
> not possible, because of inferiority of civil power. . . .
>
> The better opinion here is that the present trou-
> ble is from Texans and buffalo hunters, who, think-
> ing the regulars [troops] tied up by law, believe it
> good time to rape, steal, burn and kill. . . .
>
> In fact there is nothing to be done but make war
> upon the murderous bands. When prisoners are
> taken, let them be sent before a military commission,
> appointed to sit continuously at Ft. Stanton. In other
> words, martial law for the counties Lincoln and Dona
> Ana. The martial proclamation in the quickest time
> possible.

Wallace's soldier training made it logical for him to
turn to the military and martial law. He was favorably
impressed by General Hatch, district commander, who

was a man of stern common sense. Wallace's opinion of
Colonel Dudley, however, was vastly different: the one-
armed Chapman saw to that. One of the first of the lawyer's letters to the Governor carried a most damaging
accusation:

> I am in possession of facts which make Col. Dudley
> criminally responsible for the killing of McSween,
> and he has threatened that in case martial law is de-
> clared that he would arrest Mrs. McSween and her
> friends immediately.

Chapman then proceeded to request that a military
guard be supplied the widow in Lincoln. Without waiting to let matters cool off, Governor Wallace approved
the suggestion and passed it on to General Hatch. The
district commander bundled up the letter, together with
the formal complaint by Chapman, and shipped them off
to Colonel Dudley at Fort Stanton.

Billy was still in the Texas Panhandle when the new
Governor made his first important move. On November
13th Wallace issued an Amnesty Proclamation that was to
have a definite effect on the already muddied waters. It
read:

> For the information of the people of the United
> States and of the citizens of the Territory of New
> Mexico in especial, the undersigned announces that
> the disorders lately prevalent in Lincoln County,
> said Territory, have been happily brought to an end.
> Persons having business and property interests there-
> in and who are themselves peaceably disposed may
> go to and from that County without hindrance or
> molestation. Individuals resident there, who have
> long been driven away, or who from choice sought
> safety elsewhere, are invited to return, under assur-
> ance that ample measures have been taken and are
> now and will be continued in force, to make them se-
> cure in person and property. And that the people of
> Lincoln County may be helped more speedily to the
> management of their civil affairs, as contemplated by
> law, and to induce them to lay aside the divisions
> and feuds, which by national notoriety, have been so

prejudicial to their locality and the whole Territory, the undersigned, by virtue of authority in him vested, further proclaims a general pardon for misdemeanors and offenses committed in the said County of Lincoln against the laws of the Territory, between the first day of February, 1878, and the date of this proclamation.

And it is expressly understood that the foregoing pardon is upon the conditions and limitations following:

It shall not apply except to officers of the United States Army stationed in the said County during the said disorders, and to persons who, at the time of the commission of the offense or misdemeanor of which they may be accused, were with good intent, resident citizens of the said Territory, and who shall have hereafter kept the peace, and conducted themselves in all respects as become good citizens.

Neither shall it be pleaded by any person in bar of conviction under indictment now found and returned for any such crimes or misdemeanors, nor operate the release of any party undergoing pains and penalties consequent upon sentence heretofore had for any crime of misdemeanor.

In witness whereof I have hereunto set my hand and caused the seal of the Territory of New Mexico to be affixed.

Done at the city of Santa Fe, this 13th day of November, A.D. 1878

Lewis Wallace.

(Seal)

By the Governor,
    W. G. Ritch,
       Secretary

The amnesty definitely did not apply to those already convicted or under indictment, which classification certainly included the Kid. But no new indictments could be brought up on any charges involving the Lincoln County feud between the dates of February 1st, 1878 and November 13th of that same year. This meant that no longer could any territorial official, and particularly the District Prosecuting Attorney in Mesilla, Colonel Rynerson, hold over any man he chose the threat of an indictment for some past offense connected with the fierce war. It did not, however, exempt such transient professionals as John Kinney and other out-of-state criminals, for the amnesty provisions included only "resident citizens of the said Territory."

The clause granting a pardon to the army officers at Fort Stanton brought violent and bitter reaction from Colonel Dudley and the officers serving under him. The Colonel drafted a two-thousand-word open letter to the Governor refusing, as he stated, to accept a pardon for a crime he had not committed.

The Colonel not only blazed away at the Governor but was so angered that he broke an ancient frontier code by an unhappy and critical reference to the Widow McSween. This portion of his long letter to the Governor read:

> Having permitted yourself to be the medium of forwarding to my senior such false, grave and slanderous charges, founded, as I have reason to believe, on the representations of a notoriously bad woman, it would, it seems to me, under the circumstances have been only justice to have furnished myself, also with a copy of your letter, setting forth your disbelief of the charges in question; but instead your Excellency promulgated an official proclamation, dated on the 13th inst., granting a general pardon, among whom are included "officers of the United States Army stationed in the County of Lincoln, Territory of New Mexico during the late disorders" for misdemeanors and offenses committed in the said County of Lincoln. . . .

> Not having asked for any leniency for myself and well knowing no officer serving in the County has, and as your Excellency cannot very consistently grant a pardon to an individual, or a class or body of men who have not committed a crime, I am with other officers of my command, at a loss to correctly interpret this part of your proclamation.

> I am not aware of having done a single illegal act, one that could be construed into a violation of law

and order; neither do I know of any officer of the Army serving in Lincoln County having done so since I assumed command at Fort Stanton on the 5th of April last.

Colonel Dudley continued for a full 1500 words with his bitter repudiation of the Governor's "pardon" of himself and his officers. Accompanying the communication was a short document signed by five officers at that moment on duty at the post. It read:

General N. A. M. Dudley
    Fort Stanton, N.M.

Dear General:
    We the undersigned officers of the U. S. Army stationed at this post during the recent disorders in Lincoln County have heard read an open letter addressed by you to His Excellency the Governor of New Mexico and desire to say that the said letter expresses most fully and explicitly our feelings upon the subject in thus publicly declining to accept for us the pardon tendered by His Excellency.

D. M. Appel	Sam S. Pague
Asst. Surgeon, U.S.A.	2nd Lieut. 15th inf. &
Post Surgeon	A.A.Q.M. & A.G.S.
G. W. Smith	J. M. French
2nd Lieut. 9th Cav.	2nd Lieut. 9th Cav.
Post Adjutant	Comd'g Company "M"

M. F. Goodwin
2nd Lieut. 9th Cavalry

So it was that within six weeks after the new Governor arrived in New Mexico, instead of his amnesty proclamation acting as a bridge to peace between the two violent factions, it was starting off as a passageway to fresh violence.

But even before the publication of Dudley's letter, Chapman, the one-armed lawyer, who had now returned to Lincoln from Las Vegas, wrote Wallace his own protest against the proclamation. It was evident that the act of pardon satisfied no one, and that instead of bringing peace it was having the opposite effect. After writing of his disappointment over the fact that the Governor had not yet visited Lincoln, the lawyer continued:

When I was in Santa Fe you assured me that all persecutions should be stopped and that your proclamation of amnesty should be respected by all parties. I ventured the opinion at that time that the "ring," or Dolan party, would use it as a convenience to shield themselves and would continue their persecution of the McSween men in defiance thereof. Upon my arrival here I found that my apprehensions were only too well founded and that Peppin, aided by the military, was pursuing McSween men, while the friends of the "ring," against whom the Sheriff held warrants, were granted immunity. I know that this is contrary to your wishes and instructions, but it is hard to produce a different effect from the causes, and so long as Peppin (who is the tool of the Dolan party) and the military are kept in authority, just so long will Lincoln County be the scene of all manner of outrages and murder.

You attach much importance to the awe-inspiring influence of the military, but it would pain you to see in what contempt they are held by the people whose confidence they have so shamefully abused. These depraved specimens of humanity who disgrace the name of soldier by their debauchery and immoral conduct are little to be relied upon in any matters where they are interested.

It is a matter of surprise to me that a man like Col. Dudley, who is a whiskey barrel in the morning and a barrel of whiskey at night, is entrusted with so important a position, or even retained in the army where his debaucheries must work such a damaging influence upon younger and better officers, and thus destroy their usefulness.

Col. Dudley is continually under the influence of liquor and has used his position as commandant of Ft. Stanton to insult and abuse unoffending citizens until his conduct has become a reproach to the military service of the country and an insult to every officer who tries to maintain the dignity of his position. I desire particularly to call your attention to

the conduct of this man Dudley to the end that in
the future we may know upon whom to place the responsibility of his wrongdoings.

If Chapman had deliberately set out to bring on himself
and Mrs. McSween the hate and fury of the entire Fort
Stanton command he could not have done a better job.
It would seem he was determined to provoke Colonel
Dudley and his friends into personal reprisals, which certainly would bring on new tragedies. It is quite possible
that the letter was passed on to General Hatch and eventually found its way into Colonel Dudley's hands.

It was now evident that the new Governor, with the
very best of intentions, had within a few weeks of his arrival in the Territory reopened the old sores which he
sought to cure. The fiery Chapman had jockeyed him into
a position where unwittingly he had become the champion of the McSween side in the violent controversy. As
a result there was now brewing a brand-new feud between
the Governor on one side and the Dudley-Dolan forces
on the other.

During all this confusion Billy was enjoying himself
with gambling, horse racing, and attending the little
bailies at Fort Sumner on the muddy Pecos. At best he
was but slightly concerned with the Governor's difficul-
ties. The legal terms used in the proclamation were probably a bit over his head but he was shrewd enough to understand that frontier law was a two-edged weapon, and
that if he did not stand in with the sheriff and prosecuting attorney neither justice nor mercy would be his.

He had few illusions concerning his position, yet it is
certain that he anxiously hoped for a chance to be included in the Governor's pardon. He might even have
permitted himself to be arrested in Lincoln County to see
if he could come out clear and thus gain a fresh start in
life.

Tradition has it that word was sent the Kid by John
Chisum, still seeking safety in Las Vegas or Santa Fe, to
take his little gang to Lincoln and see that Mrs. McSween
was protected. Whether true or not, it is a fact that Billy
and Tom O'Folliard, and probably Doc Scurlock, cut
across the high mesas and followed the old government
wagon road southwest through Capitan Gap to Lincoln.

2

As usual the Kid was broke. Obviously money meant little or nothing to him, as long as he had a few silver cartwheels to jingle together or to bet on the turn of a card or on the speed of a short-distance pony. Tom O'Folliard was just as little interested in cash, but Doc Scurlock and Charlie Bowdre had to be a bit more careful: they had their New Mexican wives to support and their little adobe homes to keep up. As long as the fighting continued in Lincoln County it had been more or less understood that old John Chisum stood back of the Tunstall-McSween obligations when it came to settling with the gun-fighters aligned on his side.

Lawyer Chapman, taking over the Widow McSween's affairs, apparently had made financial promises of one kind or another to Billy. Mrs. McSween was now administratrix of the John Tunstall estate, following the murder of her husband and the clearing out of Widenmann after the killing of Major Brady. So far, not one cent that had been salvaged from the $20,000 Tunstall investment was returned to the grief-stricken father in England.

Within two months after the murder of his son, the senior Tunstall made definite steps to obtain a substantial indemnity from the United States government. On April 29th, 1878, he wrote the Marquis of Salisbury, Foreign Secretary in Disraeli's second ministry, and the matter of a settlement was again pressed when Gladstone came into power. It was claimed by the British government that the Sheriff of Lincoln County, acting through his deputies and the posse, was accountable for the murder committed in the execution of legal process. [Some months before the senior Tunstall's death on November 17th, 1882, U. S. Secretary of State F. T. Frelinghuysen suggested that the claim be referred to the Court of Claims, but the British Government would not agree. As late as 1883 a revival of the case was submitted in printed form. One paragraph stated: "Among the most active instigators and most prominent members of this 'Ring' were Mr. Brady, Sheriff of the County; Mr. Thomas B. Catron, U. S. District Attorney General; Col. Rynerson, Attorney of the 3rd Judicial District; and Messrs. Riley & Dolan,

Merchants and Post Masters at Lincoln." . . . The charge went on to state that after Tunstall was murdered, the posse "rode on to Lincoln, sacked and plundered his stores, destroying and carrying away with them goods and property to the value of fifty thousand dollars (10,000 pounds), as was afterwards proved in the Probate Court of Lincoln." This figure of $50,000, incidentally, was almost ten times the actual property damage done. . . . Eventually on June 1st, 1885, the claim was formally disallowed by the U. S. Government.]

On December 13th, 1878, a month to the day after Wallace's amnesty proclamation and about the time Billy returned to Lincoln, Lieutenant French and a detachment of soldiers from Fort Stanton made their way into the former Captain Baca's house that had been involved in the Big Fight of July, 1878. Mrs. McSween was now living there. Chapman was there, and the officer, unquestionably drunk, let loose a disgraceful tirade of abuse against the salty, one-armed man, threatening him with violence and arrest. It was proof of the deep anger and resentment the whole post of Fort Stanton felt against the lawyer and his client. It was only luck that prevented a physical attack on the attorney.

The following morning Chapman filed a charge of assault with Squire "Green" Wilson, and French was delivered by a friendly brother-officer to the court. The case was postponed, but the feud had been stepped up another notch.

To add to the general confusion, "Dad" Peppin, tired out and fearful of getting killed, resigned as sheriff. As a successor to Peppin the Governor appointed an honest enough but ineffectual citizen named Kimbrell.

For some reason, possibly to test the workings of the Governor's pardon proclamation as far as his own case was concerned, three days before Christmas Billy allowed himself to be arrested and incarcerated in the dungeon-like cell of the Lincoln jail. When no move was made to release him he escaped under his own power.

Once again Billy found the climate around San Patricio most pleasant. He had a number of old friends among the native New Mexican residents. There were gay holiday *bailies* and now and again he could deal a little monte.

On January 20th, 1879, Chapman drove off for Las
Vegas and Santa Fe in Mrs. McSween's buggy. He may
have made a definite proposal regarding pay to Billy and
Tom, and possibly to Doc Scurlock, for, soon after his
arrival in Las Crucas, he wrote the senior Tunstall, in
London, asking for additional funds for Billy and his little crowd. As far as is known nothing came of that appeal.
Yet there was something touching in the Chapman letter
regarding the neglect suffered by these young fighters:

> They were promised by both McSween and Widen-
> mann that they would receive pay for hunting down
> the murderers of your son, but they do not ask any
> pay, but think that something should be done to as-
> sist them out of their present trouble, as it would be
> a vindication of your son. If you can do anything for
> them, I think that they deserve it. They have been
> indicted for the killing of some of the murderers of
> your son, and are without means of defending them-
> selves when the trial comes on.

Chapman, courageous and fiery-tempered, now found
himself caught in the web he himself had spun. From Las
Vegas he drove to Santa Fe to confer with Wallace. He
knew he had succeeded in making himself the Number
One enemy of the Dolan-Dudley side.

Oddly enough, it was Jimmy Dolan who suddenly appeared in the role of peacemaker between Colonel Dudley and the Governor. On the last day of 1878 Dolan, in
Lincoln, wrote a friendly letter to Wallace that began:

> Dear Governor:
>   On my arrival at Fort Stanton, I repeated your ex-
> planation etc. to the Comd'g. Officer, [Gen'l Dudley]
> —he seemed pleased, and said that it was possible that
> you and him could meet and talk matters over with
> each other for an hour that he was "satisfied that you
> would be fast friends."
>   I also explained matters to Sheriff Peppin and
> many of our citizens all of whom were pleased. I am
> convinced that the explanation has caused a very dif-
> ferent feeling from that in existance before I came
> down. Mr. Delany [the post trader] has also interest-
> ed himself in giving your explanation both to the
> officers and citizens.

> Your friend [Chapman] appears to be the only man in this County who is trying to continue the old feud. I and many of our citizens feel confident that if this man was silenced the trouble would end.

To the sensitive and romantic mind of the Governor it must have been a terrible shock to read and then reread the last sentence. It was as clear and unmistakable as the tolling of a bell. A death sentence itself could hardly have been more final.

It proved beyond doubt the violence and intensity of the struggle now going on. Yet it was hard for the Governor to believe that any decent citizen could coldly and deliberately make such an inhuman suggestion.

It is possible that Governor Wallace may have warned the rash and utterly courageous Chapman of his danger when he saw him in Santa Fe some time after the turn of the year. He might even have shown him the letter, though that would have done little good.

Yet there could be no mistaking the ominous suggestion: "if this man was silenced the trouble would end."

3

It was now mid-February of 1879 and Lincoln was tense with apprehension.

Billy, with Tom O'Folliard, Doc Scurlock, and possibly Salazar, and one or two other native New Mexicans, rode boldly down the single dusty street of the county seat. The new sheriff made no move against them. He felt the dignity of his position, but he found it impossible to secure proper deputies in Lincoln. When he asked Colonel Dudley for soldiers, the Colonel refused to put his troopers under the sheriff's orders.

Due largely to the urgings of his military superior in Santa Fe, Dudley had expelled the murderous Selman and Kinney gangs from the Bonito and Ruidoso valleys. A number of the old Rustlers, however, were still living below Seven Rivers on the Pecos where Captain Carroll's detachment was scouring the County for the stolen Tunstall cattle.

On January 1st the experienced and able J. C. Lea of Roswell, financially backed by the well-to-do Texas widow he had recently married, was appointed a County Commissioner. Captain Lea had been in the county less than six months and he had scrupulously refused to be involved in the war. In that short period he had become one of Lincoln County's most important citizens, rating second only to John Chisum who had not as yet returned to the Pecos country. Lea was quietly determined that the lawlessness must end and that the almost limitless possibilities of the vast area should be given its chance at normal development.

A second noteworthy item was the fact that Tom Catron, practical dictator of New Mexico and nominal head of the Santa Fe Ring, and now the financial successor to the Murphy-Dolan interests in Lincoln County, was no longer U.S. Prosecuting Attorney. President Hayes had replaced him with Sidney M. Barnes. The new federal prosecutor, ambitious to make a reputation for himself, announced at once his determination to bring into court Jesse Evans, still out on bail on the charge of stealing of government property.

To the Rustlers it was clear that since the arrival of Governor Wallace their Rio Grande patrons no longer completely dominated the courts and the law. They, as well as Billy's men, knew that if the fighting continued at least some of them would end up in lonely, unmarked graves. It was a good time for the actual fighters to quit.

Even Tom Catron felt the effects of the thieving gangs operating in the neighborhood of his Pecos cow camp, formerly belonging to Murphy-Dolan. His brother-in-law, young Edgar Walz, was in control of Catron's affairs in Lincoln County, but Dolan remained in actual charge of the ranching and cattle end.

So bad had things become that Dolan decided to move most of the large herd from the Pecos camp to the permanent ranch called "Fairview," on the western slopes of the Capitans at Carrizozo Springs. With Dolan rode Jesse Evans, J. B. Mathews, and several old Rustlers, including a heavy-set, tough bully by the name of Bill Campbell. For a time Campbell had been hanging around Ft. Stanton and seemed to be on friendly terms with Colonel Dudley. The Catron cattle from the Pecos were safely delivered to the open ranges near the famous springs, and the men were now back in the Lincoln-Stanton country.

The Kid may or may not have instigated the idea of a peace talk between the two bitter factions. It possibly was one of the boy's friends in the Ellis store or Squire Wilson himself who made the original suggestion. Be that as it may, arrangements were completed, and on the late afternoon of February 18th, 1879, Billy and the Dolan-Evans factions came together in Lincoln to end the feud.

It was a day of some significance: exactly one year before this Jesse Evans and his gang had shot to death the Kid's idol, John Tunstall. From this had stemmed the Lincoln County War, with all its deadly results.

It was a long chance the one-time enemies were taking in meeting face to face on this anniversary. Memories were still fresh, and there were many old scores which remained unsettled.

Billy decided to take only Tom O'Folliard with him. To bring along Doc Scurlock or Salazar or any of the others of his little crowd would only have increased the possibility of trouble. Billy knew he could keep his own head and not be provoked into a wild gun fight. And he could implicitly trust Tom to follow his lead.

There were six or eight men in the Dolan-Evans contingent in addition to young Walz, who took no formal part in the talk. By nightfall there was a general acceptance of an arrangement that called for an end to the bitter grudges and conflicts.

Most of the conference was held in a little adobe bar and eating house, and there had been considerable whiskey consumed by all except the temperate Billy and one or two others. Evans and Bill Campbell and Dolan were soon drunk enough to be quarrelsome and dangerous. It was a toss-up whether the new peace would last even through this first night.

It was around ten o'clock in the evening when the Dolanites, with Billy and O'Folliard, moved down the middle of the dirt street towards the Cullun saloon, which was in the newly built Ellis structure adjacent to the ruins of the McSween home. Bill Campbell particularly was in an ugly mood. It was at this moment that Fate stepped in.

Lawyer Chapman had arrived early in the evening from the long drive from Las Vegas. It was Fate that he should have appeared in Lincoln on this day. It was Fate that sent him down the street at this very moment. And it

was Fate that, as he met the drunken mob spoiling for
some brutal sport, he was suffering from fatigue and pain.
Certainly it was Fate that from all the personalities involved in the affair this courageous, unarmed Kansan
should have been chosen for the victim.

The following day a letter was sent to the Las Cruces
Thirty-four, a newspaper published in the fast-growing
town two or three miles from Mesilla, which described
the event in stark prose. The words carry the sense of terror and utter helplessness. It was signed "Max" and probably came from the pen of a man who was helping build
the government telegraph line. It may be inaccurate in
minor details but time has substantiated most of its statements. It reads:

> Wednesday some of the leaders of the two parties had
> a meeting and agreed to bury the hatchet. They pa-
> raded the street of Lincoln arm-in-arm and had a
> regular good time.
>
> That evening early Chapman arrived from Las
> Vegas and put his horse in Mrs. McSween's corral.
> Then he went to a neighbor's to get some bread to
> make a poultice for his face. He was suffering from
> a severe attack of neuralgia.
>
> He was returning about 10 o'clock and met Jesse
> Evans, and Bill Campbell, with Billey Bonney and
> Tom O'Folliard of the McSween party. Dolan and
> his party had insisted upon their accompanying
> them, and they had assented to do so rather than
> show any unfriendliness.
>
> When they met, one of the Dolan party asked,
> "Who are you and where are you going?"
>
> Chapman answered and told them he was attend-
> ing to his business. He was told to talk differently or
> they would make him.
>
> "You cannot scare me, boys. I know you and it's
> no use. You have tried that before."
>
> "Then," said Campbell, "I'll settle you," and fired
> his pistol, the ball going in at the breast and coming
> out the back. Dolan shot him with his Winchester.
> Then they set fire to his body. It is thought they
> soaked his clothes with whiskey to make them burn.
>
> When they first met, Kid tried to get away and ran

around an angle in the lane wall, but Evans held the other fast and made him look on during the entire affair.

Next day a coroner's jury was held, and the Dolan party was in town armed and the people so bulldozed no evidence could be brought out.

These are the facts as near as I can get at them, but no one dares to speak of them except in whispers. If it were known I am writing to you, my life would not be worth insuring two hours, and I don't think you will be safe in publishing this letter. I want to get away as soon as possible and don't want any more Lincoln County in mine.

P.S. Chapman was unarmed. He never carried arms.

It was a terrible test for Billy and Tom when the drunken Campbell whipped out his pistol and shot the brave but foolhardy lawyer. Billy and Tom were outnumbered four to one. The slightest false move on either man's part and both would have been killed instantly.

When Evans stopped Billy from turning from the outrage he must certainly have shoved his gun into the boy's middle. Tom unquestionably was also covered. Neither dared show the slightest disapproval of the brutal act.

There was nothing for the two to do but go on to the Cullun saloon with the murderers. It seems to be well authenticated that Campbell cooled down a bit and was heard to remark: "I promised my God and General Dudley that I'd kill Chapman, and I've done it."

Caution and not remorse dictated the killer's next move. Knowing the potency of the old-time plea of self-defense, Campbell asked young Walz to go back to where Chapman's body lay and put a gun in his hand. When Walz begged off, the Kid quietly volunteered to do the job. Campbell and Evans, interested in their drinking, agreed. When Billy left the crowd Tom O'Folliard waited a moment and then slipped out. They both had played their part perfectly. They had kept cool and saved their own lives.

They had horses tied over in the Ellis corral and they hurried there, tightened cinches and mounted. Their next stop was their hide-out over in the Ruidoso country near San Patricio.

Instead of peace there would now be violent open war. It was hard luck for Billy. He'd hoped to get a chance at a fresh start in life. But he knew that this would be no longer possible in Lincoln County.

There is sound evidence that he definitely planned to leave for Old Mexico with Tom O'Folliard as soon as their horses were rested up.

4

The four men personally involved in the killing—Campbell, Evans, Mathews, and Dolan—rode on to Fort Stanton late that night. Some time the next day they were on their way to the Carrizozo ranch, some forty miles to the west. They had no fear of arrest by the incompetent Sheriff Kimbrell.

In the morning a coroner's jury sat over the body of the one-armed lawyer. The best it could do was to fall back on the time-worn phrase that the deceased had come to his death from a bullet fired by a person or persons unknown to the jury. So heavy hung the threat of reprisal, by both the mob and the military against anyone opposing them, that no citizen of Lincoln dared appear as a witness against the murderers.

The confused and impotent sheriff secured six soldiers from Fort Stanton and went through the motions of trying to arrest Billy in the San Patricio country. He might as well have sent a mule team to catch butterflies.

The second day, February 20th, the unfortunate Chapman was buried in the plot just to the east of the old Tunstall store, next to the grave of the murdered young Englishman. A year before, to a day, John Tunstall had been equally brave and equally foolhardy. The little row of wooden headmarkers was lengthening. Already Tunstall and McSween lay here; and Harvey Morris, the young law student killed on the day McSween died; and Charlie McNab who had met death in the ambush at the Fritz ranch. Now Chapman joined them.

Governor Wallace was shocked and angry when the telegraphed news reached him. A day or two later he received a letter from his personal and professional advisor at Las Vegas, Judge Ira E. Leonard. It is worth quoting:

> You have undoubtedly learned ere this of the assas-
> sination of H. I. Chapman at Lincoln on the night of
> Feby. 18th. He left here for Lincoln Wednesday,
> Feby. 12 about noon, and from a letter received from
> Sidney Wilson, an attorney at that place, it seems
> that Chapman had just arrived in town when he was
> assassinated.
>
> The morning Chapman left here I had a long talk
> with him concerning his course down there, and ad-
> vised him to be careful and more discreet in his con-
> duct—if not, he might have trouble. He said he had
> no reason to apprehend trouble from any source than
> through Col. Dudley and Lieut. French. From what
> he revealed to me I came to the conclusion that he
> had undoubtedly had good reason to fear from that
> source, and I cannot shake the conviction from my
> mind that if the truth should be reached about this
> dastardly assassination that it could be traced close
> to the door of these two officers.
>
> When I see you I can give you some circumstances
> that fasten that conviction on my mind and consti-
> tute to me "proof as strong as holy writ" of their im-
> plication in it.
>
> I hope, Gov., you will go down to Lincoln when
> the court convenes there. I intend to go.

Apparently Colonel Dudley had fallen back on his old
prescription of a display of military force as a cure all for
civil disorders. A day or two after Chapman's murder the
post commander himself rode into Lincoln at the head of
two companies of troops. As he had done in his disastrous
appearance during the Big Fight in Lincoln on July 19th
of the previous year, he came with a Gatling gun. His
dramatic entrance only added to the fear and intimida-
tion of the cowed and frightened citizens.

Governor Wallace was now inclined to accept Judge
Leonard's general feeling that Dudley was at the root of
the new trouble. Wallace had made his first request to
General Hatch for the removal of Colonel Dudley from
Fort Stanton on December 7th. The request had been referred to General Sherman, head of the Army, who had
curtly turned it down with the suggestion that if the Gov-

ernor so chose he could make formal military charges against Dudley.

Wallace could no longer put off giving Lincoln his personal attention. He and General Hatch saw eye to eye on the need for drastic action, and the General agreed to accompany him to Lincoln. They left Santa Fe on March 1st, 1879, and on a late afternoon four days later they separated at the forks in the Lincoln road where the right-hand branch led off to Fort Stanton. General Hatch proceeded to the army post while the Governor drove on east to Lincoln and the Montano home where he was to stop.

Almost from the moment of his arrival the Governor was dumfounded at the complete paralysis that had gripped the machinery of civil government, and at the fear and apathy of the citizens. Two weeks had gone by since the Chapman assassination, and though the murderers and their whereabouts were well known not a single arrest had been made. The citizens appeared to be more terrorized by fear of reprisals from the military than from the killers themselves. All respect for the soldiers was completely gone.

On the day following his arrival the Governor called a mass meeting of the citizens. More than seventy-five adults attended and applauded his promise to clear up the mess and once again request General Hatch to remove Colonel Dudley. Following the meeting Wallace called in a dozen of the most prominent citizens and conferred confidentially with them, one at a time. He found the same story repeated over and over again; fear of reprisals by Colonel Dudley and the military if anyone brought on their displeasure.

The day following the citizens' meeting Wallace renewed his written request for the removal of Colonel Dudley on the grounds that the officer was so compromised in the county that "his usefulness in the effort being made to restore peace is now gone." Shocking and specific charges were boldly made against Dudley in the report the courageous Wallace now sent to Secretary of the Interior Schurz:

> The intimidation under which really well-disposed people are suffering, and which prevents my securing affidavits as the foundation of legal proceedings

against parties already in arrest, results in great part
from fear of misdirection of authority by him.

It is with the greatest regret I add that if I am to
believe the information which had come to me, the
dread referred to is not irrational. In justice to Col.
Dudley, and that he may take such action as your
sense of duty may suggest under the circumstances,
I will state in general terms that Lt. Col. Dudley is
responsible for the killing of McSween and the men
who were shot with that person. I have information
also connecting him with the more recent murder of
H. I. Chapman; to the effect that he knew the man
would be killed and announced it the day of the
night of the killing, and that one of the murderers
[Campbell] stated publicly that he had promised
Col. Dudley to do the deed. I am informed that another man [Scarce, Mrs. McSween's detective] was
driven in fear of his life from Lincoln to Fort Stanton; that a band of armed men (among whom was
Campbell) followed him there and hunted for him
about the Trader's store, vowing a purpose to kill
him; that the party pursued appealed to Col. Dudley
to give him protection, was turned away, and escaped
with difficulty; that there was no investigation of the
affair by Col. Dudley and that the would-be murderers were not interrupted in their hunt, which was
reported through two days, but were permitted to
leave at their leisure and within a night or two after
engaged in the killing of Chapman in the town of
Lincoln.

It was about as scathing an indictment as could be conceived being made by a Territorial Governor to the Secretary of the Interior regarding the conduct of a high
army officer. Certainly the information which had come to
Wallace's hand shocked his fine sense of decency and
honor. Obviously he was amazed by this sequence of actions on the part of Colonel Dudley.

Billy and Tom O'Folliard, with two or three others
who remained of the old Regulators, were able to follow
the turn of events from their hide-outs. Billy's sources of
information unquestionably included such sympathizers
as Squire Wilson and the former Tunstall clerk, Sam Cor-

bett, as well as members of the Ellis family, all faithful believers in the McSween cause. Some unsuspected native New Mexican would slip out of Lincoln and a couple of hours later Billy would have the latest news, along with advice from his older friends in Lincoln.

He was delighted when he heard that Governor Wallace had asked General Hatch to arrest Campbell, Mathews and Jesse Evans, who were enjoying life at Catron's Carrizozo ranch. They were swooped up without trouble and lodged in the Fort Stanton guard house.

The Governor, suspicious of the security of the set-up at Stanton, requested that the trio be sent up north to Fort Union for safe custody until the April term of court. His request was not followed. But soon orders were issued transferring Lt. Colonel Dudley from Fort Stanton to Fort Union. In protest against this transfer, Dudley immediately asked for a Court of Inquiry.

Billy probably did not know the exact meaning of the words "Court of Inquiry," but he did know that he personally was in grave peril from enemies who would stop at nothing to remove him from the scene. He could survive only if he were constantly on the alert as he rode the dangerous trails and camped in hidden canyons.

[Many years after these troublesome times a gracious, silver-haired lady in her seventies used to rock on the porch of her home at Globe, Arizona, and talk to a young artist by the name of Ross Santee. She was called "Mrs. Van" by all her friends, but her real name was Jennie Van Wagnan, and as a girl she had attended school in Silver City, New Mexico, with a boy she had known as Henry Antrim. She would always insist that until his mother died he was the kindest sort of a boy and always helped wash and wipe the dishes for her, and not many boys did that in those days. . . . Then she would tell about the time when her family moved to the tiny village of Ruidoso in the mountains of western Lincoln County; and how on one of the first nights after she got home from school at Silver City, she and two boys started down the canyon to a native's house to get some potatoes, and how they raced their ponies through the gathering darkness. Jennie who was fifteen was in the lead, her long, brown hair trailing straight behind her like a trooper's guidon snapping in the breeze. Suddenly she ran into several

mounted men, and one shouted, "Don't shoot! It's a girl!"
The night-riders pulled up their ponies and a young man,
who apparently was the leader, rode up. A band of gray-
ish light from the open door of a native hut cut through
the darkness. The young man pushed back his wide-
brimmed hat as he surveyed the situation. "Why—hello,
Jennie," he said in a friendly voice, when he recognized
the girl. "What in the world are you doing here? It's bad
on these roads at night." And then he talked of the old
days back in the little mining camp of Silver City, and of
his brother Joe and his stepfather. He warned her once
again in gentle tones to be careful and not ride the roads
at night because it was unusually dangerous just at this
time. Then he tipped his hat and touched his horse with
his spurs and rode off with his men. . . . The little episode
had happened during these wild days when Billy was hiding out, following the Chapman murder.]

5

Two days after the arrest of Campbell, Mathews and
Evans, the hard and elusive Jimmy Dolan voluntarily surrendered. Wallace promptly took his parole and confined
him to the limits of the post. Within forty-eight hours
Dolan violated his parole by appearing in Lincoln, and
Governor Wallace immediately demanded that he be
held in close confinement at Fort Stanton.

Billy's original glee over the arrest of his chief enemies
lasted but a single day. Then a messenger rode to him
with the news that Sergeant Murphy and nine troopers
were being sent to arrest Tom and himself. The Governor
had learned that, while Billy was in no wise directly involved in the actual killing of Chapman, he was a key
witness and might aid materially in the conviction of the
quartet. Wallace communicated at once with General
Hatch:

> I have just ascertained that the Kid is at a place
> called Las Tablas, a plazita up near Coghlin's ranch.
> He has with him Tom O'Folliard, and was going out
> of the Territory, but stopped there to rest his horses,
> saying he wanted to stay a few days. He is at the
> house of one Salazar.

You will oblige me by sending a detachment after
the two men; and if they are caught, send them to
Fort Stanton for trial as accessories to the murder of
Chapman.

If the men are found to have left Las Tablas, I
beg they be pursued until caught.

There is no way of knowing just how accurate was the
Governor's information that Billy "was going out of the
Territory, but stopped there to rest his horses." It is a
point of some importance, because, as the Kid later stated,
he was tired of the eternal fighting and wanted peace. He
might well have concluded that this was the time to pull
out for good.

It seemed that about everything Billy tried sooner or
later built up evidence against him as a man outside the
law. The few hours of peace with the Dolan-Evans gang
had ended in the brutal assassination of poor Chapman.
The Kid's own murder had been prevented only by his
cool behavior that night.

He had taken no part in the killing but nevertheless he
now had soldiers after him again. It probably occurred to
him that people figured he knew too much. Fate wouldn't
let him quit; none of the men on either side would let
him quit. He was on everybody's black list.

With a tip in advance of the arrival of the army detachment, Billy took to the hills. He was safe enough in his
hide-out, when suddenly a fresh complication arose.

The next messenger who arrived from Lincoln brought
the disturbing news: the new Governor had verbally offered a $1,000 reward for the arrest of the Kid.

Even in the eyes of the new Governor he was a criminal with a price on his head.

PART THREE

The Outlaw

14

While Billy was playing hide-and-go-seek with the Fort Stanton soldiers, the Governor saw the need of a well armed and well mounted body of local men who would swiftly carry out his bidding. Don Juan Patron, the energetic twenty-five-year-old Speaker of the Assembly at Santa Fe, agreed to become the captain of a detachment to be called The Lincoln County Mounted Rifles.

Some thirty volunteers were enrolled in the militia company, and the Governor personally took time out to drill them. They were primarily native New Mexicans and were the victims of considerable amusing comment. Opposition papers over in Las Cruces and in Santa Fe referred to them as "the Governor's heel flies." Nevertheless, they did serve a very useful purpose.

There is some evidence that it was Squire "Green" Wilson who fathered the idea of a secret interview between Billy and the Governor. A spy who kept Billy informed of the various moves in Lincoln and Fort Stanton may well have carried the idea to the boy, who was still dodging the rather clumsy detachment of troopers, hard on his trail. Billy was tired of being eternally on the dodge. And the prospect that the Governor might somehow or other be able to wipe out the murder indictments held against him was worth any try.

On either the 14th or 15th of March a messenger handed the Governor a letter that bore neither a date nor place mark. It was in Billy's handwriting, and save for a little individuality in punctuation it was above the average in frontier scholarship:

> To his Excellency the Governor,
>   Gen. Lew Wallace
> Dear Sir:
>   I have heard you will give one thousand $dollars for my body which as I understand it means alive as a Witness. I know it is as a witness against those that Murdered Mr. Chapman. if it was so that I could appear at Court I could give the desired information but I have indictments against me for things that happened in the late Lincoln County War and am afraid to give up because they would kill me. the day Mr. Chapman was murdered I was in Lincoln at the request of good Citizens to meet Mr. J. J. Dolan to meet as Friends. so as to be able to lay aside our arms and go to Work. I was present when Mr. Chapman was Murdered and know who did it and if it were not for these indictments I would have made it clear before now. if it is in your power to Annul those indictments I hope you will do so as to give me a chance to explain. please send me an answer telling me what you can do You can send answer by bearer I have no Wish to fight any more indeed I have not raised an arm since Your proclamation. as to my Character I refer to any of the Citizens for the majority of them are my Friends and have been helping me all they could. I am called Kid Antrim, but Antrim is my stepfathers name.
>
> > Waiting for an answer, I remain
> >   Your Obedient servant,
> >   W. H. Bonney

The romantic Wallace must have been touched by the lonely cry "I do not wish to fight any more." Certainly the letter showed a definite straightforwardness in the attitude of the boy. Instead of being a vicious little killer mocking the law, Billy showed himself to be a young man who wanted the turmoil to end, and to be given a clean slate so that he might start life anew.

The Governor, deeply impressed and full of hope, immediately answered Billy's letter. The whole affair had an aroma of mild intrigue and drama that appealed to the Hoosier writer and lawyer-soldier. He wrote:

LINCOLN, MARCH 15, 1879

W. H. Bonney;

Come to the house of old Squire Wilson (not the lawyer) at nine (9) o'clock next Monday night alone. I don't mean his office, but his residence. Follow along the foot of the mountain south of the town, come in on that side, and knock on the east door. I have authority to exempt you from prosecution, if you will testify to what you say you know.

The object of the meeting at Squire Wilson's is to arrange the matter in a way to make your life safe. To do that the utmost secrecy is to be used. *So come alone.* Don't tell anybody—not a living soul—where you are coming or the object. If you could trust Jesse Evans, you can trust me.

Lew Wallace.

The sentence, "I have authority to exempt you from prosecution" must have rung like a bell in Billy's mind.

Despite the stern warning to tell no one, it is probable that he discussed the Governor's terms with the tall Texas boy who looked up to Billy in worship and affection, just as a year before Billy himself had looked up to John Tunstall. It would be hard to believe that Tom O'Folliard did not ride with Billy that Monday night of March 17th. He must have stood guard over the two horses in some hidden arroyo in the hills to the south of Lincoln, while Billy alone and on foot made his way through the night to Squire Wilson's residence.

Some time later the Governor recalled in an interview the singular meeting of the boy of nineteen and the distinguished soldier and executive of fifty-one. They were at the opposite poles of the earth in family background, environment and position.

It was exactly 9 o'clock when Billy rapped on the east door of the adobe building. The Governor called out, "Come in!"

Billy carried his rifle cradled in the bend of his left arm. A Colt rested lightly in its holster on his right hip. A coal oil lamp on the table at the far end of the room dimly lighted the scene. Two men sat at the table.

Coming into the room from the outer darkness the Kid could not immediately identify the figures across the room.

"I was sent for," he began with a smile and a friendly nod, "to meet the Governor at 9 o'clock. Is he here?"

"I am Governor Wallace," the bearded man answered, half rising and motioning the boy to come forward.

"Your note gave promise of absolute protection."

"Yes, and I have been true to my promise. This man here, whom of course you know, and I are the only persons in the house."

Billy nodded in approval. Carefully he lowered the hammer of his rifle, and set the gun against the wall near the door. With quiet dignity he walked towards the table, and the Governor rose and they shook hands.

He must have appeared a young and slender boy to be carrying such terrible secrets and memories. To the sensitive and imaginative Lew Wallace, hardened as he was by four years of service in the Civil War, it seemed as though he had suddenly turned back the clock of time and stood face to face with a figure out of another age. It was almost as if he were witnessing the birth of a legend; a scene from some ancient play that created mood in place of reality.

The boy in front of him surely could not be the cruel and senseless young killer of whom Tom Catron and Dolan and the others in Santa Fe had told him. This could not be the monster who was said to have killed a man for every year of his life. Surely not this soft-spoken boy, with the blue-gray eyes and the quick, disarming smile. Even the famous upper teeth did not disfigure him but seemed to add to the unique and definite personality now filling the Governor's eye.

It was not a brusque and threatening conversation that followed. Instead, it was the friendly meeting of a wise

and gentle man of the world and a young boy of talent
and exceptional intelligence, who somehow had had a
wrong start and didn't seem to be getting along too well
with life.

Lew Wallace was a man of genuine compassion and,
while his primary motive for the meeting was to make use
of the boy's testimony in the coming trial of the men who
had killed the defenseless one-armed lawyer, he was deeply touched by the honesty and the obvious handicaps of
this unusual boy. Certainly he possessed a gift of leadership and was a past master of the fine art of self-preservation.

"Testify," Wallace quietly urged, "before the grand
jury and the open court, and convict the murderers of
Chapman, and I will let you go scot-free, with a pardon in
your pocket for all your misdeeds."

It was the one thing that Billy wanted more than anything else in the world. But even a full pardon did not
mean safety. Billy, cool and unemotional, surveyed his
chances for life once he had been given complete immunity from legal prosecution. He hesitated before answering.

"Governor," he finally said, "if I were to do what you
ask, they would kill me."

"We can prevent that," Wallace argued patiently.

He slowly unfolded his plan. Billy was to be arrested at
night while he was apparently asleep. To all appearances
his arrest would be genuine. Every detail would be carefully worked out.

The boy was alert and impressed. He suggested just
how the arrest should be made and who should be included in the posse. There was always grave danger of some
enemy killing him at the moment of arrest and safeguards
must be built up against this possibility. He even suggested that he be kept in manacles and leg irons, to help
build up the illusion of reality.

But Billy still was not quite ready to give his final word
to the arrangements. He would think it over and in a
couple of days send his formal decision to the Governor.

He had been talking for an hour and a half with Wallace when he shook hands and courteously bade him good
night. It must have seemed a long time to the Texas boy
waiting for him back in the arroyo.

2

On Wednesday, March 19th, two days after the meeting
with the Governor, Billy heard the shocking news that
Evans and Campbell, who had taken part in the actual
killing of Chapman, had been permitted to escape from
the guard house at Fort Stanton. A soldier sentinel known
as Texas Jack pulled out with them but was later captured. The two murderers, however, were still at large.

Billy, wise beyond his years, had few illusions regarding
any interest officials might have in him save to use him.
He figured that for his own safety he should find out
whether the sudden turn of events had changed his own
status. He wrote a note at once but did not send it directly to the Governor. His letter, dated San Patricio, was
addressed to his old friend, Squire Wilson:

San Patricio

THURSDAY, MARCH 20TH, 1879

Friend Wilson:
    Please tell You know who that I do not know what
to do, now as those Prisoners have escaped. to send
word by bearer, a note through You it may be that
he has made different arrangements if not and he
still wants it the same to Send "William Hudgins,"
as Deputy. to the Junction tomorrow at three o'clock
with some men you know to be all right. Send a note
telling me what to do.

W. H. Bonney

P.S. Do not send soldiers.

The four-word postscript showed Billy's hate and dis-
trust of Dudley's soldiers. He made no bones over his
worry that the Governor might no longer choose to go
through with the deal. Maybe the happy prospect of going scot-free "with a pardon in your pocket" had now
turned into so much moonshine. *Quien sabe?*

The Governor had alerted Capt. Juan Patron and his
Mounted Rifles and then left for Fort Stanton to take
charge of the searching parties for the escaped murderers.
There was consequently some little delay in getting the
Kid's letter to him. Wallace immediately sent back a note
and enclosure to Squire Wilson. It read:

I enclose a note for Bonney. Read it and forward at
once. I presume the messenger is waiting. If you
should know why Kimbrell should not go rather
than Hudgens, hold on until I get over this evening.

Squire Wilson now studied the Governor's open note
addressed to Billy. It was blunt and to the point:

The escape makes no difference in arrangements.
     To remove all suspicion of understanding, I think it
better to put the arresting party in charge of Sheriff
Kimbrell, who will be instructed to see that no violence is used. If I don't get other word for you, the
party (all citizens) will be at the Junction by 3 o'clock
tomorrow.

Billy was fully satisfied with the Governor's reply. He
even went so far in his answering letter as to give the
Governor advice on how he might catch the two escaped
men. Apparently, however, he did not know that the
sheriff's posse would be made up of members of Patron's
Lincoln County Mounted Rifles, who were almost to a
man friendly to Billy and the Tunstall-McSween side.
     The Kid's answer to the note received through Squire
Wilson was dated Thursday, March 20th, and sent from
San Patricio:

General Wallace,
Sir:
     I will keep the appointment I made, but be Sure
and have men come that you can depend on I am
not afraid to die like a man fighting but I would not
like to be killed like a dog unarmed. tell Kimbal to
let his men be placed around the house and for him
to come in alone; and he can arrest us. all I am
afraid of is that in the Fort We might be poinired or
killed through a Window at night, but You can arrange that all right. tell the Commanding Officer
to watch Lt. Goodwin (he would not hesitate to do
anything there Will be danger on the road of Somebody Waylaying us to kill us on the road to the Fort.
You Will never catch those fellows on the road
Watch Fritzes, Captain Bacas ranch and the Brewery
they Will either go to Seven Rivers or the Jicarillo
Mountains they will stay around close until scouting

parties come in. give a Spy a pair of Glasses and let him get on the mountain back of Fritzes and watch and if they are ther ther will be provisions carried to them. it is not my place to advise you, but I am anxious to have them caught, and perhaps know how men hide from Soldiers better than you. please excuse me for having so much to say and I still remain,

Yours truly,

W. H. Bonney

P.S. I have changed my mind Send Kimbal to Gutieres just below San Patricio one mile, because Sanger and Ballard are or were great friends of Camels Ballard told me yesterday to leave for you were doing everything to catch me. it was a blind to get us to leave. tell Kimbal not to come before 3 o'clock for I may not be there before.

At three o'clock that next morning everything worked out according to schedule. It was early in the forenoon when the posse rode into Lincoln with Billy and Tom O'Folliard mounted and with their hands manacled. Their horses were led and there was every evidence that the arrest was a bona fide one. Governor Wallace hurried off a message to the authorities at Ft. Stanton:

Sheriff Kimbrell and a posse of citizens have just come in with the Kid and Tom O'Folliard, captured about a mile below San Patricio. I will keep them under guard for a couple of days; then send them to the Fort.

Billy may have had something to do with the fact that he and Tom were never sent to the uncertainties and dangers of the post guardhouse. Apparently they were taken directly to the miserable jail that was little more than a deep, square cellar with a small house built over it. Juan Patron claimed it really was only a $300 job, although the county paid Sheriff Peppin $3000 to build it. Billy was turned over to his friend, Deputy Sheriff Tom Longworth. Ash Upson, the somewhat unreliable scribe of Roswell, writing three years later, drew a picture of the scene of Billy's entrance into the underground prison, and the boy's conversation with Tom Longworth:

"Tom, I've sworn I would never go inside that hole

again alive." There was no smile playing around the Kid's mouth as he addressed the deputy.

"I don't see how either you or I can help it," the deputy sheriff answered quietly. "I don't want to put you there—I don't want to put anyone there. But that's orders, and I have nothing to do but obey. You don't want to make trouble for me."

The Kid is reported to have walked gloomily towards the door which led to the lower cell-room and then stopped to address Longworth again. "Tom, I'm going in here because I won't have any trouble with you, but I'd give all I've got if the son of a b— that gave the order was in your boots."

He slowly walked along the passageway to his own cell. The wooden door was open and, taking a pencil from his pocket, the Kid wrote out on the panel:

> William Bonney was incarcerated first time, December 22nd, 1878; second time, March 21st, 1879, and hope I never will be again.
>
> W. H. Bonney

Something apparently had gone a little wrong with the Governor's arrangements. Here was the star witness, who had voluntarily submitted to arrest, undergoing unnecessary hardships and indignities. A day later the Governor ordered Billy transferred to the back room of Juan Patron's store and held there in arrest.

Court would not open until the second week in April, in this year of 1879, and the Kid was permitted to pass away the bright spring days in fairly pleasant surroundings. His friends were allowed to drop in on him. There seems some authority for the legend that Billy was endowed with heavy wrists but very small hands, and that he enjoyed freeing himself from his handcuffs when he "entertained." It may be, of course, that his "jewelry," as he called the steel bracelets, were very loosely put on his wrists so that it was simple for him to slip his slender hands through them.

It was all a little too much for the Hoosier Governor, trained to respect the sanctity of the law and its various processes. He had been intrigued by the boy and touched by the handicaps he had been brought up under, but he could neither quite understand him nor condone him.

It was while Billy was still held under loose arrest that
Wallace wrote Secretary of the Interior Schurz of his
great disappointment at the turn of affairs and at his complete lack of confidence in the local citizens:

> My expectation of a revival of courage and confi-
> dence on the part of the better people of the county
> is far from realized. The escape of Campbel[1] and
> Evans shook their faith in the soldiers. As jurors and
> witnesses they are singularly unreliable on account
> of their fear of retaliation. . . .
>
> To still further weaken my confidence in juries as
> instruments of the law in this county, I have been
> forced to take account of the fact that everybody of
> any force or character has been in some way commit-
> ted to one side or the other in the recent war, and is
> yet all alive with prejudices and partialities. A pre-
> cious specimen named "the Kid" whom the sheriff is
> holding here in the Plaza, as it is called, is an object
> of tender regard. I heard singing and music the other
> night; going to the door I found the residents of the
> village actually serenading the fellow in his prison.

Instead of exercising his sense of humor the good Governor could only fall back momentarily on his own high
code of dignity and honor. Certainly it was an outrageous
exhibition that was taking place down the street.

But the romantic old soldier could not long hold out
against the warm and magnetic charm of the strange boy.
After all, the Governor's real quarrel was with the apathy
of the people and not with this oddly talented and unfortunate young man.

3

On Sunday, the third day after the arrest, the Governor
had a long talk with Billy in the back room of the Patron
store. He questioned him at length about the gangs that
had been depredating the County, and about trails and
hide-outs, and various cattle thieves. There still exists the
memorandum that the Governor wrote out in his own
hand and labelled "Statements by the Kid." It bears the
date of March 23rd, 1879, and one particular section gives

an insight into Billy's fine capacity for accurate reporting
and analysis:

> The "Rustlers," the Kid says, were organized at Fort
> Stanton. Before they organized as "Rustlers" they
> had been Peppin's posse. They came from Texas.
> Jake Owens was conspicuous amongst them. They
> were organized before the burning of McSween's
> house, and after that they went on their first trips
> down country as far as Coe's ranch and thence to the
> Feliz, where they took the Tunstall cattle.
>
> Martin (known to Sam Corbett) was in charge of
> the Tunstall cattle and was taken prisoner and saw
> them kill one of their own party. On the same trip
> they burnt Lola Wise's house, and took her horses.
> Coe at the time was ranching at the house. On this
> trip they moved behind a body of soldiers, one com-
> pany, and a company of Navaho scouts. They moved
> in sight of the soldiers, taking horses, insulting wom-
> en. Gregorio Trujillo, Juan Trujillo, Jose M. Gui-
> tierres, Pancho Sanchez, Santos Teojoya are witnesses
> against them. They stopped on the Pecos at Seven
> Rivers. Collins, now at Silver City, was one of the
> outfit—nicknamed the Prowler by the cowboys.
>
> At Seven Rivers there joined them Gus Gildea
> (wanted at San Antonio for killing Mexicans.) Gil-
> dea is carrying the mail now from Stockton to Seven
> Rivers—James Irvin and Reese Gobles (rumored that
> their bodies were found in a drift down the Pecos)—
> Rustling Bob (found dead on the Pecos killed by his
> own party)—John Selman (whereabouts unknown)
> came to Roswell while Captain Carroll was there—
> The R's stayed at Seven Rivers; which they left on
> their second trip via the Berenda for Fort Stanton.
> On their return back they killed the Chaves boys and
> the crazy Lorenzo, and the Sanchez boy, 14 yrs. old.
> They also committed many robberies. They broke
> up after reaching the Pecos, promising to return
> when some more horses got fat.

The Kid, apparently, was more than willing to tell
everything he knew to his new friend. The long memorandum in the Governor's handwriting continues with reports of Shedd's Ranch, Mimbres, San Nicholas Spring,

and the Jones family. In each case Billy gave a clear and frank account. The Governor had his complete confidence, and it is obvious that the Kid constantly advised him as to his best chances of capturing Campbell and Jesse Evans.

Returning to Lincoln from Fort Stanton one night the Governor's army Doherty wagon, or converted ambulance, was fired on. It was rumored that Jimmy Dolan, held at the Fort in loose arrest, had a part in the affair. On March 29th Dolan addressed a letter to the Governor disavowing any connection with the outrage. With pained concern Jimmy added that there were unscrupulous men loose in the country who would kill anyone in their way, and that "you can't be too carefull."

Early in April Judge Leonard of Las Vegas arrived in Lincoln as a special assistant to the Governor, to aid him in the prosecution of the men he was gathering in. Wallace had settled down at the army post so that he could personally direct the work of searching for Campbell and Evans and assist in the bringing in of new prisoners.

He was beginning to feel alone in his fight against the powerful Santa Fe Ring. He saw now that it was a loosely knit but deadly effective organization. Against it, he counted more than ever on the help of the Kid. He asked Judge Leonard in Lincoln to contact the boy. A little later Wallace wrote his friend Leonard:

> You have no idea how pleasant it is to have one hearty assistant and sympathizer in my work. To work trying to do a little good, but with all the world against you, requires the will of a martyr.

But Governor Wallace's initiation into Lincoln County vagaries was only beginning. On April 3rd District Judge Bristol, who would preside at the term of court at Lincoln, wrote Wallace asking for protection of the court. On Sunday the 13th the Mesilla judicial contingent arrived at Fort Stanton. It consisted of Judge Bristol, District Prosecuting Attorney Rynerson, the clerk and attorneys Thornton, partner in Catron's law firm, and Newcomb, and Colonel Fountain. The fourth attorney who would appear at court, Sydney Wilson, resided at Lincoln and most of the men held under indictment were Wilson's own clients.

The Kid, outwardly gay and unconcerned, must have
been considerably worried over what might happen to
him at the court sessions which would start on Monday.
He had in good faith staked his life on the promise that
the Governor had made to him that if he would "testify
before the grand jury and the open court, and convict the
murderers of Chapman, I will let you go scot-free with a
pardon in your pocket for all your misdeeds."

He knew that the Governor, for all his good intentions,
had never stood up against the hard and unscrupulous
giant, Colonel Rynerson. Nor had Wallace ever sharpened
his wits against the uninhibited mind of Judge Bristol.
The investigator Angel had told Wallace in Washington
that Judge Bristol seemed honest and reliable in all matters save the Lincoln County troubles. Nor had the Governor ever tried to operate in a court under the handicap
of a sheriff who was not to be trusted.

The regular court and grand jury actually got under
way on Tuesday, April 15th. That same day John Chisum,
who had finally screwed up enough courage to return as
near to Roswell as Fort Sumner, wrote the Governor sug-
gesting the desirability of stationing guards at Fort Sumner and two hundred miles to the south at Horsehead
Crossing, so that the upper and lower entrances to the
great Pecos valley could be blocked off from thieves and
criminals. Chisum continued that one Pat Garrett of Fort
Sumner would be just the man to have charge of the upper station.

The tall, lean buffalo hunter, cowboy and gambler thus
first appears in important Lincoln County history. It is an
item worth remembering. John Chisum thus was washing
his hands of any obligations he might have owed the Kid
and the few living Regulators who had fought on the
Chisum-Tunstall-McSween side. The outsider, Pat Garrett, had now replaced them as far as Uncle John was concerned.

But Governor Wallace had other fish to fry than those
caught in the muddy waters of the Pecos. He felt that he
had already been away too long from his duties at the
Palace in Sante Fe. And he had a date to meet his wife
at the new railhead pushing down into New Mexico
through the Raton Pass.

So it was that four days after the court opened in Lincoln the Governor started on the long drive overland to the capital. Judge Leonard, assisted by a young man named George Taylor, a distant relative of President Hayes, could handle the court affairs and the delicate matter of the men indicted by the grand jury who were now pleading the Governor's pardon.

There was also the little item of the Kid turning State's evidence. The fact that both Campbell and Evans, murderers of the Lawyer Chapman, had escaped arrest might very possibly cancel the Governor's promise to the Kid to give him a pardon if he would turn State's evidence. At least it might ease the official's conscience.

The boy duly appeared before the grand jury and testified against the men involved in the Chapman murder; Campbell and Evans for the actual murder, and Dolan as accessory to the crime. He had now done his part. His own case for the killing of Sheriff Brady would soon be heard. A simple motion by the Prosecuting Attorney, Colonel Rynerson, could throw out the case and then, as the Governor had promised, Billy could walk out of the court scot-free.

Tom O'Folliard had been indicted for stealing horses from the Fritz ranch, and there had been no less than twenty-five men held by the grand jury for the murder of McNab. A string of men, including John Long, Marion Turner, and Buck Powell, pleaded the Governor's amnesty, and Col. Rynerson agreed to their release. Dolan, Peppin, and Mathews asked and were granted a change of venue to Socorro County, above Dona Ana on the Rio Grande.

And now came the case of the Territory of New Mexico against the Kid for the murder of Sheriff Brady, based on the indictment found by the Grand Jury in April, 1878. Governor Wallace was en route to Santa Fe but his representative, Judge Leonard, was on hand.

Suddenly the Kid realized that something had gone wrong with the arrangements he had made with the Governor for his release. Judge Leonard quietly explained to the boy that the Governor had not been able to make good his promise because of the stubborn and unreasonable refusal of Colonel Rynerson, the Prosecuting Attorney, to withdraw the charges against the Kid. The legal power and influence of even the Governor was not enough to throw out an indictment for murder unless the Prosecuting Attorney acquiesced. Wallace had simply been blocked and frustrated in the fulfillment of his pledge to the boy.

The next blow for the Kid was almost as deadly. Colonel Rynerson asked the Court for a change of venue to Dona Ana County. Presiding Judge Bristol immediately granted the request.

So it was that in a matter of minutes the unfortunate boy found that Governor Wallace had not only been checked in his attempt to carry out his side of the bargain, but a change of venue had been granted to Rynerson; thus Billy would not even be tried in the friendly atmosphere of Lincoln, where he might have had a reasonable chance at acquittal. Instead, he must face a jury hand-picked by the unfriendly Sheriff of Dona Ana County and Prosecuting Attorney Rynerson, with little chance of securing adequate defense witnesses. He would swiftly be framed and headed for the gallows—and he knew it.

The deputy sheriff led Billy back to his jail room in the rear of the Patron store. Never for a single moment did he show his terrible disappointment. He joked with his jailers and shrugged off his fate with the Spanish phrase, "*No es importante.*"

Even the dire prospect ahead of him could not break down the boy's iron nerve and his cheerful disposition. Bad luck had once again caught up with him. So what? He took life as it came. He asked for little, therefore he never permitted himself to be completely overwhelmed by disappointment.

As far as this change of venue to Mesilla was concerned, he simply didn't expect to be on hand for the trial. He was too shrewd not to realize fully the certain outcome.

With his almost uncanny ability to judge people the Kid apparently had no illusions as to the true character of the bitter prosecutor, Colonel Rynerson. He knew that he could expect nothing but harsh and crooked justice from this roaring, ill-tempered giant, with his great, hairy paws and his exaggerated sense of his own importance. [Rynerson was known all his life as a man of violent rages. In December of 1867 he shot and killed Judge John P. Slough, in the office of the old Exchange Hotel in Santa

Fe, when Slough started to draw his derringer. A lonely man, with no gift for making money, Rynerson married the wealthy widow of one of his close friends who had been killed, along with fourteen other citizens, in the disastrous Republican political riot in Mesilla in 1871. He had no daughters by this marriage, but he was the father, by an attractive Mexican woman, of an illegitimate girl whom he named Cosetta Rynerson. When she was a child he took her from her mother and sent her to boarding school in Indiana. She returned as a polished young lady, with considerable talent in music and art. She was the only gracious and lovely thing in his life and, although he obviously loved her, he was strict and unbending, and he completely failed to understand her. She lived in constant fear of his outbursts. . . . A young physician from the East fell in love with her and, until he heard of her true ancestry, wanted to marry her. When another young man was attentive to her Rynerson ordered him out of the house, on the threat that he would run him out of town with a gun if he ever showed up again. . . . Eventually Cosetta taught music at a nearby college and became organist at the Presbyterian Church there. Tragedy overtook her when she fell in love with the minister, a married man with three children. The couple fled to Mexico. Some years later they returned to the Rio Grande and settled in Socorro where the onetime minister tried to practice law. Upon his death she taught music and tried to sell her paintings. Long before this time she had known the meaning of poverty, and the hard road of the transgressor. Never did she return to her father's home nor did she ever see him again.]

Billy wasted little time on his personal resentment against even this hard, unconscionable man. He knew he could break jail here at Lincoln at any time he wished. But he wasn't quite ready to go. He still wanted to square accounts with Colonel Dudley before he pulled out for good. Dudley had returned to Fort Stanton from Fort Union at the beginning of the court term. He had been indicted by the grand jury on a $25,000 arson charge for the burning of the McSween house and had secured a change of venue to Socorro County.

But it was the coming Dudley court of inquiry at Fort Stanton that interested Billy. The Kid would be held in

custody here in Lincoln until his own case was called at
Mesilla in July. The Dudley court of inquiry would come
in May, and that was what he was waiting for. For the Kid
to testify against the pompous, hard-drinking old soldier
would be worth risking big chances on his own neck.

In the meantime Tom O'Folliard was held with the Kid
in what was actually little more than an informal house
arrest.

15

The spring term of court at Lincoln ended May 1st, 1879. Ten days later the Governor with Mrs. Wallace arrived at Fort Stanton from Santa Fe. He was to be the star witness against Colonel Dudley at the opening of the court of inquiry.

For five straight days the Governor was grilled by the U.S. District Attorney General Barnes, who was acting as Colonel Dudley's chief counsel. Over and over again Wallace was forced to admit that he had acted on hearsay and not positive evidence when he had made his charges against Colonel Dudley. Judge Leonard, serving as attorney for the Governor, found himself powerless before the three-man court of senior officers who were definitely prejudiced in protecting their brother officer and the good name of the Army.

Among the several charges involved in the court of inquiry that Colonel Dudley had requested was the specific one that he had conspired with the Dolan-Riley party to aid and assist them in measures of violence against McSween. The result had been to afford the Dolan crowd protection in their actions in the burning of the McSween house and in the subsequent killing of the lawyer and three others.

A key point in the trial was whether or not the soldiers

whom Dudley had brought in helped the Peppin-Dolan gang: first, in setting fire to the house; and, second, in the killing of McSween and the others when they had tried to escape from the burning trap. The Governor, who had not even been in the Territory at the time, obviously could not testify regarding the exact events of the afternoon and night of July 19th. But the Kid could.

On May 28th, 1879, the nineteen-year-old boy stood in front of the long table that served the President of the Court, Colonel Pennypacker, his two fellow judges, Major N. W. Osborne and Capt. H. W. Brinkerhoff, and the Recorder, Capt. H. H. Humphreys. They were all of the 15th Infantry, stationed at Fort Bliss, Texas. Billy raised his right hand and repeated the oath.

Every officer there was old enough to be his father. Each wore his dress uniform and sword, and there was behind them the fearsome dignity and power of the United States Army. But the boy was not the least over-awed. He was as cool and self-controlled as if he were attending a cockfight or a horse race.

Captain Humphreys, the Recorder, swore Billy, then motioned him to take the stand. The examination of the witness proceeded:

The Recorder—Q. What is your name and place of residence?
A. My name is William Bonney. I reside in Lincoln.
Q. Are you known or called Billy Kid? Also Antrim?
A. Yes, sir.
Q. Where were you on the 19th of July last, and what, if anything did you see of the movements and actions of the troops that day?
A. I was in Mr. McSween's house in Lincoln, and I seen the soldiers come down from the Fort with the sheriff's party—that is, the sheriff's posse joined them a short distance above there—that is, McSween's house. The soldiers passed on by; the men dropped off and surrounded the house—that is the sheriff's party. Shortly after, three soldiers came back with Peppin, passed the house twice afterwards. Three soldiers came down and stood in front of the house in front of the windows. Mr. McSween wrote a note to the officer in charge asking him what the soldiers

were placed there for. He replied saying that they had business there; that if a shot was fired over his camp or at Sheriff Peppin or any of his men, he would blow the house up; that he had no objection to his blowing up if he wanted to his own house. I read the note. Mr. McSween handed it to me to read. I read the note myself. I seen nothing further of the soldiers until night. I was in the back part of the house when I escaped from it. Three soldiers fired at me from the Tunstall store, from the outside corner of the store. That is all I know in regard to it.

Q. Did the soldiers that stood near the house in front of the windows have guns with them there?

A. Yes, sir.

Q. Who escaped from the house with you, and who was killed at that time, if you know, while attempting to make their escape?

A. Jose Chavez escaped with me; also Vicente Romero, Francisco Zamora, and Mr. McSween.

Q. How many persons were killed in that fight, if you know, and who killed them, if you know?

A. I seen five killed. I could not swear as to who it was that killed them. I seen some of them that fired.

Q. Who did you see that fired?

A. Robert Beckwith, John Kinney, John Jones, and those three soldiers. I don't know their names.

Shortly the Recorder stated that he had finished with the witness. Billy now faced the inquisition of Colonel Dudley himself. The boy was cool and collected and completely in hand. Not even this hard old soldier accustomed to command, and nearly three times the boy's age, could break through his quiet reserve and self-confidence.

One of the early questions brought an objection from the Court and the room was cleared while the matter was thrashed out. Colonel Dudley then resumed his cross-examination:

Q. In what direction did you go upon your escape from the McSween house?

A. I ran towards Tunstall's store; was fired at and then turned towards the river.

Q. From what part of the McSween house did you make your escape?

A. The northeast corner of the house.

Q. How many soldiers fired at you?

A. Three.

Q. How many soldiers were with Peppin when he passed the McSween house each time that day, as you say?

A. Three.

Q. The soldiers appeared to go in companies of three's that day, did they not?

A. All that I ever seen appeared to be three in a crowd at a time, after they passed the first time.

Q. Who was killed first that day, Bob Beckwith or the McSween men?

A. Harvey Morris, McSween man, was killed first.

Q. How far is the Tunstall building from the McSween house?

A. I could not say how far. I never measured the distance. I should judge it to be 40 yards, between 30 or 40 yards.

Q. How many shots did these soldiers fire, that you say fired from the Tunstall building?

A. I don't know.

Q. How many shots did you see them fire?

A. I could not swear to that; on account of the firing from both sides, I could not hear. I seen them fire one volley.

Q. What did they fire at?

A. Myself and Jose Chavez.

Q. Did you not just now state in answer to the question who killed Zamora, Romero, Morris, and McSween, that you did not know who killed them but you saw Beckwith, Kinney, John Jones and the three soldiers fire at them?

A. Yes, sir, I did.

Q. Were these men, the McSween men, there with you when the volley was fired at you and Chavez by the soldiers?

A. Just a short way behind us.

Q. Were you looking back at them?

A. No, sir.

Q. How then do you know they were just behind you then or that they were in range of the volley?

A. Because there was a high fence behind and a good

many guns to keep them there. I could hear them
speak.

Q. How far were you from the soldiers when you
saw them?

A. I could not swear exactly—between 30 or 40
yards. . . .

Q. Did you know either of the soldiers that were in
front of the windows of McSween's house that day;
if so, give it.

A. No, sir. I am not acquainted with them.

Colonel Dudley announced that he was finished. There
were further questions by the Recorder, and once again
Colonel Dudley resumed his cross-examination. Then
suddenly it was over and Billy was dismissed.

Later testimony of Jose Chaves y Chaves, who had left
the burning McSween house almost immediately ahead of
the Kid, collaborated Billy's sworn statement that soldiers
had fired at the fleeing men.

I went slowly until I see the soldiers fire; then I went
with all my might. . . . I saw the three men when
on us. I knew they was soldiers because I saw them
in soldiers' clothes, blue pantaloons, wore caps and
black blouses. They were white men.

A few days later the testimony was ended, and the three
members of the court retired. It took them less than two
hours to arrive at their verdict:

In view of the evidence adduced the Court is of the
opinion that Lieut. Colonel N. A. M. Dudley, 9th
U. S. Cavalry, has not been guilty of any violation of
law or orders; that the act of proceeding with his
command to the town of Lincoln on the 19th of July,
1878, was prompted of the most humane and worthy
motives and of good military judgment under exceptional circumstances.

The Court is of the opinion that none of the alle-
gations made against Lieut. Colonel Dudley of His
Excellency the Governor of New Mexico or of Ira E.
Leonard have been sustained and that proceedings
before a court-martial are therefore unnecessary.

The findings were sent on to General John Pope, commanding the Department of the Missouri with headquar-

ters at Fort Leavenworth. General Pope promptly disapproved them and recommended to his superiors that Dudley be court-martialed.

A final review by the Judge Advocate General, announced some months later, held that while the principal charges had not been substantiated "it was to be granted that the presence of soldiers had given a certain degree of moral support to the sheriff's posse and stimulated them to more drastic action than otherwise had been undertaken." There was some criticism of Dudley in the final findings, but no punishment was recommended. The affair had cost the government 30,000 gold dollars.

It is charitable to assume that the old soldier had done his best—but his best was not quite good enough to meet the challenge of this complex and unprecedented situation in Lincoln County.

2

The Wheel of Fortune, spinning out men's lives and destinies, continued to turn slowly on its rickety axis. . . . Most of the Seven Rivers warriors asked for and received the Governor's pardon, and all charges that might be brought against them were thus wiped off the slate. . . . Colonel Dudley, in a travesty of court proceedings at Socorro, was eventually acquitted of Mrs. McSween's charge of arson in setting fire to the McSween house; Colonel Rynerson was forced to keep a straight face while he went through the motions of prosecuting his friend Colonel Dudley. . . . Jimmy Dolan, likewise, had no difficulty in eventually securing a dismissal in the Socorro courts of the charges that he had been involved in the murder of the one-armed Chapman. . . . Evans and Campbell made good their escape to the Fort Davis country on below in Texas.

Wallace seemingly had failed on all counts in his bitter fight; yet despite the fact that he had been mocked at and humiliated in his appearance at the Dudley court of inquiry, he had won a real victory: he had succeeded in driving Colonel Dudley out of Fort Stanton and away from Lincoln County.

In due time the case of William H. Bonney, alias Kid

Antrim, alias Billy the Kid, was called in Mesilla. But the case had to be held over for the next term of court, because Billy wasn't on hand. He had learned the hard way to trust only himself, his six-shooter, and his Winchester. He could trust his little bay mare, too, and his *compadres*, Tom O'Folliard and Doc Scurlock and Charlie Bowdre.

It seemed that big men were always busy men, with many interests. They had little time to worry over a homeless boy. This strange brand of territorial law and justice, coupled with the hidden power of the Ring, was too much even for Governor Wallace. The machine had cut the ground from under him. And now it was after the Kid. He was the one these enemies wanted. There was something about the boy that made him stand out in heroic stature in people's minds. He was a bright figure, a symbol, an unforgettable and arresting character.

It was high time he pulled out. Tom O'Folliard was still with him in partial arrest, and they sent word to Doc Scurlock to have the horses ready and hidden at the Ellis corral. Then on the appointed afternoon the Kid and Tom simply broke their arrest, and the three mounted up and headed for the Pecos country.

There was nothing more they could do for John Tunstall or for McSween, or for the cause that had once seemed so real. It had pretty much been finished off that night of July 19th of the previous year when they'd been whipped so badly at the Big Fight in Lincoln, thanks largely to Dudley's interference.

And a year later, following the Chapman killing, Billy and Tom O'Folliard had been all set to pull out of the Territory for good when Governor Wallace sent the soldiers after them. Then it was that the Kid and Wallace cooked up their deal, but Colonel Rynerson and Judge Bristol had punched it full of holes. It really had not been the Governor's fault. Rynerson was simply too tough for them all.

It would be a good time right now for the Kid to say *adios* forever to New Mexico. But it wasn't quite so easy as that. A fellow's pride got in the way. Billy simply couldn't let Dolan, or Rynerson, or even Tom Catron, run him off. It was fun to defy the whole lot; to plague them, and maybe let them think that some day he might ride in on them a little unexpectedly and leave each with

a couple of lead slugs as souvenirs. Only that wasn't Billy's
way of doing things. He wasn't a cold-blooded, calculating killer.

Then there was the question of rich, old John Chisum.
Whenever the going got a little heavy Uncle John always
managed to pull out. He'd done plenty of talking about
how he was standing behind Tunstall and McSween and
their boys in the long fight. But always when the blue
chips were down he was the busy little man who wasn't
there. He'd never directly paid any of the fighters as much
as a two-bit piece. Almost half of the original Regulators
had been killed off, so money was not bothering them any
longer. But the Kid and Tom and Doc Scurlock and Charlie Bowdre were still very much alive. Consequently they
figured that there was a little settling up to be done with
Mr. John Chisum before the Kid and the others could
pull out for good.

There was also something about the vast reaches and
the high rolling mesas, and the early mornings and the
twilights when the whole world of the Pecos suddenly became afire with color, that got into a fellow's heart. In the
upper river there were those lazy little Mexican settlements—Fort Sumner, Puerto de Luna, and Anton Chico,
and a lot of tiny spots where life was warm and honest
and ever so gentle.

Doc Scurlock had his wife over at Sumner, and Charlie
Bowdre and his wife were nearby at Yerby's, and the Kid
had a girl or two on his own hook. The one named Celsa
was the one he liked best. Of course, Tom O'Folliard
didn't mind where he was as long as he was with the Kid.

So, towards nightfall of June 17th, 1879, when Billy
and Tom broke out of their loose jail confinement and
picked up Doc and the horses behind the Ellis corral, it
felt good to the Kid to have the bay mare under him
again. And to be outdoors and breathe deep of this mile-
high air did something to a fellow who'd been cooped up
for weeks. It made him feel like the real thing, as big as
anybody in the world—just riding along free and young
and brave—a man on horseback.

Billy could take it easy now; he had plenty of time.
And he had nothing special to do and nowhere special to
go. Of course it would be mighty fine to see his girl Celsa

again. He'd been thinking quite a lot about her lately. She was the one for him.

3

He probably thought that it might be a good idea to drop in at the little settlement of Roswell and get the latest news of the Pecos from Ash Upson. Ash was now a Justice of Peace. The odd old character had successfully managed to last through the war and to keep on friendly terms with all factions.

Billy heard that Captain J. C. Lea, the new owner of the old Smith & Wilburn store, had some big ideas of developing a sheep ranch on the range to the east of the river. Lea had been made one of the County Commissioners and already saw great possibilities in the future of the Pecos country. He was an ambitious, formidable man with unlimited vision.

John Chisum might soon be returning to his South Spring headquarters, five miles south of Roswell. Billy was anxious to talk over a little matter of business with Uncle John. Forty miles below him was Seven Rivers, and there might be important news from that section, too. So, all in all, an hour or two could be profitably spent gabbing with old Ash.

Ash liked the Kid and he caught Captain Lea just before he was leaving and introduced the boy to the new owner of Roswell. The Kid was courteous and pleasant and most willing to explain the state of affairs in Lincoln and how the Dudley court of inquiry had ended at Fort Stanton. Billy and his two companions ate their noon dinner at the stage-stop and listened to Ash while their horses fed and rested.

[A dozen years later, when Roswell had become a booming town with its own weekly newspaper, Ash wrote a short series on the early history of the community. He related how the Kid would drop in at the little two-house cow-town and come into the store and cordially greet any of the farmers and neighboring ranchers who happened to be there and ask them to join him in refreshments. Then Ash went on in his rather florid style:

Bold, daring and reckless, he was open-handed, gen-

erous-hearted, frank and manly. He was a favorite of
all classes and ages; especially was he loved and admired by the old and decrepit, and the young and
helpless. To such, he was a champion, a defender, a
right arm. He was never seen to accost a lady, especially an elderly one, but with his hat in his hands;
and did her attire, or appearance, evidence poverty,
it was a poem to see the eager, sympathetic, deprecat-
ing look in Billy's sunny face, as he proffered assistance, or afforded information. A little child never
lacked a lift over a gutter, or the assistance of a
strong arm to carry a heavy burden when Billy was
in sight.]

4

It was somewhere near John Chisum's old ranch headquarters at Bosque Grande, north of Roswell, that Billy
met the young Englishman, T. B. Townsend. The incident is described in some detail in Townsend's autobiog-
raphy published in 1924 under the title, *The Tenderfoot
in New Mexico.*

The Kid and his *compadres* riding up the Pecos encountered a band of a hundred or more horses and mules
being herded by several Mexicans. They carried brands
unfamiliar to the Kid, Tom O'Folliard or Doc Scurlock,
and this meant they had been driven in from a distance
and consequently were fair prey.

Off to one side Billy caught a glimpse of a camp, and
the three riders headed that way. The young Englishman
met them at the cook-fire where a Mexican was preparing
dinner. Townsend asked them to dismount and eat with
him.

With the meal finished the worried young owner rode
off with the three visitors towards the herd. Billy suggested that he might want to make a deal for the outfit and
questioned him as to where he had secured the animals,
what he had paid for them and how he was going to dispose of them. He inquired especially if he had any race
horses in the lot.

The young Englishman answered that he hoped to sell
the band to the miners of Leadville, and that while they
would only be worth $25 a head here on the Pecos they

might fetch $50 or $60 at the mines. Townsend reports
Billy as saying:

"Twenty-five dollars a head! You'll have to give me
time on them, of course. Don't you think you could say a
trifle less?"

At this juncture the now frightened owner heard one of
the trio address the smallest of the visitors as "Kid." Several days before this he had camped for some time below
on the Pecos with one Hugh Beckwith, while he was
gathering his stampeded and scattered herd. As he was
leaving the old man scribbled out a little note addressed
to Billy the Kid which Townsend was to give him if he
encountered the young outlaw. Now from his shirt pocket
where he carried his most valuable papers, he brought out
the folded sheet and nervously handed it to Billy. It was
a crude request to the Kid that he take good care of his
young friend, the bearer.

It must have been the recollection of just such another
brave, young Englishman as this horse dealer which now
touched the inner heart of the Kid. There might also have
been memories of how kind Hugh Beckwith had been to
him when he had first ridden into the Pecos country.
Somehow the old rancher held no personal resentment
against the Kid for the death of his son, Bob, at the Big
Fight in Lincoln. Billy finished reading the note and
handed it to Tom O'Folliard.

"Well, sir," Townsend reports Billy as saying, "you
don't seem to jump at my offer to take the herd on credit.
So I'm afraid we can't trade, but I wish you luck. I hope
you'll get 'em safe to Leadville and a good price foi 'em
when you get 'em there."

Billy waved a farewell to the Englishman and led the
way on up the Pecos. He had, as he told his companions,
"business elsewhere."

5

They made Fort Sumner late that next afternoon and
headed for Beaver Smith's all-purpose bar and eating
place. Smelly old Beaver explained that Pat Garrett was
odd-jobbing around Anton Chico, some eighty miles or
so up the Pecos towards Las Vegas.

There was big news from Las Vegas, Beaver allowed.

The first train was pulling in there on July 4th; that would be the following week. Vegas was booming, and you could feel prosperity seeping on down through Anton Chico and Puerto de Luna and even as far below as right here at Sumner.

Great days would be coming soon, old Beaver predicted. The freighters would only have to haul from Las Vegas now, instead of all the way from Trinidad, Colorado. That would make things cheaper. Why, all New Mexico would be booming. Civilization! Progress! Good times! Everything would be different around here.

Billy must have felt a little sad when he heard of Pat Garrett's hard luck. Pat had married that pretty little Juanita Martinez at a Justice of Peace's office, there being no priest at Fort Sumner. Pat and Juanita had kept right on going to the *bailies,* but things began to weight a little heavy on the young wife. She was going to have a baby and she was worried because she hadn't been married by a priest. Late one night when she and Pat came home from a dance, she was suddenly taken violently ill. It had to do with the premature birth of her baby, and before Pat could get help his little wife was dead. That was the reason Pat had gone to Anton Chico.

Doc Scurlock found his own half-Mexican wife waiting for him in one of the adobe buildings of the old reservation. She and Doc were deeply in love with each other; no foolishness there. Charlie Bowdre and his wife were living on the Yerby ranch, twenty miles northeast of Sumner. Tom O'Folliard could get work there any time he wanted it.

Billy probably dropped in to see Pete Maxwell and his mother, Dona Luz, that first day he arrived in Sumner. Dona Luz had an open heart for the boy, although she might have been a little worried lest her youngest girl fall in love with him. Pete, who was old Lucien Maxwell's only son, told Billy to take any of the empty rooms he wanted and settle himself down. Altogether there were two or three hundred people living in the one-time army post originally built for six companies. In addition there were numerous barracks and warehouses, and a hospital for the Indian agency. The old reservation lay here at the strategic gateway into the valley of the Pecos, and there was always more or less excitement around the place.

The Kid probably didn't have a pair of silver dollars to his name, but he had plenty of friends among the natives. They were always proud to share their simple meals with him. There was, for instance, the old Apache retainer, Deluvina, who had been bought by Lucien Maxwell for $10 from her Navaho captors when she was eight years old. An immense, square old woman, with a complexion like wrinkled saddle leather, she fairly worshipped the boy. He was *muy simpatico* to her, and she called him endearing Spanish names and fussed over him and was always ready to get him a meal any hour of the day and night. He could do no wrong in her eyes.

In many ways this wind-swept, dusty, isolated com-

munity here at the abandoned fort was home to the Kid.
It was five times bigger than San Patricio over southwest
on the swift little Rio Ruidoso, and almost the same size
as the county seat of Lincoln County. And it was actually
outside the borders of the battle-scarred Lincoln County,
thus giving a certain margin of safety for Billy.

On special days he could deal monte on a percentage
basis at one or another of the store-saloons, and when
there were *fiestas* at Puerto de Luna or Anton Chico, or at
one of the little settlements nearby he'd mount up and
take off for the holiday. Sometimes Tom would ride with
him, but often he'd go alone.

Gambling and horse racing was what he liked most. He
never cared for cock fighting, but he'd dance most of the
night if he had a chance. Then he liked just to sit around
in the evenings and listen to the strumming of a guitar,
and now and again to join in some old Mexican ballad sung
in a minor key.

Most of the time he was gay and humorous, but he
could slip into the mood of these gentle, kindly people
when he was with them. It was easy for him to be one of
them. Life had been tough for him, too, just as life had
been for them.

For a hundred years and more they had escaped peon-
age only because they lived out their little isolated existence in tiny settlements far removed from even the sluggish life-stream of the Rio Grande. Lonely-hearted and
filled with an ancient racial longing for some touch of
romance, their women looked upon this young outlaw as
a bright knight, an *hidalgo*, a dashing, fearless *caballero*.

They were to prove themselves the makers and the
keepers of the deathless myths and imperishable legends
built around him, which they would tell and retell a thousand times over. It was they who would give life and depth
to endless tales of this unaccountable boy, who lived
among them for a while and was their true hero. For only
plain people and not writers or even singers can give
vitality and permanence to the little saints and sinners of
their own making.

There is some proof that the girl Celsa was older than
the boy, and that she was married to a man named Saval
who was considerably her senior. Apparently he had left
her, but the church did not recognize divorce. So it was

that her own uninhibited instincts of protection and compassion for the motherless, homeless "Beelie" filled her passionate heart. Hers were qualities and gifts natural and inherent in the women of her gentle race.

Surely it gave her an abiding peace of mind to wash his few clothes and darn his socks and try to give him solace and protection from the evil destiny that seemed always to pursue him. In the full meaning of the beautiful phrase, each was *muy simpatico* to the other.

And they were both fatalists, touched by wisps of mysticism that were as elusive as the soft winds or the haunting notes of a guitar floating across the little plaza when the stars were out.

6

By fall Pat Garrett came back from Anton Chico and went to work for Pete Maxwell, but some slight difficulty arose and Pat quit. He had saved some money and he now opened a small bar-restaurant in Fort Sumner. Soon he went into partnership with Beaver Smith. Before long the Kid was spending most of his time at their place, dealing monte whenever he could find customers. Some people thought he and Pat had a sort of loose partnership, and Pete Maxwell is reported as having said with a broad grin: "They are carrying on the same line of business."

It was along about this time that the Kid began his open feud with John Chisum. There is no way of knowing whether Uncle John had ever actually promised the old Regulators that he would see that they got their pay for fighting on the Chisum-Tunstall-McSween side of the Lincoln County War. At least the four men of the Regulators who were left figured that, since both Tunstall and McSween were dead and the fighters had never received one cent of pay from the two principles or their estates, it was up to Chisum to make some sort of settlement with them.

But the war was over and the practical Chisum believed that everybody should call it a day and forget it. There is a legend that along about this time the Kid and one or two of his followers ran into Uncle John in a bar at Fort Sumner, and that the Kid drew his six-shooter and shoved it into Chisum's face. Either Chisum must lay $500 on the line or he'd stop a .44 slug.

Old John is supposed to have talked the boy out of his demands. It could well have been true, for it was not out of line with Billy's character. He would never have killed the unarmed old cowman; but it would have delighted his deep sense of humor to have forced slick Uncle John to beg for his life. There can be no question that the boy felt that Chisum still owed a substantial sum of money to the men who had risked their lives for him and Tunstall and McSween and had never been paid a cent on account.

Billy's resentment against Chisum continued to grow until it became an obsession with him. Eventually the relationship between the man and the boy became a matter of considerable concern.

By October of this year of 1879, the Kid with Doc and Tom and a native or two decided to make their own purely financial settlement with Chisum. They jogged down the Pecos, cut out 118 head of his fattest steers, then drove them north to Yerby's ranch, where their old brands were blotched and new brands burned in. Up near Alamo Gordo they were sold to a Colorado buyer, who apparently was not particularly concerned with questionable brands. But one of John's brothers and his men overtook the herd and its new owner, and drove back the stolen cattle.

Doc Scurlock and his wife quietly took stock of the changing situation that was coming over the Territory and concluded that the time had come for them to pull out for the open spaces of South Texas and start life over again. Pete Maxwell helped them get away. So the Kid's gang was now down to three—Tom O'Folliard, Charlie Bowdre, and himself.

He could see Pat Garrett getting somewhere. Pat had a new girl named Polinaria Gutierrez, and he was going to marry her. There is a legend that she was a sister of the girl Celsa, but Billy wasn't figuring the least on marrying Celsa. He just wanted to be free as the wind, to race horses and play monte, and go to *bailies,* and once in a while slip away on some little adventure that paid off in a few head of cattle or horses. It was fun to have a girl who was as kind and affectionate as Celsa. Pat was the marrying kind. But the Kid wasn't cut out for that kind of life.

That August of 1879, down below in the Lincoln country, a hundred miles to the southwest, there was a big gold strike. Almost overnight the boom town of White Oaks blossomed in a sweet valley, rimmed by mountains that were fairly studded with gold, or so it seemed. Boom mining towns meant good markets for beef and good gambling. Both of them interested the Kid.

The limitless sea of grass, unfenced and inviting, over northeast of Sumner in the Panhandle of Texas, was filling up with big ranches. In winter hundreds of head of cattle drifted south and southwest before the blue blizzards. It was no trick to gather up a little batch of strays, drive them across the high mesas that stretched from the Pecos southwestward to booming White Oaks, and sell them to local butchers. Or he might drive steers on to Tularosa and turn them over to Pat Coghlin, who now held a beef contract for Fort Stanton. Ten dollars a head was good money for the strays that drifted down from the Texas Panhandle to the Pecos valley when the deadly northers blew south from Kansas.

The Kid was only mildly interested. He much preferred making the few dollars he needed by gambling. There is little question but that he did some stealing, largely horses, but it wasn't long before he was blamed for ninety percent of all the thieving jobs that were done. Within a year after he came to the Pecos his notoriety had grown to enormous proportions. Certain other incidents added to the unsavory fame that was centering around his slender figure.

On a night in early January of 1880, Joe Grant, a silly braggart and general nuisance from Texas, ran into the Kid in Bob Hargrove's saloon at Fort Sumner. Jim Chisum, Old John's younger brother, also was in the bar with two or three of his cowboys, including a young fellow by the name of Jack Finan, who was packing a very fine, ivory-handled Colt. Grant, too drunk for safety, snatched Jack's pistol from its holster and substituted his own.

Grant was known to have bragged that he intended to kill Billy the first chance he got. Billy figured now that he better play it safe with the young fool, so he casually remarked about what a beautiful gun it was and asked Joe if he could see it. He took the six-shooter from Joe's hand and, while pretending to examine the inlay on the barrel,

slowly spun the cylinder and saw that there was one unloaded chamber. Deftly he set the cylinder so that when
the double-action gun was cocked and the trigger pulled
the firing pin would hit the empty chamber. Then he returned the gun to the drunken Grant.

"Pard, I'll kill a man quicker'n you will for the whiskey," Grant is reported to have said.

"What do you want to kill anybody for?" the Kid answered. "Put up your pistol and have a drink."

Grant now stepped behind the bar and with the gun in
his hand started knocking over glasses and whiskey bottles.
Billy pulled his own gun as if to help him. Grant, glaring
at *Jim* Chisum, remarked that he wanted to kill *John*
Chisum, anyway.

"You got the wrong pig by the ear, Joe," the Kid
argued in a friendly way. "That's not John Chisum."

"That's a lie!" Grant shouted.

In a flash he swung his gun from Chisum flush into
Billy's face and pulled the trigger. It snapped on an empty
chamber. The hammer was halfway back for a second shot
when Billy cut him down.

He was dead when he crumpled up on the floor behind
the bar.

[It is recorded in the Las Vegas *Optic* that in describing
the killing to a young man named Rudolph Minor at nearby Sunnyside, the Kid modestly explained, "It was a game
for two—and I got there first."]

7

The Kid probably had rather mixed feelings when **Pat**
Garrett was married for the second time. It meant a slight
rift in the close relationship between the tall, reserved,
thirty-year-old man and the slender, gay twenty-year-old
boy. Between the two extremes in age and size stood a
mutual friend, Barney Mason, who decided to throw in
with Pat in a double-marriage ceremony. The nearest
priest lived at Anton Chico, and this time Pat was determined on a formal church wedding.

So it was that a happy little caravan of men on horseback and women in a two-seated hack and a buckboard,
borrowed from Pete Maxwell, pulled out from Fort Sum-

ner early on a January morning. They took the rough
road to the north which paralleled the west bank of the
river.

The parents of Pat's youthful little Polinaria were
Dolores and Valdez Gutierrez. Barney's sweetheart bore
the lovely name of Juana—the Spanish for Jane—and she
rode with her parents, Anna Maria and Santos Madril.
Manuel Abreu and Alejandra Madril, who were to be
witnesses for both marriages, completed the list of travellers. They all stopped for a night at Puerto de Luna. The
unique little settlement was set on a high bench in a bend
of the Pecos at the entrance to a deep, terrifying canyon.
It was halfway on the eighty-mile journey from Fort
Sumner to Anton Chico.

They reached the live little *placita* of Anton Chico late
in the afternoon. It, too, was set in a bend of the Pecos,
with a good crossing to the north of the *plaza* and at the
foot of a long slope. The church stood at the east end of
the town, and there were stores and saloons and a blacksmith shop and large wool warehouses occupying the
sides of the dirt square.

This was a rich country around Little Anton, with
orchards and irrigated fields, and on back from the river
the sparse grazing lands held numerous bands of sheep.
At each water hole and spring was a semi-permanent hut
of rocks or adobe. The native shepherds would take out
their bands at dawn and bring them back to water at
twilight. Often their families would come to live with
them. The tiny shelters seemed almost as much a part of
the vast, lonely solitude as the stars and the warm moon.
They were as home to Billy.

Six months before this the railroad had finally reached
Las Vegas, twenty miles or so north of Anton Chico. Al-
ready the small community was experiencing the influx
of hard citizens and jailbirds who had been run out of
Vegas. Most of them were known as the Dodge City
Toughs, and they had been forced to leave the Kansas and
Colorado frontier towns in a series of end-of-rail moves.
Pat had met some of them at poker tables and monte
games and at *fiestas* when he hung out around Anton
Chico for a while, following the tragic death of his first
wife. But Pat was having no truck with them on this 14th
day of January, 1880, when the gentle Father Redin

stretched a point by marrying the pair of Anglos to these two devoutly religious girls.

He was a wise *padre,* this noble Father Redin. He knew and loved his people. He could even understand the lonely heart of the Kid. He often talked with the happy-go-lucky boy in the little dirt *plaza* in front of his church.

In later years the good Father used to say: "Billy did not have a bad heart; most of his crimes were those of vengeance."

16

Back at Fort Sumner the ambitious Pat played a little less poker and kept his eye peeled for the big chance.

John Chisum had already shown an interest in him, and had painted in glowing colors the opportunities that soon would be opening up around Roswell. Chisum figured that he and the energetic Captain J. C. Lea, and the other big cowmen of the middle Pecos and Hondo country, could use a man who kept his mouth shut and was handy with a six-shooter and wanted to get ahead. Pat filled all three of these specifications.

The Kid apparently wasn't concerned if Pat seemed to be pulling away from him. There is good evidence that Billy actually was figuring on starting a little ranch of his own, which eventually would grow into a stage station at a big spring called Los Portales in the arid country to the east of Sumner. It was near the western edge of the Staked Plains, and the boy and Charlie Bowdre planned to take up homesteads there. Cool, fresh water flowed from the bottom of a ledge, and off to one side was a cave that could give protection on cold and stormy nights.

It must have been a rather odd dream that Billy was nurturing: he'd stock his future ranch with cattle and horses and someday settle down there, and when the new mail route came by he'd open up a stage-stop. Garrett might have given him his inspiration, for Pat was already beginning to talk ranches and cattle.

From the practical and immediate side, the big spring and the cave also offered a fairly safe hide-out and an ideal place to hold little batches of cattle which Billy might accumulate one way or another. The spot was soon to have some bearing on affairs already shaping up.

It was along in March or April of 1880 when Billy met a lad by the name of John P. Meadows. The Meadows boy had ridden across the parched and waterless Staked Plains with a young fellow named Tom Norris. A day or two before their tired ponies carried them into Fort Sumner, the high cutting winds had whipped off John's hat and carried it away like a scared kite. The boy was suffering from sunburn and windburn that had fairly cooked the skin on his face and neck. Billy first caught sight of him as he lay on the ground under a leafless tree near one of the half-occupied adobe barracks, his face covered with a red bandanna.

A half century later John Meadows told a Pioneer Day gathering in Roswell of his first meeting with Billy. John had lived in the community all the subsequent years and had enjoyed a reputation for honesty and high character. A half century is a long time to carry exact memories, but there is an undeniable essence of truth in his spoken words, carefully taken down, that wins them the right to permanency. They are given here exactly as John Meadows spoke them February 26th, 1931:

> After while some fellow come along and give me a kick in the foot, and I took the handkerchief off my face, and he said, Say, pardner, you look like you were up against it. I said, Yes, that's the way it feels. He said, What's the matter with your face; so I told him my troubles and about my hat. He said, You can't lay here in the hot sun and wind in that fix. I said, I say so, too. He said, Get up and come on and I'll give you a room and a cot to lay on. I thanked him and said I thought I'd better stay right where I was at.
>
> You see, Tom and me had just crossed the plains and I had got plumb full of creeping vermin and I didn't want to go into his room and I told him so, and

he said, Oh, I've had a million on me, come on in. So he picked up my bed, walked in and laid it on an old iron cot that was there. I went in and laid down on it. He went and saw old lady Maxwell, and she was a good lady, and he told her what he had there, so she come over and looked at me. The Kid brought over a sponge and washed off my face and she doctored me back to health again. I think I was about five or six days, more or less, laying there with this face.

That was the first time I met him. I had never heard tell of the Kid, much less saw him before, and finally I began to get pretty well acquainted with him. Tom come around and said, So help me God, I can't find no hat here. Looks like they don't even wear 'em out here. The Kid says, I'll give him one and he did—an old Stetson hat he had.

So far, so good. He and the old lady Maxwell kept on feeding me and greasing my face until I got well, and finally I got up and began to mosey around.

Now, the day I got to Fort Sumner the Kid come in from White Oaks. I got there about nine or ten and he got there about eleven, he come from Cedar Canyon up to Sumner, and I went from Sunnyside down to Sumner.

I got to talking with him and the more I talked to the boy the better I liked him. I didn't care how many men he had killed, I didn't know he had killed any and I didn't care either, I liked him and I do yet.

But time went on and there was a big *fiesta* taking place at Puerta Luna and he said, I have just come over from White Oaks and I want to go to the *fiesta* and deal monte to them fellows. I been dealing monte at White Oaks and made some money. Well, the time come for him to go up to Puerta Luna and he had just forty-two head of cattle, yearlings, calves, cows and two-year-olds—I don't know how many of each he had, but whatever it was he had them forty-two head, and he said, How would it suit you to work for me a little while. I said I'd work for anybody, if he would give me something to eat. He said he'd give me something to eat and a dollar a day if you'll help me take them cattle to Los Portales, that was

where he wanted to start a ranch. I said, All right,
I'll go, just so I get something to eat.

So I helped the Kid take his little bunch of cows
over there and things didn't look good to me, not
enough of them some way. Only forty-two head. And
we got there, stayed all night, and the next day he
went back and on up to Puerta Luna. I was there
and I just don't remember how many days it was,
but in a few days a man named Pankey come in. I'll
bet a dollar some fellows here remember old Pankey.
He lived on Plaza Largo between Fort Sumner and
old Fort Bascom. He was the man and the Kid wrote
a note saying, John, I have sold that entire outfit and
brand and all to Mr. Pankey, in case he likes it, and if
he does, count them out, tally it out and collect so
much—there was a price on cows, one on calves, steers
and so on. And I did just what he told me to do.
Pankey liked the cattle and I tallied them out and
collected so much, what the Kid said. I hadn't been
there long enough to earn money enough to buy a hat
yet and I helped Pankey drive them back to Stinking
Springs with his boy, and we stayed all night there
and the next day Pankey pulled out home across to
what we called Hubble Springs in them days. That
was the way he was travelling and I went on to Fort
Sumner and got there between sundown and dark.

I don't believe I ever saw a rougher bunch of men
than was in Fort Sumner that evening, and all playing poker, and drinking, and there I was with $420
of the Kid's money in the saddle pocket. Uncle
George Fulgum was running a little restaurant there,
and I thought I would hate awful bad to have this
money took away from me, and I asked Uncle George
if he didn't have a cigar box and he dug around and
found one, and I put the money in the cigar box,
with a slip of paper that told how many cows, how
many calves—the tally list; and as I went down in the
bend of the Pecos River there was a whole lot of
stumps, there was one big one and a bunch of
zaccatone grass growing around by it. I slipped that
box in there and then went and got a rock and laid it
on top of the stump, and went back and told Uncle
George all about it. He said, You acted wise, them

men is over in the Kid's room now drinking and playing poker, there must be eight or ten of them and they have been there two or three days now. They were a tough bunch all right.

The next morning I got up and by an hour by sun that bunch of men just evaporated—I don't know where they went, but they just slipped off and I was awful glad they was gone. The next day or the next day after that—I don't want you to think I am going to be just exact, I might make a mistake in the days, but shortly anyway the Kid comes in from Puerta Luna. I was sitting on the bench in front of the old man's restaurant, and he got off his pony and asked me about them cattle and I told him. Yes, I sold them and have got the money down here in the bend of the river. Well, he says, what's it doing there, and I told him all about these men and he said about who they was—Tom Cooper, Charlie Bowdre, O'Folliard and Billy Wilson and others, I don't know who all.

And he said, I don't think you was in any danger from them. But I found my cigar box where I put it, set it up on the stump and pulled out the paper and said, Here's how many cattle you had and here's how much they brought. He went over the tally list and said, You have got one two-year-old steer too many. Well, I says, you got the money and there's no kick coming. Well, he says, I don't have no kick, but I didn't have but one two-year-old steer. Well, folks, I run in the long yearling for a two-year-old steer. He kind of laughed and said, That's a pretty good stunt and you made yourself a $10 bill, and he said, I'll give you this, you need it and I think you deserve it, if you can make a cowman like Pankey take a long yearling for a two-year-old, you deserve it.

Well, that brought a warm spot in my heart for that boy and it's there yet.

2

The Kid apparently had pretty much a regular gambling route he followed during these pleasant days of early 1880; Fort Sumner to Puerto de Luna—then on up the Pecos to Anton Chico—then southwest across the high mesa to booming White Oaks—and then back home to Sumner and his sweetheart. Next to Fort Sumner itself, he probably spent more time in Anton Chico than anywhere else.

One of the important figures of Anton Chico at this time was a short, slightly built, dark-complexioned, heavy-mustached man about thirty, who ran a freighting business between that town and White Oaks. He also owned a store and stage-stop and freight yard on the high mesa halfway between the two places. His name was Jim Greathouse and he was Texas-born, and from the time he was a small boy he had followed the rolling wagons of the frontier freight lines.

Greathouse was on intimate terms with several of the Las Vegas toughs who had left the booming new railroad town of Las Vegas for the benefit of their health. On the Kid's journeys to and from Anton Chico and White Oaks he invariably stopped at the Greathouse stage station, which carried the name of the Greathouse & Kuck ranch. Jim, however, spent most of his time in his depot and outfitting yard in Anton Chico.

It was some time around April or May when Jim introduced Billy to a well-known character from Vegas, who had made quite an unsavory reputation for himself. His name was Dave Rudebaugh, and although a Missourian by birth he had been raised in Kansas. By the time he was eighteen he was living by his wits and his Colt and Winchester. Soon he was a full-fledged bad man wanted by the frontier detectives. He showed up at Wichita and in the Black Hills gold camps and then at Fort Griffin, the haven of the buffalo hunters. By early January of 1878 he was back in Dodge City country on the Kansas prairies. Along with five other desperate men, he pitched camp at Wolf Creek, near Kinsley on east of Dodge. They muffed an attempt to rob an express car, and the six men were arrested by a posse headed by Bob Matherson and tried in the spring term of court in Edwards County, Kansas. Rudebaugh turned State's evidence and betrayed his five pals who were each sentenced to three years in the state penitentiary.

Rudebaugh's reformation was short lived. Soon he was throwing in with an extraordinary frontier character named John Joshua Webb, who was born in Iowa and was seven years older than Dave. When the better ele-

ment started to clean up Dodge City there was a general
exodus of the toughs and jailbirds. To date Webb had
been on the side of the law, but once again the frontier
was to be plagued by the dual personality of a bad good-
man who was also a good bad-man.

Such characters as Hoodoo Brown, Mysterious Dave
Mather, Billie Wilson, Tom Pickett, and scores of other
Dodge City toughs and adventurers followed Webb and
Rudebaugh to the new railhead. Webb now was town
marshal and Dave a policeman, and through the fall and
winter of 1879 the gang practically ruled Las Vegas.

Finally they overplayed their luck in a vicious plot to
murder a man looking for a ranch to buy, and Webb
found himself arrested, tried, and sentenced to be hanged.
Dave Rudebaugh, faithful to his friend, plotted a jail delivery. On March 7th, 1880, he and another desperado
named John Allen talked their way inside the jail and
approached the cell where Webb was held. When the
jailer, Antonio Valdez, refused to surrender the key to the
cell, Allen shot him dead, took the keys from his pocket
and tossed them to Webb. Hoping to receive clemency
from Governor Wallace, Webb refused to leave the jail.
Rudebaugh managed to escape and make his way south to
Anton Chico. Here he found sanctuary in the freighting
depot of his old Dodge City friend, Jim Greathouse.

It was some time after this that Greathouse introduced
the Kid to Rudebaugh. Dave's reputation had preceded
him, and for some odd reason the boy found himself attracted to this strange character, who at one moment could
turn State's evidence against his companions in robbery
and in the next moment chance his life in an attempt to
rescue his friend Webb.

It may well have been the professional audacity of
Rudebaugh, or the breadth of his experiences and reputation, that drew Billy to this man who was four years his
senior. Likewise, the older man apparently found some
stalwart qualities of leadership and magnetism in the
young outlaw who had not yet reached his twenty-first
birthday. Certainly whatever it was that drew Billy to
Rudebaugh was a far cry from the loyalty and affection
that had tied him to John Tunstall, McSween, and Dick
Brewer. They were all dead now, and the Kid had only
Tom O'Folliard and Charlie Bowdre left to remind him

of the wild, brave days of the seemingly long-ago Lincoln
County War.

His only other new friend was Pat Garrett.

3

It may be that the Kid now turned to the companionship
of Rudebaugh and Jim Greathouse, and shortly to that of
Billie Wilson and Tom Pickett, because he must intui-
tively have felt that Pat Garrett would soon cease to be an
intimate. He could see that the tall, lean, ex-buffalo hunter was sort of outgrowing him and their friendship. There
was already gossip around Fort Sumner that Pat was planning on taking up land down the Pecos, three or four miles
north of Roswell, to develop a cattle ranch there.

Captain J. C. Lea had been host on Pat's several trips
to his new property some eighty miles on south. Lea had
a clear vision of this strategic spot of Roswell developing
some day into an important trading center. It lay at the
junction of the great north-and-south trail along the Pecos
and the western road up the Hondo, that led through the
mountain passes and settlements to the Tularosa Basin
and on beyond to the Rio Grande. To Lea it was clear
that the day was coming when Roswell would be a booming railroad town and fortunes would be made there by
men of courage and imagination. But first there must be
peace and order. And Garrett was the very man to bring
the present lawlessness and terror to an end.

It was early summer when the rumor came to the Kid
that Lea and Chisum and several other big ranchers of
Lincoln County had put pressure on Sheriff Kimbrell of
Lincoln to appoint Garrett his deputy for the Pecos area.
If he made good as deputy sheriff the secret plan was that
they would then run him against Sheriff Kimbrell in the
fall elections.

So that was it. Pat was to be backed in his ranch operations if he would take the job of deputy sheriff and do
the bidding of the big fellows. Yet here in Ft. Sumner and
Anton Chico it had looked for a time as if the ex-buffalo
hunter would end up as a two-bit gambler and barroom
proprietor. But he was always quietly planning on getting
ahead, while the Kid took life as it came. No driving

ambitions bothered Billy; he wasn't after either money or power. He just wanted to be left alone.

Legend has pictured the boy as a daring leader, killing men without conscience or reason, abetted in this career by a score of fighting rustlers riding under his banner. Many years later the great Panhandle cowman, Charles Goodnight, testified concerning the Kid at this period in a letter to the Lincoln County historian, Maurice G. Fulton. Colonel Goodnight had been the moving spirit in the Canadian River Cattlemen's Association in the early '80s, and he was deeply concerned over the depredations of the professional rustlers. A single sentence in his letter to Fulton was all that was needed to describe the boy's true place: "We had other bands of lawless men in the Panhandle who gave us more real trouble than Billy the Kid."

But there is no minimizing the fact that the figure of this boy, riding the river valleys and high mesas under the bright New Mexican sun, did cast a dark shadow over the southwest. In the late summer of 1880 a curious little incident occurred in the Fort Davis section of western Texas that illustrates the mysterious quality of the boy's reputation.

When Jesse Evans and Bill Campbell escaped from the Fort Stanton guardhouse in February of the previous year, following their murder of the one-armed lawyer Chapman at Lincoln, they joined up with a band of outlaws, robbed a store, and killed the proprietor. Later, in a fight with Texas Rangers, they killed one of the men of Company E, commanded by Lieutenant C. L. Nevill. Evans and most of his gang were captured and were soon to be tried and sent to Huntsville prison.

Jesse Evans was desperate. Judging from the character of his guards and the manner of his confinement, he felt that he could be rescued, but there was only one man he knew who could do it. That was the twenty-year-old Kid from the Pecos.

Billy and Evans had been sworn enemies for two and a half years, yet the boy had so deeply impressed Evans with his shrewdness and valor that the older man, now in grave trouble, decided to appeal to him. The story of the intercepted letter from Evans unfolds in a report the young lieutenant of Rangers wrote to his superior:

FORT DAVIS PRESIDIO CO., TEX.
AUGUST 26, 1880

Gen. John B. Jones,
Austin, Texas.
Sir:

The prisoners are getting very restless. I have a letter they wrote to a friend of Evans in New Mexico
calling himself Billy Antrim to cause their rescue,
and to use his words he was "in a damned tight place
only 14 rangers here at any time, ten on the scout and
only four in camp now," and that Antrim and a few
men could take them out very easy. And if he could
not do it now to meet him on the road to Huntsville
as he was certain to go. I understand this man Antrim is a fugitive from somewhere and is a noted desperado. If he comes down and I expect he will, I will
enlist him for a while and put him in the same mess
with Evans & Co.

Twelve days later Lieutenant Nevill wrote a second
letter to General Jones in Austin, stating that he had reliable information that "Billy Antrim, alias Kid" and his
gang from New Mexico would arrive in a day or two.

But the young Ranger lieutenant misjudged the Kid
almost as badly as did the killer Evans. Billy would hardly
have been concerned over the plight of Jesse Evans, even
if the message had reached him. Evans was no longer his
headache. The Kid would probably have been interested
in the outcome had he lasted long enough to learn the
final score in the long contest between Evans and the law;
after a year's imprisonment and with a twenty-year sentence in prospect, Evans managed to escape from the
Huntsville penitentiary and vanish forever into the land
of lost and forgotten men.

4

The Kid was completely aware that grave danger to himself would result from the new appointment Pat Garrett
now held. Pat had moved to his ranch just north of Roswell and already was serving as a deputy sheriff. His sponsors had fully carried out their pledges to him and were

openly backing him in his race against Sheriff Kimbrell in the coming November elections.

Billy wasn't quite sure what he could personally do about it, but he was willing to take the chance and ride into Lincoln County alone. At least he could appeal to some of his native New Mexican friends to vote against Pat. He was by no means angry, nor did he probably feel in any way that Pat was double-crossing him. This running for sheriff was Pat's business. It was the Kid's business to try to keep him from being elected. It was more of a game than anything else, and apparently there was little or no bitterness on either side.

The Kid quietly saddled his bay racing mare and headed down the river. The days were cool and lovely, and on the first night he stopped at Dan Dedrick's ranch near Bosque Grande, a little more than halfway to Roswell. Dan was one of three Dedrick brothers who were known to be more or less associated with Jim Greathouse in his various and at times shady enterprises. Sam Dedrick ran a livery stable at the edge of White Oaks, in partnership with a man named West. The youngest brother, Mose, divided his time between the two properties. The ranch at Bosque Grande was known as a friendly spot for itinerant outlaws on the dodge. It was a matter of some importance that Garrett was well acquainted with that fact.

After spending the night at the Dedrick ranch Billy caught the trail that led on west to the north side of the Capitan Mountains, and towards twilight he pulled in at the Three Block Ranch. The outfit was owned by Dowlin & Delaney, post traders at Fort Stanton, and the temporary manager was a striking young man named George Curry. [As a boy he had ridden out of Louisiana to an adventurous career with trail herds, Kansas cow towns, New Mexico ranches, sheriffs' offices, Roosevelt's Rough Riders, then as Chief of Police in Manila in the Philippines, finally ending up as Governor of the State of New Mexico.]

When Billy stepped down from his tired pony at the ranch house young Curry invited him for supper and to stay for the night. George made no inquiry as to the stranger's name or business. When his host had cooked the meal and the two had washed up the few dishes, Billy proposed that they ride to a little settlement a few miles away where he had been informed there was to be a *bailie*.

George courteously declined, explaining that his bosses
had instructed him to do some electioneering that evening
in behalf of Pat Garrett. The election was to be held the
following day, November 3rd.

"Do you know Garrett?" Billy is reported to have asked.

"No, I don't, but from all I hear he is a splendid man,"
Curry answered.

"Do you think he will be elected?" Billy questioned.

"I don't know," Curry admitted with a grin, "but I'm
sure he'll carry this precinct. I've got a gallon of whiskey
here, and I think that will help carry it."

Bill rode in one direction that night while George
Curry took another. A faint glow was beginning to show
in the east when Billy pulled in. He fed his mare and then
lay down for a couple of hours' sleep. George did not call
him until the coffee and the flapjacks were ready. When
Billy had eaten he thanked his host for his hospitality, and
while he was shaking hands he broke out in a characteris-
tic little laugh.

"You're a good cook and a good fellow," he said, "but
if you think Pat Garrett is going to carry this precinct,
you're a damned poor politician."

Some time that day, while young Curry was busy getting
his few widely scattered neighbors to the polls, he learned
the identity of his visitor. Several days went by before
George heard the news that Pat Garrett had indeed been
elected sheriff.

He always figured that when he next met Billy he'd twit
him about what a poor politician he was—but George was
never to see him again.

It must have been a blow to the Kid when he fully realized the consequences of Pat Garrett's election as sheriff.

On January 1st, 1881, Pat would formally take office. The House, which had been built seven years before for the Murphy & Co. store in Lincoln, had recently been purchased from Tom Catron by the County Commissioners as a courthouse and would serve as Garrett's headquarters when he took over.

As a matter of fact, Garrett had energetically started his offensive operations from the day in September when he was appointed Deputy Sheriff. In the interim before he came into full authority, he was assigned the eastern or Pecos section of the sprawling county that stretched some 200 miles north and south and 150 miles east and west. The extreme southeastern portion of Dona Ana County, that touched Texas on the east and south, had in 1878 been added to the area of the original Lincoln County.

The newcomer, Captain J. C. Lea of Roswell, apparently assumed the leadership in the move to bring order to Lincoln County and to kill or drive out the Kid and the even tougher Pecos outlaws who operated below his townsite. But behind Lea was the shrewd and calculating hand of John Chisum. As usual, Uncle John Chisum pulled the strings while other men took the credit or the discredit. He had been the first to pick Pat Garrett for the danger-

ous task to which he was now assigned, but it was Captain
Lea who had made the actual deal with the tall sheriff.

It was Captain Lea, too, who must have interested the
powerful Tom Catron in the plan. For some reason or
other, Catron had never once set foot in Lincoln County
during this violent time, but his large interests there were
well represented by his young brother-in-law. It might
have been Catron who put sufficient pressure on U. S.
Marshal John Sherman of Santa Fe to have him appoint
both Pat Garrett and Bob Ollinger as Deputy U.S. Marshals.

The Kid certainly understood how vitally important
this move was, because as U. S. Marshals the two officers
could travel freely north of the Lincoln County border
into San Miguel County, or even over into Texas, or anywhere else they chose to go. He knew that both a federal
indictment for the killing of Roberts, presumably on Indian Agency property, and the old charge of killing Sheriff
Brady still hung over him and his two remaining *compadres,* Charlie Bowdre and Tom O'Folliard. Fort Sumner, Puerto de Luna, and Anton Chico all lay in San
Miguel County, north of Lincoln County, which now was
open hunting country for Garrett and Ollinger.

In a single turn of the screw of Fate the Kid was suddenly faced with this new and deadly threat. With the involved loyalties that were so common on the frontier, he
held Bob Ollinger his deadly enemy partly because Bob,
acting as bodyguard for Old Man Pierce, had killed
Johnny Jones. Johnny was the favorite son of Ma'am
Jones, who had befriended Billy when he rode into Seven
Rivers back in the fall of 1877.

Billy recognized that Ollinger was a brave and resourceful officer, but he also looked upon him as a braggart and
a bully. And throughout his short life the Kid had in-
stinctively been hostile to men who belonged to either of
these categories.

Pat Garrett had been his friend since Billy first met him
at Fort Sumner almost a year and a half earlier. But now
Pat had shifted his allegiance. Fame and fortune were to
be his—if he did his job. That job was to get rid of the
symbol as well as the actuality of lawlessness in Lincoln
County.

If the Kid stayed on Pat would have to go after him—

keep after him—follow him—plague him—run him off or
capture him and kill him. Eliminate this symbol and the
lesser men could be destroyed or driven off. Over and
over again Pat's sponsors drove in the argument that there
could be no peace or security in Lincoln County as long
as the Kid rode his secret trails between the camps and
little settlements, a wild, free figure living outside the
hard and fast limits of the law. These men left no alternative to Pat: he could make good with them only if he
eliminated the troublesome boy who had assumed such
gigantic proportions in their eyes.

Certainly Billy must have thought long and deeply over
the possibility of leaving the country and trying to start a
new life. There was always Old Mexico, and there were
the almost endless high plains of the grass world that
stretched east of the Rocky Mountains from New Mexico
and Colorado and western Kansas far above the Canadian
border. And of course there were Texas and Arizona. But
always the shadow of the tall figure of Pat Garrett seemed
to fall across the outbound trails.

[A curious proof of the relationship between Pat and
the Kid came to light in the talk John Meadows delivered
at that Old-Timers meeting in Roswell in 1931, mention of
which has already been made. Meadows' exact words were:

> When Garrett was elected Sheriff, he told me this
> time and again, he said, My first object was to try and
> get this thing settled without any bloodshed and I
> figured out how to do it. Before I was elected Sheriff,
> I saw the Kid and talked to him, played poker with
> him and told him the best thing he could do was to
> get up and be gone three or four years, and then
> come back and there would be nothing said about it,
> there would be no trouble. And Pat told him, If you
> fellows don't do this, I am going to arrest you or kill
> you, or you are going to kill me if you stay here.
> But the Kid would not see the point.]

It is clear enough that as far back as March of 1879, at
the time of the Chapman murder, the Kid had contem-
plated pulling out with Tom O'Folliard, before Governor
Wallace sent the soldiers from Fort Stanton after him.
And even several months before that at Tascosa he had
thought a good deal about leaving with Fred Waite and

John Middleton, when they with Henry Brown and Jim
French rode away from the New Mexican scene forever.

Billy could recall, too, when pressure was put on Tom
O'Folliard to leave him. After the publication of Governor Wallace's amnesty proclamation Tom's uncle, the
famous Texas ranger Thalis Cook, rode the long distance
from Uvalde to New Mexico. He tried his best to get his
favorite nephew to leave and come back home to his grandmother. But the quiet, loyal boy only stubbornly shook
his head.

"I can't quit now," he told his uncle. "They'd think I
was a coward. When our side gets things settled I'll leave
here and come back to Grandma. You tell her that."

Of course Billy had no grandma to go back to, nor a
great-hearted uncle who was willing to ride a thousand
miles on horseback just to plead with him to come home.
This untamed Pecos country was the only home he knew.

No one can ever be sure just why the Kid did not settle
his few affairs at Fort Sumner and drift on over to the
Rio Grande and then perhaps south to Chihuahua. Or cut
across the southeast corner of Arizona to be swallowed up
in the vast and beautiful Sonora land. Probably, as usual,
he was broke. Or maybe he just couldn't quite get around
to it. Or maybe it was largely pride that held him.

He wasn't going to leave now. He'd accept the challenge. He wasn't afraid to draw pistols with Pat Garrett,
or anyone else. The *ricos* had killed off all those who had
been close to him—all save Tom O'Folliard and Charlie
Bowdre. And now they had hired Pat Garrett to kill him
or run him off.

These men who were behind Pat were not unlike the
high army officers in New Mexico and Arizona, who in
these very days were running down the last free Apaches
and killing them or driving them back to their reservations. The army would have failed in this plan if the
officers had not stumbled on the idea of using renegade
agency Apaches as scouts and ferrets. These betrayers of
their brothers knew the hide-outs and the water holes and
all the Indian tricks and secrets. They understood how to
trail and ambush and how to help rub out the last of the
exhausted little bands of their own brave and confused
tribesmen.

In a way, Pat had now put himself in somewhat the

same class as these bought Indian scouts. He knew the
water holes and hide-outs and the secrets of the Kid. He
could track him down and either capture or kill him. He
who had once been the boy's close friend was hired now
to follow him until his death.

It is probable that the girl Celsa pleaded with Billy to
leave while there was still time. But he could only answer
in the words of the refrain of the old Seventh Cavalry
song, The Wild Missouri—"I cannot leave these muddy
waters." Lonely troopers used to sing it in a haunting
minor key during the long nights on the banks of the
great river at Bismarck, Dakota Territory, before Custer's
luck ran out.

Neither could this strangely talented boy, in love with
life and danger, leave these muddy, reddish waters of the
wild Pecos—River of Sin, Graveyard of Hopes.

2

But there was still one small chance left for him to gain
his legal freedom. Mrs. McSween's lawyer, Judge Leonard,
might once again take up his case with Governor Wallace.
Leonard was close to the Governor, and there was a rumor
that Colonel Rynerson, who had blocked the Kid's former
attempt to gain a pardon, was about to be replaced as
Prosecuting Attorney. With Rynerson out of the way, the
Governor might possibly get the new District Attorney to
drop the indictments against Billy.

It was a long shot, but it might be worth a trip to White
Oaks to talk matters over with Judge Leonard. The Judge
had opened a law office in the boom mining town, forty
miles northwest of Lincoln.

It would be dangerous for the Kid to step foot in Lincoln County, even though Garrett had not been installed
as the new sheriff. Yet Pat was already pretty much the
active head of the office. Kimbrell, the incumbent, had
been defeated, so Pat was practically in control. The orders may already have gone out to arrest Billy on sight,
or kill him if the chance came.

But the Kid probably figured he should take the risk
in order to talk personally with the kindly Judge Leonard.
The boy could still remember the exact words Wallace
had used that night at Squire Green's house when the

older man had given his solemn pledge: "Testify before
the grand jury and the open court, and convict the murderers of Chapman, and I will let you go scot-free with a
pardon in your pocket for all your misdeeds."

The boy had carried out his end of the bargain. By permitting the Lincoln County sheriff to arrest him he had
stuck his head squarely in the hangman's noose. However,
he had been smart enough to pull it out before they
dropped the trap door.

Everything always seemed to go against him. He doubt-
ed if the Governor was concerned about him any longer.
But it would be worth a last try, no matter how dangerous
White Oaks was for him.

3

Charlie Bowdre was still running the Yerby ranch, twenty
miles or so northeast of Fort Sumner, and Tom O'Folliard
was over there with him. They now had a third man
named Tom Pickett riding the unfenced range for the
outfit. He was a six-footer from Decatur, Wise County,
north of Dallas, Texas, and he was more an imitation
bad-man than the real article.

Pickett's father, a Kentuckian and former Confederate
officer, was a member of the Texas Legislature, and when
Tom was seventeen the boy got himself involved in a cattle-stealing charge. His heartbroken mother pleaded with
the father to intercede with the sheriff and the county
judge. The senior Pickett mortgaged his home in order
to settle for the cattle and to pay the heavy fine. For a time
Tom ran straight and even served as a Texas Ranger.
Then he joined a trail herd going north, and soon he was
bucking the moving Kansas railheads and cow towns.

At Dodge City Pickett became acquainted with Dave
Rudebaugh and his gang and followed them into Las
Vegas. Webb and Hoodoo Brown wangled him a job as a
policeman in the Old Town, but following a big drunk
Tom slipped down to White Oaks where he was taken on
as a special merchant police or night watchman. In time
he drifted east to the Fort Sumner country where Charlie
Bowdre hired him as a cowboy on the Yerby ranch.

The Kid rode alone to Anton Chico. Even his carefree
nature must have been depressed by the latest turn of

events. No longer could he ride gaily into the little towns on their *fiesta* days, open a monte game, race his bay mare, bet on the cock fights, and then dance until dawn broke. Since he had pulled out of Lincoln in July of 1879, there had been no rewards posted for his arrest, and as long as he spent most of his time in San Miguel County, or used a fair amount of caution when he visited in Lincoln County, he had felt reasonably safe.

But now everything would be different. The fact that Pat Garrett and the tough Bob Ollinger were out to get him or drive him off, and that both men held warrants as Deputy U.S. Marshals, changed the whole picture. The easy-going days were over. It was a natural reaction for the Kid to be drawn to the tough Dave Rudebaugh.

As far as the record went Dave had never actually killed a man although he had often been an accomplice to murder. And there was about the man an aura of bravery and intense loyalty, and of reckless fatalism. He had, as well, a cheerful, humorous side that must have matched the Kid's own lighthearted disposition.

Along with Dave was a less hardened outlaw named Billie Wilson who had been associated with the former in several shady ventures. For some months Wilson had hung around White Oaks and then Fort Sumner, where he became friendly with the Kid. He and Rudebaugh were hiding out in the Greathouse freighting yards at Anton Chico when the Kid rode in. Pat Garrett's avowed campaign against the Kid had made it dangerous for him longer to receive letters, so the only safe way to get in touch with Judge Leonard at White Oaks was to contact him personally. Rudebaugh and Wilson volunteered to go along.

To help pay expenses and make the trip interesting, the trio decided to pick up a few head of horses belonging to the rich Grzelachowski of Puerta de Luna, with his big store and two or three ranches and his easy way with women. Horse brands were always small and easy to vent or blotch, and for men with murder indictments hanging over them, as was the case with the Kid and Rudebaugh, the lifting of a few head of horses belonging to a man whom they mistrusted and cordially disliked was a very small matter.

It was around the middle of November when they

rounded up eight head, and after picking out two for their
own use trailed the remaining six across the dry, high, rolling country to Jim Greathouse's stage station, halfway to
White Oaks. Jim agreed to take four of the six. The last
two were simply turned loose to shift for themselves.

For a day or two the Kid and the two men from Vegas
hung around the combination station and store of Greathouse & Kuck—the latter name being pronounced and
often spelled Cook. Around daybreak on November 20th
they started on the forty-mile ride south to the Oaks, and
towards evening pulled up at the livery stable and corrals
of West & Dedrick on the outskirts of the mining town.

The Kid immediately inquired as to Judge Leonard's
whereabouts and learned that he had recently left for Lin
coln. From later evidence it is clear that Billy figured he
would chance riding the forty miles on southeast to the
county seat in order to see the lawyer. He could stop at
one of the little ranches this side of the *placita*, and send
a New Mexican friend on ahead to spy out the land and
arrange for an appointment.

That Saturday night Sam Dedrick was asked to make
several purchases in town, including a sack of groceries
and a pair of warm gloves for the Kid. The weather having turned bitterly cold, with flurries of snow, Sam and
his younger brother Mose turned over extra overcoats
they owned to the Kid and one of the other visitors.

Billy and the others were still lounging in the warm
office of the livery stable when Barney Mason, who was
living with his wife in Fort Sumner, walked in. He was
a long way from home, and after the Kid greeted him he
asked Barney what brought him here to the Oaks. Barney
glibly concocted a story about locating a bunch of horses
nearby that he proposed to steal.

The Kid was well aware that Barney was completely
untrustworthy and invariably played both ends against
the middle. Since Barney and Pat Garrett had gone
through their double marriage ceremony at Anton Chico,
Barney had more or less followed Pat's fortunes. And now
Pat was out to capture or kill the Kid. Barney was his tool,
and his appearance here might well involve the Kid's
safety.

There was quiet talk of forcing a confession out of the
slippery Mason. It was even suggested that he had better

be killed out of hand, but Sam Dedrick vetoed that with the argument that it would ruin his business.

As a matter of fact, Mason's visit had no relation whatever to the Kid. Two weeks or so before this a federal agent named Azariah F. Wild, from the New Orleans office of the Treasury Department, had arranged to meet Pat Garrett at Lincoln. He related to Pat that a considerable amount of counterfeit money had been sent to New Mexico and on to Lincoln County. Garrett suggested to the government agent that Barney Mason be hired to join the suspected gang. Pat was told to go ahead and negotiate matters with Barney. Immediately Pat wrote Barney, then at Fort Sumner, to meet him at his ranch near Roswell.

Barney had a strange tale to tell when he reported back to Pat: stopping for the night at Dan Dedrick's ranch at Bosque Grande, Dan had shown him a letter he had just received from W. H. West, his brother Sam's partner in the livery stable at White Oaks. West wrote in the letter that he had $30,000 in counterfeit bills with which he planned to buy cattle in Mexico, then quickly drive them north across the border. He wanted a man to go along who could negotiate for the cattle and secure bills of sale. If caught, West could then pose as the innocent purchaser. It was indeed a strange coincidence that Mason had thus been selected as an accomplice by both the crooks and the law-enforcement elements.

Garrett immediately returned to Lincoln with Mason, and the federal agent hired Barney to go straight to White Oaks to work in with the crooks. The presence of the Kid at the West & Dedrick stables when Barney arrived had changed Barney's plans and he returned to Lincoln and Roswell five days later, without once broaching the subject of the counterfeit money to West.

On this first night in White Oaks, following the violent argument regarding Mason and the lame excuse he gave the Kid for his being there, Barney was glad to get back to his friends in White Oaks with his whole skin. He looked up J. W. Bell, a soft-spoken, fairly slender man in his early thirties, whose left cheek had been slashed by a knife from one ear to his mouth. Barney told Bell that the Kid and two men were at the livery stable, and that Pat Garrett was determined on capturing Billy, running him out of the country, or killing him. Bell passed the word about the Kid's arrival to Deputy Sheriff William N. Hudgens, who at once alerted a number of citizens, good, bad and indifferent, to act as a posse. One of the members was Hudgens' own brother, John, who was his partner in a saloon and had recently been involved in the killing of a miner. In the group were two men named Tom Longworth and Jim Redmond, who had both been against the Kid's side in the Lincoln County War.

There is a certain amount of conjecture as to just what happened during the next forty-eight hours. Apparently Billy and his two companions, with possibly two recruits, pulled out of the Oaks that first night and made camp five miles to the northwest at an abandoned sawmill near Coyote Spring. An unsuccessful attempt to steal several horses belonging to one J. B. Bell is reported. And there is a tradition that the Kid and one or two of his companions rode brazenly into the Oaks. As they galloped out the Kid is said to have taken a wild, good-natured shot at Jim Redmond, who was standing in the doorway of the Hudgens' saloon.

Early the following morning the White Oaks posse started for Coyote Spring. On the way they encountered Mose Dedrick, a sort of renegade brother of Sam's, and a man named Lamper, and promptly arrested them. As the posse approached the abandoned sawmill the men were suddenly fired on by the Kid's crowd. In the mix-up the Kid's and Billie Wilson's horses were killed under them. Two recruits to the Kid's gang promptly pulled out, and the Kid was forced to abandon his camp.

The White Oaks party found the sack of provisions, the overcoat belonging to Mose Dedrick and the Kid's new gloves. The gloves were promptly appropriated by a young blacksmith named Jimmy Carlyle and later were to play a part in the fateful drama.

The posse of nine was technically the victor in the brush, but the men were glad enough to pull back to the Oaks and the warmth and security of the local bars. The Kid, Rudebaugh and Wilson somehow secured another mount, and with only two horses for the three of them they took turns riding double, and managed to make their way back to the Greathouse & Kuck stage station, thirty or forty miles away.

Shortly after dawn the second morning following their late arrival at the stage-stop, the temporary cook and roustabout of the outfit, a young man named Joe Steck, left the house to feed his team which was staked out some distance from the house. Nine years after the event Joe Steck sent to the Lincoln County *Leader* of White Oaks his own story of how he was grabbed by the White Oaks posse of thirteen men and forced to take part in the subsequent happenings.

Steck makes no mention of the generally accepted supposition that it was the sight of the Kid's gloves, picked up at the Coyote Spring camp and now sticking out of Carlyle's hip pocket, that aroused the Kid's anger. Despite this omission the Steck piece is the only completely unbiased report that is in existence:

> When about 300 yards from the house somebody hollered "Halt!" I naturally turned around to see what was up, when to my great surprise two men had their guns pointed at me. I went like a little man. When I got to them they got behind me and ordered me to march towards what I supposed was a bunch of fallen timber. And so it was, but there were men behind it, two bold, bad, ferocious looking men with plenty of guns and ammunition. When I got amongst them one of my captors said, "Captain, we have got one of the s. of b's.," and I did not resent it even a little bit.
>
> They ordered me to lie down with them, and I did so. They wanted to know if Billy the Kid, Billie Wilson, or Dave Rudebaugh were in the house. I told them I did not know. They doubted my word, and I didn't allow myself to get mad. They gave me a description of the men they were after, and I told them that three such looking men were in the house. Then they told me they were a sheriff's posse from White Oaks and would have the notorious trio dead or alive. After a consultation among themselves, more coming from different posts around the house, they decided that perhaps I was not so hard a citizen as I looked, and if I would give 'em my word of honor to come out again I could carry a dispatch into the house telling the boys to surrender, as a posse of 13 men from White Oaks had come in during the night,

surrounded the house on all sides, and large parties
from Lincoln were enroute with provisions and
everything necessary for a siege, and they had better
surrender at once as there was no show for escape.

I took the note in and delivered it to the one I
knew to be Billy the Kid. He read the paper to his
compadres who all laughed at the idea of surrender.
They told me also to rest easy and not to be alarmed
as no harm would come to me from them. They sent
me out with a note demanding to know who the
leader of the party was and invited him into the
house to talk the matter over. Carlyle, the leader of
the White Oaks party, at first objected, but Greathouse putting himself as hostage for his safety while
he was in there, he took off his arms and walked into
the trap. In the meantime I was backward and forward between the two parties, carrying dispatches.

Getting hungry, about 11 o'clock, I went into the
house to rustle up a dinner. I found Carlyle getting
under the influence of liquor and insisting on going
out, while the others insisted on his staying. While I
was getting dinner Mr. Cook, Greathouse's partner,
carried dispatches between the camps. For some reason the White Oaks boys became suspicious; things
were not as they should be with their leader, and
they decided to storm the fort. Therefore they sent
me word by Mr. Cook to come out as war would com-
mence in earnest. I stepped outdoors to go to some
safe place and witness the bloody conflict. After being
out, Cook stopped and turned, when with a crash a
man came through a window. Bang, bang, the man's
dying yell, and poor Carlyle tumbles to the ground,
with three bullets in him, dead.

I started to run away from the house, with Cook
behind me, and towards a barricade of the White
Oaks boys when they commenced to shoot at us, and
so did all the boys behind the different barricades.
About 60 or 75 shots were fired at us, bullets flying
all directions. . . .

We crawled out amongst the boys when they told
us it was all a mistake; that they thought we were
making a feint to cover the retreat of the desperadoes.

In the general excitement Greathouse slipped away from his captors, located one of his hobbled ponies, and with young Steck and Kuck made good his escape. [From now on Greathouse was a marked man, hounded by suspicion and eventually driven out of the district. A year or two later he was shotgunned to death by a desperado named Joe Fowler, at the man's ranch near Socorro, on the Rio Grande.]

Some time after dark the posse at the Greathouse station gathered up all the horses they could find and started back for the Oaks, leaving the dead Carlyle where he had fallen. On the return journey the posse met a contingent that had been recruited by the sheriff in Lincoln, which was bringing in food and supplies. But the White Oaks warriors had experienced all of the Kid they wanted.

It was towards midnight when Billy and his companions cautiously surveyed the situation. They discovered that the house was no longer surrounded. The trio made their way on foot to Old Man Spencer's small ranch ten miles away, arriving for a dawn breakfast. They were still afoot when they started the long trek to a sheep camp at a water-seep in the direction of Anton Chico.

Two or three days after the killing of Carlyle a noisy and revengeful mob from the Oaks returned to the Greathouse & Kuck stage-stop and burned the station. Then the posse rode on to Spencer's ranch and burned it in senseless retaliation against the old man for having fed the outlaws.

Billy had pretty well made monkeys out of the White Oaks braggarts, but it was a costly victory. Soon the whole country was aroused and every arm of law and all the power of the Ring was raised against him.

4

It was Thursday, November 25th, 1880, when Barney Mason on his return trip reached Pat Garrett's ranch house, four miles north of Captain J. C. Lea's privately owned town of Roswell. He told Pat of the Kid's arrival at the West & Dedrick livery stable in White Oaks and that a posse was being organized to raid his camp at Coyote Spring.

Barney could not possibly have known at the time he

hurriedly left the Oaks of the fight at the Spring or the subsequent killing of Carlyle at the Greathouse & Kuck stage station. The elaborate plan for Barney to join the gang of men passing the counterfeit money had been abandoned because of the Kid's sudden appearance.

Even from the scanty information which Mason brought him it was clear to Pat that the Kid would soon be driven out of White Oaks and that in all probability he would return to his old haunts around Fort Sumner. Pat would not actually take the office of sheriff until January 1st, but if he could either capture the Kid or drive him out of the country before that date it would be a fine feather in his cap. It was logical to conclude that once he got rid of the Kid most of the other outlaws would pull out.

He knew that Billy was not guilty of a fifth of the crimes of which he was accused. He knew, too, that the Kid was no drunken braggart and that there were many men in the Territory who were infinitely more vicious and criminal. But the Kid was enjoying a growing reputation which appeared to be almost a direct challenge to law and order. Somehow there was a dash and a romantic flare to everything he did. His fine art of daring and his youth and warm, sympathetic nature set him apart in popular imagination from the cheap thieves and killers. He was already becoming a legend.

And Pat had to think about his own best interests. He had turned thirty back on June 5th. He'd been poor all his adult life, and now he was married and there was a baby coming, and he was in debt for his holdings near Roswell. And here was the first real chance he had ever had in his life to win a big stake, to succeed, to make a name for himself. Capture Billy or dramatically run him out of the country and overnight he'd be known from one end of the Southwest to the other. He'd be going places. He could really get somewhere then.

There can be no doubt that he had kindly feelings for the boy. The last thing Pat wanted was to shoot it out with him. He knew how deadly the Kid was. Pat wasn't afraid of him, but he knew this was a game Billy could play quite as well as he could. But he had to make his move now or Captain Lea and the others might think he lacked the plain nerve to go after the young outlaw.

There was a second consideration that possibly helped

Pat to make his decision to start north at once. A tip came to him that John Joshua Webb, under sentence of death as the leader in a Las Vegas jail delivery in which three men had been killed, was hiding out in the Dan Dedrick ranch at Bosque Grande on the Pecos north of Roswell.

This same Webb had refused to leave the Las Vegas jail when Dave Rudebaugh was an accomplice in the killing of the jailer back in April. Webb's exemplary action at that time had brought a delay in his execution; some months later, however, he was in a far more bloody escape plot which had resulted in the killing of the three men. There was a substantial reward offered by San Miguel County for Webb's arrest, and Pat figured that he might have a good chance to capture him. He might even pick up the Kid at the same time.

As soon as Barney Mason reported to him Pat gathered up a posse in the Roswell district. Late that same Thursday night he and Barney, with twelve deputies, rode up the river. Bob Ollinger and Tip McKinney, who later were each to have his moment of fame, were members of the party.

At daybreak the men surrounded the Dedrick ranch house and swooped up Webb and another escaped prisoner named Davis, who was awaiting trial for mule stealing. Heavily guarded, the pair were mounted. By riding most of that night the posse pulled in at Fort Sumner around daybreak on the 27th. It was almost exactly the same day and hour that the White Oaks posse surrounded the Greathouse stage-stop some fifty or sixty miles on west.

From A. H. Smith, who ran the livery stable at the old army post, Garrett heard that the immediate whereabouts of the Kid were unknown but that Charlie Bowdre, Tom O'Folliard, and Pickett were at the Yerby ranch, twenty miles on to the northeast. Pat immediately left four men to guard his prisoners and, with the remaining eight possemen, rode off to gather in the trio. Both Bowdre and O'Folliard were under federal indictment for murder, and Pickett was wanted by the Vegas authorities on a minor charge. The Kid, of course, was Garrett's Number One target and it would badly cripple the young outlaw if he lost the last two members of his old Regulators.

Tom O'Folliard, mounted on a fast horse, barely missed

being intercepted on his way to the Yerby ranch, but he managed to elude the posse and warn Bowdre and Pickett in time for them to pull out before Pat reached the house. The only game the posse found was Bowdre's New Mexican wife and a second native woman who was frightened half out of her wits.

Empty-handed, Pat and his crowd returned to Fort Sumner and then took off for what was reported to be the Kid's hide-out at Los Portales, sixty miles to the east and near the Texas line. Arriving at the fine spring and cave Garrett found no evidence of Billy having been there in recent days. In place of sixty or seventy head of stolen cattle which Pat had expected to find, he located only two old cows and a yearling. Pat shot and butchered the yearling, and that night the posse ate beef straight, seasoned with salt found in a moldy sack in the cave.

Once again Pat turned back towards Fort Sumner with no game in his bag. The posse and mounts were tired out when they reached the Wilcox ranch, twelve miles east of Sumner. While the men and horses were being fed Wilcox told Garrett that the Kid's side-kick, Charlie Bowdre, was anxious to have a talk with Pat and find out if, in giving himself up, he would be allowed to make bond while awaiting trial.

Pat arranged to have Wilcox carry word to Bowdre that he would meet him alone and unarmed, at two o'clock the following afternoon at a fork in the road near Sumner.

Back at Fort Sumner Pat dismissed all his posse except Barney Mason and sent them on down river to Roswell. Previously he had written Sheriff Desiderio Romero at Las Vegas, telling him of the capture of Webb and Davis, and asking him to send men to take them back to Las Vegas.

The following morning Pat received a letter from Captain Lea at Roswell with the report of the killing of Carlyle at the Greathouse & Kuck stage station, and stating that the Kid, with Rudebaugh and Wilson, were set afoot and were making their way towards the Pecos. A second letter from Lea, now a Lincoln County commissioner and practically the new boss of the county, advised Pat that, if Bowdre would make a clean break of his association with the Kid, Lea would help him make bond and try to get him out of his indictment for murder.

Garrett showed this letter to Bowdre when he met him that afternoon. Charlie knew how Billy had been double-crossed when he had surrendered and turned State's evidence, and he was skeptical about these newest promises. He did, however, assure Garrett that he would have nothing more to do with the Kid.

Garrett waited two or three days at Sumner for word from Sheriff Romero and, when none came, he decided to go on to Vegas and personally deliver the prisoners. Before he reached Puerto de Luna he encountered the large and noisy posse from Vegas. The prisoner Webb explained to Pat that he had only $10 to his name but that he would gladly give it to him if he would see him to the jail, as he feared this undisciplined gang. When he pleaded that he had surrendered to Garrett and not to this wild mob, Garrett refused to take his money but agreed to stay with him on the 100-mile ride to Las Vegas.

Luck was now suddenly to break in Pat's favor. At Hay's ranch, on above Puerto de Luna, he received word that Frank Stewart, the newly arrived New Mexico representative of the Canadian River Cattlemen's Association of the Texas Panhandle, was now at or near Anton Chico. Garrett knew of the decision of the big Texas ranchers to send Stewart and two round-up wagons with riders to help break up the cattle stealing in New Mexico and capture or kill the Kid and any cow thieves they could find. Pat immediately dispatched Barney Mason to contact Stewart and ask him to come to Las Vegas for a conference.

Garrett knew the type of Texans who had been chosen by the Cattlemen's Association to embark on such a strange and dangerous mission into a neighboring territory. They were sure to be hard and resourceful men who were afraid of neither God nor the devil—nor of cold, hunger, nor fatigue. They would do to ride the rivers with. With six or eight of such Texans at his back Garrett would have a good chance of settling final accounts with the Kid.

Pat's neighbors from down around Roswell frankly weren't tough enough to do the job. The Kid's reputation was a little too overpowering for them, too. But the Texans simply weren't concerned with tall stories. They had cut their teeth on six-shooter barrels and the lead bullets of .44 cartridges.

5

There is no record of how the Kid spent the humiliating
days following the killing of Carlyle on November 27th.
Eventually he secured horses for himself and Rudebaugh
and Wilson, and late one night they rode into Fort Sumner.

Here he learned of the adventures of Garrett and his
prisoners and of Pat's visit to Los Portales, and of his interview with Charlie Bowdre. Billy contacted Charlie and
Tom O'Folliard and the latest recruit, Tom Pickett. The
Kid was well supplied with loyal spies, but he was smart
enough to realize that among the several Anglos around
Sumner there were one or two who would willingly act as
agents for Pat Garrett.

The Kid's sweetheart, Celsa, always saved for him copies
of the Las Vegas and Sante Fe newspapers, and when he
came to her now he eagerly scanned the pages for notices
recording the events of his little world. The Las Vegas
Gazette on November 30th, three days after the killing of
Carlyle but before word of the incident had reached
Vegas, carried a short piece that caught his eye:

> As is well known, there has been a gang of horse
> thieves along the Pecos who have run off stock from
> many ranches and who are believed to have com-
> mitted other depredations. The headquarters of the
> gang are at Fort Sumner, and their market for stolen
> stock is White Oaks. Last week three of the crowd,
> Dave Rudebaugh, "Billy the Kid," and Billy Wilson,
> went to the Oaks to dispose of some of their surplus
> stock and while there Sheriff Kimbrell of Lincoln
> County, who learned of their whereabouts, came
> with a posse expecting to corral them. They skipped
> out before the sheriff reached the camp and were met
> at Coyote Springs, seven miles away. They refused to
> surrender and showed resistance; a sharp fight fol-
> lowed. The gang seemed to have the best of the fight
> and drove the attacking party into the Oaks, follow-
> ing them up all the way. In the struggle Rudebaugh
> and "The Kid" both had their horses shot from
> under them.

Possibly it was certain little inaccuracies in the item that aroused the Kid to address a letter to Governor Wallace. This letter, along with one that Pat Garrett later claimed the Kid wrote to Captain J. C. Lea at Roswell, seem to prove that Billy had not altogether given up the idea that he might avoid shooting it out with Garrett. In his book Pat stated that the Kid wrote Lea that if he were given a chance to rest up his horses and not be harassed, he would leave the country for good. However, if the Kid were pursued he would "start a bloody war and fight it out to the fatal end."

The Kid's letter to Governor Wallace was written in red ink on ruled tablet paper. It read:

Fort Sumner

DEC. 12TH, 1880

Gov. Lew Wallace
    Dear Sir
I noticed in the Las Vegas Gazette a piece which stated that Billy "the" Kid, the name by which I am known in the Country was the Captian of a Band of Outlaws who hold Forth at the Portales. There is no such Organization in Existence. So the Gentlemen must have drawn very heavily on his Imagination.

My business at the White Oaks the time I was waylaid and my horse killed was to See Judge Leonard who has my case in hand. he had written to me to Come up, that he thought he could get Everything Straightened up I did not find him at the Oaks & Should have gone to Lincoln if I had met with no accident. After mine and Billie Wilsons horses were killed we both made our way to a Station, forty miles from the Oaks kept by Mr. Greathouse. When I got up next morning The house was Surrounded by an outfit led by one Carlyle, Who came into the house and Demanded a Surrender. I asked for their Papers and they had none. So I Concluded it amounted to nothing more than a mob and told Carlyle that he would have to Stay in the house and lead the way out that night. Soon after a note was brought in Stating that if Carlyle did not come out inside of five minutes they would Kill the Station Keeper)Great-

house) who had left the house and was with them.
in a Short time a Shot was fired on the outside and
Carlyle thinking Greathouse was Killed he jumped
through the window, breaking the Sash as he went
and was killed by his own Party they thinking it was
me trying to make my Escape. the Party then with-
drew.

they returned the next day and burned an old
man named Spencer"s house and Greathouses, also
I made my way to this Place afoot and During my absence Depututy Sheriff Garrett Acting under Chisums
orders went to the Portales and found Nothing. on
his way back he went by Mr. Yerbys ranch and took
a pair of mules of mine which I had left with Mr.
Bowdre who is in Charge of mr Yerbys Cattle. he
[Garrett] claimed that they were Stolen and Even if
they were not he had a right to Confiscate any Outlaws property.

I have been at Sumner Since I left Lincoln making
my living Gambling. the mules were bought by me
the truth of which I can prove by the best Citizens
around Sumner J. S. Chisum is the man who got me
into Trouble, and was benefited Thousands by it
and is now doing all he can against me There is no
Doubt but what there is a great deal of Stealing going
on in the Territory, and a great deal of the Property is
taken across the Plains as it is a good outlet but so
far as my being at the head of a Band there is nothing of it in Several Instances I have recovered Stolen
Property when there was no chance to get an Officer
to do it.

one instance for Hugo Zuber Postoffice Puerto De
Luna. another for Pablo Analla Same Place, if Some
impartial Party were to investigate this matter they
would find it far Different from the impression put
out by Chisum and his Tools,

Yours Respect
William Bonney

It is possible that the mail carrier's buckboard, with
Billy's letter aboard, had not yet left Fort Sumner for the
north when Governor Wallace announced in Santa Fe
an award of $500 for "the apprehension and arrest of said

Bonney and his delivery to the sheriff of Lincoln County at the county seat." Obviously the Governor had received the official word of the killing of Carlyle.

The Kid was now joined in Fort Sumner by Tom O'Folliard and Tom Pickett, and finally by Charlie Bowdre.

There is true pathos in the failure of Charlie Bowdre to pull out before the killing started once again. Charlie certainly pondered long and seriously over the advice that Pat Garrett gave him. There seems little doubt but that he tried his best to get Billy to leave after the young leader returned from the desperate affair at the Greathouse station. But as always the Kid postponed his decision.

Worried and apparently urged by his wife and his own good sense, Charlie now took the big step of writing directly to Captain Lea at Roswell. By some strange set of circumstances the letter is still preserved, and it helps explain the motivations and the strength of the binding friendships of men who fight together against heavy odds and for lost causes, worthy or otherwise.

FORT SUMNER DEC 15TH 1880

Capt. Lea,

I have broke up housekeeping and am camping around, first one place & then another on the range, so that no one can say that Yerbys ranch is the stoping place for any one. So no party will have any excuse for going there unless they are after me. I thought this a duty due Mr. Yerby, for if there is nothing to eat at the ranch no one will go there & there will be no chance for a fight coming off there & Mr. Yerby's property injured. If I don't get clear I intend to leave some time this winter, for I don't intend to take any hand fighting the territory, for it is different thing from what the Lincoln Co war was. The only difference in my case & some of the officers in Lincoln Co. is that I had the misfortune to be indicted before the fight was over & did not come under the Gov's pardon. It seems to me that this would come to their minds once & a while, when they are running around after me, but I suppose it is human nature to give a man a kick when you have the upper hand.

I saw the two Billies the other day & they say they are going to leave this country. That was my advice to them for I believe it is the best thing they can do. Don't you think if you can get the Gov interested in my case, that it could be thrown out by the Dist Att'y without my appearing at court. I don't doubt your good intentions, but during the present state of the country I think there is some danger of mobing. For my name has been used in connection with a good many things that I have had nothing to do with, which outside parties can't know. I have taken your advice in regard to writing to Mr. Yerby & have no doubt but what he will do all he can for me. I know of nothing to urge in my favor, now than that others were pardoned for like offences. Experience is a good but slow teacher & I think if I keep my mind, I will let every man do his own fighting so far as I am concerned & I will do my own.

Respt
Chas Bowdre.

There was no time for an answer before the swift turn of events changed the entire picture. Pat Garrett had now contacted the Texas gun-fighters. Bowdre must have almost at once joined up with the Kid again. It was a proof of the quiet power of the boy's leadership, and of the pure magnetism of his nature. This gave his side a total of six men, the Kid and his last two old Regulators, and three new men who had belonged to the Las Vegas Toughs.

By the time the news of the Governor's reward offer reached the Kid he had information that Pat Garrett, Barney Mason, and Stewart had left Las Vegas. There were vague rumors that two round-up wagons with their accompanying crews from the Panhandle had reached Anton Chico and were now heading for White Oaks.

The final showdown would come at any time now. No longer did the Kid have the slightest hope of any help from Governor Wallace, nor from any of the others whom he had once served so faithfully. John Chisum had completely deserted him, and Pat Garrett had been hired to kill him.

And now these hard men from Texas might soon be riding with Pat.

18

It was shortly after noon dinner on Monday the 14th of December, 1880, when Pat Garrett and Barney Mason, and the Texan Frank Stewart rode out of Las Vegas. They ate their supper at Hay's ranch, eighteen miles southward, and then pushed on until one o'clock in the morning when they stopped at the camp of a Mexican freighting outfit. At daybreak they mounted again and rode on southwestward.

Frank Stewart, who was acting independently of the rest of the Texans, explained the general situation to Pat. The LX spread near Tascosa in the Panhandle had furnished one wagon and outfit and put it in charge of Charlie Siringo; besides the cook, who also drove the four-mule team, there were Jim East, Lee Hall, Lon Chambers and Cal Polk. A second wagon to help in the rounding up of the New Mexico thieves was fitted out by Major Littlefield's LIT and the men who rode with it were Tom Emory, George Williams, Louis Bausman and Bob Robinson.

Charlie Siringo was apparently more or less in general charge of the two wagons. He was given an LX check for $300 to buy provisions and horse feed at Las Vegas. Since it would save a good deal of extra hard travel Siringo sent the two wagons straight on to Anton Chico to wait for him while he rode into Vegas to arrange for the grub. But Siringo lost the check and his own few dollars bucking a monte game that first night.

When Siringo reached Anton Chico, crestfallen and apologetic, he found that the Texans had squandered such pocket money as they had brought with them on the pleasures of the bright little town. A friendly merchant, however, accepted Siringo's order and stocked up the two wagons for the long, cold drive through the snow to White Oaks, where they would make their headquarters while they turned cattle detectives. This winter of 1880–81 was to go down in local history as one of the most severe ever recorded in the country.

It was nine o'clock in the morning when Pat, with Mason and Stewart, rode up to where the two Texas outfits were camped in the outskirts of Anton Chico. Cautiously Garrett and Stewart explained that a bunch of stolen Panhandle steers had been located near Fort Sumner and that there was a good prospect of a fight with the Kid. Those who wanted to go along could volunteer. Six men saddled up. With Barney and Frank Stewart, this gave Pat eight experienced men as the hard core of his posse. Despite the cold each man carried only a single blanket tied behind the cantle of his saddle.

Men and horses were almost exhausted when they pulled up at a poverty-stricken Mexican ranch at nine o'clock that night. At daylight the men mounted and slowly made their way southward towards Puerto de Luna. A bitter wind blew down from the northwest and at times the men dismounted and led their horses. It was a test of pure endurance and fortitude, with Garrett setting the killing pace. It was almost as if some obsession had seized him. Nothing could stop him from closing with the Kid.

It was somewhere between eight and nine that morning when they reached Grzelachowski's long, adobe store and home at Puerto de Luna. A hot breakfast and bottled cheer welcomed the men, while their horses were given a double ration of grain. Pat was persuaded that there was a limit to the physical drain on both men and animals, and he agreed that the outfit must stop here that day and night.

The tall, restless leader took advantage of the forced lay-over by dispatching a spy, Jose Roibal, who was highly recommended by the Pole, to ride on south to Fort Sumner. He was to pretend that he was a herder looking for lost sheep, while he found out as much about the Kid and his gang as he could. He was then to return north and intercept the Garrett party somewhere on the road the following afternoon.

It was around eight o'clock that next evening when Jose contacted Pat's party at Pablo Beaubien's ranch, just north of Gearhart's. Pat's posse was now reinforced by two young Americans and Jose Roibal's brother Juan. Jose reported that the Kid and his gang of five were still at Fort Sumner but were very much on the alert. They kept their horses saddled and were momentarily prepared to fight or make their get-away. George Farnum, the mail carrier, apparently had told Billy that Garrett and Mason were on their way towards Sumner, riding alone.

When Jose pulled out of Fort Sumner O'Folliard and Pickett overtook him at the edge of the old army post and severely questioned him. He stuck to his sheepherder story and was turned loose. After getting the report Garrett rewarded the lad, and then he and his posse rode south to Gearhart's ranch.

It was a situation made to order for Pat. Twenty-five miles down the river the Kid and his five men were taking it easy, totally unaware that Garrett and his posse of eight gun-fighters were riding down on him.

Pat waited at Gearhart's until men and horses had been fed and rested. At midnight the party turned their backs to the biting winds and pointed on down the river.

Daylight was barely breaking when they pulled in at one of the abandoned buildings above the *plaza* at Fort Sumner. Garrett took Mason with him, and the two men silently made their way on foot to the A. H. Smith corral and stable. The outlaws' horses were not there, so Smith was awakened and questioned.

The Kid and his party had pulled out the previous night. Pat missed his quarry by a matter of six or seven hours.

2

It was now the morning of December 18th, and Garrett ordered all his men to remain concealed excepting Barney

Mason whose wife and father-in-law were living here and who consequently had a reason for being at Sumner. Pat, cautiously circulating around the little community, ran into one Iginio Garcia, who lived a dozen miles down the river. Garcia claimed he was in search of a lost cow. Pat was fully aware that Garcia was very friendly with the Kid and would send him word that he and Mason were at Sumner. As he was anxious for this very information to reach Billy, he made no effort to restrain Garcia.

The New Mexican pledged he would tell no one of Pat's presence and then hurried on south. Near his own home he ran into Bob Campbell and Jose Valdez, who were driving north a small bunch of cattle that A. H. Smith had purchased at Bosque Grande. Garcia, knowing that Campbell was a Kid adherent, told him that Garrett and Mason were in Sumner, but that apparently they had no posse with them. Campbell immediately hired a native boy and dispatched him with a note to the Kid whom he was sure was at the Wilcox & Brazil ranch, twelve miles east of Sumner.

There was considerable hilarity at the ranch house when the messenger came in with the note. The shoe was now on the other foot; Garrett and Mason were the two who were now in danger of being surprised and overwhelmed.

But the Kid was fully aware of how shrewd and resourceful the lean and hard Garrett really was. He was taking no unnecessary chances. Wilcox had a stepson named Juan, and Billy quickly sent the lad into town with instructions that he was to find how many men Garrett had and as much of his plans as he could.

Once again Pat played in luck. He encountered the Kid's undergrown spy almost as soon as the boy reached the *plaza*. Pat knew the lad, and soon he was explaining to Pat the true nature of his mission. The sheriff-elect was sure that Wilcox the stepfather and his partner were both law-abiding citizens and would be willing to help him. It was an easy job to talk the boy into a promise of strict obedience.

The native named Jose Valdez, who had been with Bob Campbell when Campbell had learned of Garrett's presence in Sumner and had sent the note of warning to the Kid, was now back in town. Garrett encountered

Valdez and forced him to write a note to the Kid stating that Garrett and his small party had pulled out for Roswell and that there was no longer any danger.

He instructed the Wilcox boy to give this note to the Kid, and when he was alone with his stepfather he was secretly to hand him a second note. In this Pat explained that he had a posse totaling thirteen men and that he would never give up until he had captured the Kid, killed him, or run him out of the country.

With the boy safely on his way, Pat arranged that come nightfall he would plant his men in one end of the old Indian hospital, at the eastern edge of the post. Mrs. Charlie Bowdre and her mother occupied rooms in the long structure. It was logical for Pat to assume that, as it was located squarely on the road from the Wilcox & Brazil ranch, the Kid with Bowdre and O'Folliard and the three recruits from Las Vegas would drop in here en route to the *plaza*.

He had now set and baited his trap for the Kid.

3

The boy Juan accurately played his role, delivering the right notes to the Kid and his stepfather, and answering all questions.

Apparently there was no suspicion on Billy's part. He could ride into Sumner when and how he chose. There was even talk that they might follow Garrett on south and shoot him up a little, and then utterly disgrace him by setting him afoot. To kill him would only add to their troubles.

Billy had planned to take in a wagon load of beef that evening, but that idea was now dropped in favor of riding into Fort Sumner along about eight o'clock. He probably figured on seeing his sweetheart Celsa, and Charlie Bowdre could stop off with his wife at the old Indian hospital, while the remaining four could pursue such simple pleasures as Beaver Smith's or Bob Hargrove's bar offered in drink and gambling.

Apparently it appeared completely unnecessary to the Kid to send in an additional spy to check on Garrett. Pat would undoubtedly be well down toward Bosque Grande by the time the Kid rode into Sumner. It was only customary caution to wait until nightfall before appearing in the settlement.

Mrs. Wilcox fixed supper and there was good-natured banter when the six men saddled up and started off. It was still snowing a little, and it was cold.

The men rode bunched up, but a mile or two from the old army post the Kid and Tom O'Folliard took the lead, while the rest followed in sets of twos. Of the five it was Tom whom the Kid loved the best. He had taken the half-Cherokee Fred Waite's place in the Kid's affection, and only the young Englishman, John Tunstall, had ever been as close to the boy's heart.

From time immemorial horsemen approaching a settlement have invariably pulled up on their reins and touched their mounts into a smart trot or gallop. This happened now as the men in front saw the dim outlines of the old Indian Hospital building looming up in the snow ahead.

For some unaccountable reason Billy turned his horse to one side and let Tom O'Folliard ride on ahead. Pickett spurred up his horse and took the Kid's place. It might have been the result of some premonition, some slim hunch of the Kid's which can never be explained; some intuition that had to do with the primeval instincts of self-preservation. This was not the Kid's night to be killed.

At that moment the Texan Lon Chambers, who was standing on guard outside the old hospital building, caught a faint glimpse of the little cavalcade down the white road. He rushed to the door of the big room and shouted the news to Pat, Bob Williams, Barney Mason, and Tom Emory who were playing poker on a blanket in the corner. Jim East had just spread out his blanket on the floor for a little sleep.

The men jumped to their feet, grabbed their Winchesters, and hurried outside to their assigned places. Pat hugged the back wall of the overhanging porch, partially hidden by a set of harness which hung from wooden pegs. Chambers was to his right.

The party of six riders turned at the corner of the building and rode up close to the porch. Garrett shouted an order, "Halt!" Apparently he and Chambers both opened fire on O'Folliard in the lead, before Tom could make a move to pull up his horse or throw up his hands.

The two possemen pumped in fresh shells and fired at

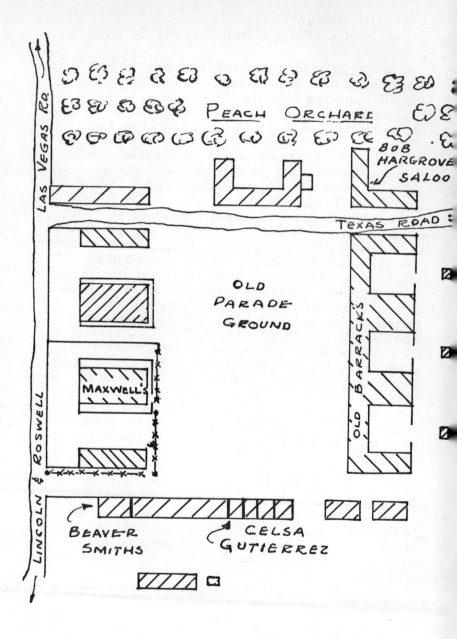

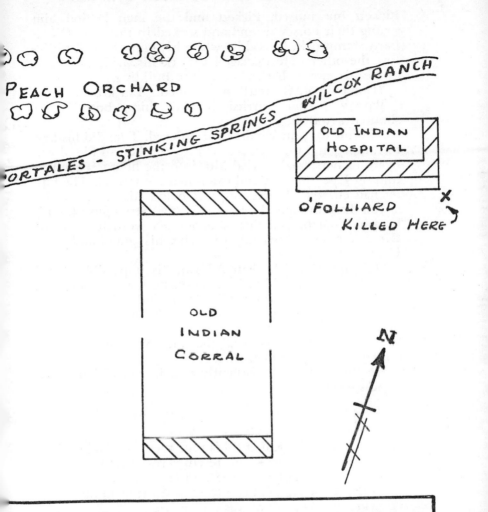

PEACH ORCHARD

PORTALES - STINKING SPRINGS WILCOX RANCH

OLD INDIAN HOSPITAL

O'FOLLIARD KILLED HERE X

OLD INDIAN CORRAL

N

FORT SUMNER, NEW MEXICO 1881
1955© R.N. MULLIN

Pickett but missed. Pickett and the men behind him swung their horses around and socked in the steel. O'Folliard slumped in his saddle while his horse turned to follow the others. He managed to jerk his bridle rein and guide his mount back close to the building.

"Don't shoot, Garrett!" he pleaded. "I'm killed."

Barney Mason hurried towards him, but Garrett shouted a warning.

"Throw up your hands!" Pat ordered. Tom did his best to comply, and the men reached up and helped him down from his horse and carried him into the house. They laid him on East's blanket and examined his wound. The bullet had entered his left side just below his heart.

Jim East brought him some water. Struggling for his breath, Tom begged that someone get word to Tip McKinney, a family friend, to write his grandmother in Uvalde, Texas.

"Oh, my God," he half sobbed, "is it possible that I must die?" He wouldn't be twenty-one for a few months.

"Tom, your time is short," Garrett said to him, perhaps reminded of the death of the boy he had shot in the buffalo hunters' camp three years earlier.

"The sooner—the better," the tall boy gasped. "I'll be out—out—of my pain—then."

He seemed to shake violently as if in convulsion. Then he was dead.

4

Off to the east the Kid and his four men who had escaped death were riding with the terrible realization that they had let themselves be trapped and ambushed. They knew Tom had been shot and captured, but they had no way of knowing whether he was dead or alive.

Rudebaugh's horse had been hit, and it gradually weakened and finally fell. Dave got up behind Billie Wilson, and the beaten little party made its way to the Wilcox & Brazil ranch. They took turns standing guard the rest of the night.

Of all the Regulators who had volunteered that long-ago February morning following the killing of Tunstall, only Charlie Bowdre now remained with Billy.

The Kid rode on ahead alone. He had never been

known to loosen the tight rein he held on his inner feelings or betray the secret pain in his heart. He spoke to no one.

No longer would he be riding stirrup to stirrup with the brave and faithful Tom—tall, light-hearted, half Irish and half Texan, and wholly loyal. He must have felt certain that it was Garrett who had killed his dearest friend.

He himself was in great danger. Never in his life, save only on the tragic night when McSween was killed and escape from the burning house had seemed all but impossible, had he been in such deadly jeopardy as he was at this moment.

5

It snowed hard late that night and on into the next morning. By the time Garrett and his posse saddled up and cautiously rode east to reconnoiter, the Kid's trail was well covered. A mile out of town they came upon a dead horse, and Pat figured that at least two of the outlaw gang had been forced to double-up.

They rode further on for a mile or two towards the Wilcox & Brazil ranch. But it was obvious the Kid would have posted guards, and they themselves might run into a trap. Pat turned his horse around and motioned for his men to follow him back to Fort Sumner. Neither man nor beast could last long in such terrible weather.

On beyond the Wilcox house there was a vast emptiness. The nearest ranch on east was fifteen or twenty miles distant. It was the edge of the barren Staked Plains, whose lonely infinity daunted the heart of even the staunchest traveller.

Back at the old army post Garrett's men helped in the burial of Tom O'Folliard. But he was not the one they wanted.

The day and early night wore on. Some of the men played poker for small stakes, and there was a little drinking. It was as if the storm had dropped down as a barrier between the two parties, the very fury of the weather rendering both immobile.

The next morning Brazil, the junior partner in the ranch, rode into Fort Sumner and looked up Pat Garrett. He reported that the Kid and his four remaining men had sent him to spy out the land. The Kid and his gang were a little suspicious of Wilcox and had dispatched Brazil in his stead. He explained that both the Kid and Rudebaugh were despondent and worried. For once they had lost their bright quality of optimism and humor.

Brazil did not start back for his ranch until early Tuesday morning. He had been thoroughly drilled in the report he was to make: Garrett had only Barney Mason and the three recently acquired natives with him; it was pure luck that had let him intercept the Kid's gang and kill O'Folliard; Pat was scared and anxious to start down the river for Roswell, but the storm had made him fearful of leaving the *plaza*.

These were the instructions Brazil was given: if he found that the outlaws had pulled out, or if they did leave shortly, he was to return at once to Sumner; under any circumstance, if Pat did not hear from him by two o'clock the following morning, the deputy sheriff and his posse would start for the ranch and surround it.

It was close to midnight that same night when Brazil showed up again in Sumner. It had stopped snowing, but it was so bitterly cold that the rancher's beard was dripping with icicles. He reported that the Kid and his four men had left soon after they had eaten their supper.

Garrett ordered his men to move out immediately; they had kept their horses saddled and ready in a nearby stable. Brazil was told to go directly to his ranch, and if he found that the Kid's party had returned there he was to backtrack and let Garrett know.

The sheriff-elect led his own men on a side trail to a small house known as Lake Ranch, where he figured the Kid might have gone for shelter for the night. He cautiously surrounded the cabin but found no one there.

Brazil contacted Garrett about three miles from his house. He quietly piloted the posse to a trail in the snow that led towards Stinking Springs. An abandoned one-room, stone shack was known to be near. At best it could serve the Kid only as a temporary refuge.

It was now a little after 3 o'clock of the morning of Thursday, December 22nd. The men could make out the shack on ahead, as eerie and indistinct as if it were the ghost of some haunted house adrift in a gray, uncertain world. A small arroyo curved halfway around the square structure of rock.

Garrett quietly studied the situation. Back in a low spot in the terrain and out of sight of the shack, he left the horses with Juan Roibal, who had joined up with him at Puerto de Luna. The group quietly approached the house on foot.

With two hundred yards still to go, Pat told Lee Hall, Ed East, and Tom Emory to follow him. [Tom Emory's real name was Armun and he was an escaped convict travelling under the alias of Emory. He had been playing poker on a blanket on the floor of Mrs. Bowdre's room the night previously when O'Folliard was killed, and for the balance of his life he was called "Poker Tom."] The remainder of the men with Garrett were ordered to conceal themselves in a depression well back of the stone house but to keep on the alert. Pat knew that the shack had no windows and that the only door was on the far side.

With his three men following him, Pat noiselessly made his way in the gray darkness on up the little arroyo that led to the front of the hut. They carried blankets, and reached a spot hardly more than thirty feet from the open doorway when they spread them out on the snow-covered bank. If they crouched down, or lay on their blankets, no bullet fired from the house could reach them.

Soon it grew lighter and Garrett could count the outlines of three horses, their halter shanks tied to the round *vegas* that stuck in front to support the flat, dirt roof. The two remaining horses, probably the Kid's bay racing mare and one other animal, obviously had been taken inside for protection from the biting winds.

To Pat and his men, shivering from the cold as they lay sprawled out on their blankets against the side of the shallow arroyo, it seemed that daylight would never come.

6

It had been a terrible night for Billy and his four followers. The wooden door of the shack had long disappeared, leaving this unprotected opening in front.

While the crude stone shack offered some small defense against the storm, it was cold and dark and hopeless within its crumbling walls. Each man had untied the blanket behind his saddle when he had loosened the cinch and slipped the chilly steel bit from his horse's mouth.

There was little sleep, with no prospect of a fire or a warming cup of coffee. One or two of the Kid's men had taken a quarter-filled sack of oats from the Wilcox ranch when they pulled out after dark. In such emergencies horses always came before men. Charlie Bowdre also had found a feed bag and, filling it, tied it to the pommel of his saddle.

Light was breaking when Bowdre stepped out of the open doorway with the feed bag in his hand. Each horse would be given a few mouthfuls of oats, and soon the men would tighten their saddle cinches, adjust their bridles, and move out with the dawn. They could head for the Yerby ranch and after a hot meal and a little rest ride on from there.

But they wouldn't dare stop for long. They knew now that Garrett was really after them. He would never give up. They would have to leave the country this time. It wouldn't be so hard to do if this weather would only change and give them a chance to move out fast. They'd make a start at dawn.

Suddenly Pat's shout of "Hands Up!" broke the silence. Simultaneously came two shots so close together it was hard to distinguish them apart.

Bowdre cried out, and backed into the house, his arms clutching his chest. The Kid pulled him away from the open doorway and located his wounds. He could see that Charlie was finished.

He jerked the dying man's pistol from its scabbard and pushed it in his right hand. He closed the fingers tight around the butt.

"Go on out there, Charlie!" the Kid urged. "You're done for! Go on and get one of them sonsabitches! Go on, Charlie!"

There was silence now as Bowdre staggered out of the doorway and walked bent-over towards the rim of the arroyo. He was bleeding at the mouth. No one fired at him.

He tried to lift up the pistol and pull the trigger. But he couldn't make it.

"I wish—I wish—I—I," he managed to utter.

Then he tumbled down the slope into the arms of Lee Hall. They laid him on a blanket and in a minute he was dead. The two slugs from the rifles of Garrett and Hall had ripped through his breast.

No one can ever know what he was thinking when he stammered out the words, "I wish—I wish."

He might have been wishing that he had followed the advice of Pat Garrett and Captain Lea and quit the Little Capitan for good.

It was too late now.

7

Garrett and the three men with him on the open side of the stone hut took turns at laying their rifles in the snow on the lip of the arroyo and drawing a bead on the open doorway. They fired a few times at the edges of the opening just to show the men within that anyone venturing to take aim would be killed.

Garrett, figuring that by accurate shooting he might cut the halter shanks of the three horses outside, suddenly saw the rope of the animal nearest the door shake and then become taut. He realized that someone inside the shack was pulling at the rope. Slowly the horse moved towards the opening.

Garrett waited until the horse was halfway inside before he took careful aim and fired. It was a perfect shot through the heart. And now the single exit was blocked. The two horses inside were trapped.

With superb marksmanship Garrett cut the halter shanks of the two remaining horses tied to the *vegas*. They galloped off, to be picked up by the men at the back of the house. The animals inside the shack were now useless, for it would be impossible for a mounted man to jump his mount over the dead horse blocking the doorway without being dragged off his own animal by the top of the low opening.

Garrett presently opened up a conversation with the Kid. Most of the time it was friendly banter. The Kid had already recovered his good nature and anyone listening in might have thought he and Pat were the best of friends and were only playing a game of banter. Garrett later recorded one small part of the dialogue that followed his question as to how the besieged men were fixed:

"Pretty well," the Kid answered, "but we haven't any wood to get breakfast with."

"Come on out and get some," Pat suggested. "Be a little sociable."

"Can't do it, Pat," the Kid replied. "Business is too confining. No time to run around."

It was nine o'clock when Pat cautiously made his way down the arroyo and arranged to take half his men to the Wilcox ranch for breakfast. When he returned the second half went after their hot meal. Figuring that the Kid might hold out for some hours, Pat arranged with the ranch owners to send a wagon with food and firewood, and he prepared for a night of siege.

At various times during the day Pat had both serious and humorous conversations with the Kid. He explained to Billy that he had a dozen men who had the stone shack so completely surrounded that there was no possibility of escape. The Kid had better surrender and get the agony over with. The Kid would banter in return, "Come on in and get me, Pat! That'll be easy."

In the middle of the afternoon the Kid turned loose his own pet mare and the other horse that had been stabled inside the house. They were picked up some distance from the shack.

It was about this time that the outlaws were discovered in the act of tunnelling a hole through the stone wall at the rear of the house. A few rifle shots put a stop to that business.

The wagon from the Wilcox ranch arrived towards four o'clock, and a fire was made on the blind side of the house. Before long the enticing smell of cooking meat and boiling coffee seeped through the open doorway and assailed the senses of the cold and famished men inside. The tough Dave Rudebaugh apparently was the first man to break under the temptation. He found a stick, tied to it what had once been a white handkerchief and stuck it up through the low chimney.

Apparently the Kid let Rudebaugh go out alone and make the arrangements for the surrender. The men were to leave their weapons behind and to come out one at a time, with their raised hands above their head.

The Kid was the last to come out. He raised one hand,
and then lowered it when he pushed up the other. He
made silent fun of the orders. Nothing could break down
his self-control.

It was a bitter business, but the good-humored grin
never left his face. Even Garrett could not conquer him.
He could capture him and even kill him—but he could
never dominate him. Nor could Pat crush his sense of
humor.

8

The Kid and his three companions were carefully herded
over towards the fire. Pat's men kept their cocked rifles
in their hands as they stood off a way while the prisoners
were fed. Then they were handcuffed, mounted, and
taken to the Wilcox ranch. A wagon was sent back for the
body of Charlie Bowdre.

The captors and captives alike were chilled and tired
out, and badly needed the rest Pat allowed them at the
ranch. At daybreak the Kid and his three Las Vegas toughs
were put in the wagon that carried the body of Charlie
Bowdre.

Never for a moment did the Kid seem to lose his iron
nerve. All his old gang were gone. Of the original score
and more he alone remained. It was almost as if he had
the whole world against him now. He'd sure miss Tom
O'Folliard and Charlie Bowdre. But he wasn't quitting
yet.

He talked with Pat Garrett as casually as if nothing had
occurred to mar their old friendship. He said that he knew
the game was up at the stone house when Pat shot the
horse so that it blocked the only exit. If the Kid could
have led this third horse through the doorway, even
though the two animals outside were gone, he would have
waited for night and then tried to get away.

He would personally have covered the attempt of his
three remaining companions, two mounted double, to
escape through the darkness. Then he would have made
his own final dash for life on his swift and durable mare.
He was cool and unemotional as he and Pat reviewed
those terrible hours.

The Kid had been friendly with Frank Stewart at

Tascosa in the Panhandle days, and when the party reached Fort Sumner he turned over his beloved mare to the Texan. Jim East had been another friend of his gay Texas adventures, and he told Jim to keep his rifle as a souvenir. [In May of 1920, forty years later, East wrote a long letter to Charlie Siringo, pilot of the two Texas wagons to White Oaks at the time six of the Texans had ridden off with Garrett. The letter to Siringo read in part:

> We took the prisoners and the body of Charlie Bowdre to the Wilcox ranch, where we stayed until next day. Then to Fort Sumner, where we delivered the body of Bowdre to his wife. Garrett asked Louis Bausman and I to take Bowdre to the house to his wife.
>
> As we started in with him, she struck me over the head with a branding iron and I had to drop Charlie at her feet. The poor woman was crazy with grief. I always regretted the death of Charlie Bowdre, for he was a brave man, and true to his friends to the last.
>
> Before we left Ft. Sumner with the prisoners for Santa Fe, the "Kid" asked Garrett to let Tom Emory and I go along as guards, which, as you know, we did.
>
> The "Kid" presented me with his Winchester rifle, but Old Beaver Smith made such a roar about an account that he said "Billy" owed him, that at the request of "Billy" I gave old Beaver the gun. I wish now I had kept it.]

The unfortunate Barney Mason of Pat's group got nothing out of the cold and harrowing experience save the added hatred of the Kid. Barney is generally credited with having been a brother-in-law of Pat Garrett but there is no evidence to sustain this. [There is, however, some proof that a few years after these events Pat was forced to arrest Mason for illegally branding one of Garrett's valuable black yearling heifers, and his one-time trusted aide and deputy was sent to the penitentiary. Returning home impoverished, Barney tried dry-farming in the country near Tucumcari. He did not have money enough to build a house, so he settled his family in a dugout. One night in a heavy rain the roof caved in, and Barney and his wife and one or two children were killed by the fall of earth.]

9

The sun was well up in the winter sky when the four prisoners, handcuffed and bound in pairs by leg irons, were put in a wagon, and with three mounted men riding alongside began the long journey to Las Vegas. Here they would take the train to Santa Fe. The Kid, Rudebaugh and Wilson were all under federal indictment and thus could be delivered to the safety of the jail in the Territorial capital. There was only a minor indictment against Tom Pickett so he would be left at Las Vegas.

The first stop was at Gearhart's ranch, twenty-five miles north of Sumner. It was midnight when the half-frozen party arrived there and got something to eat. They rested until eight the next morning. It was around two on Christmas afternoon by the time they had covered the next eighteen miles and pulled up in front of the long *portales* of the Grzelachowski store and headquarters at Puerto de Luna.

An immense wild turkey with all the trimmings was about to be served to the big family, and the visitors were assured there was plenty for all. The Pole, who years before had changed his priest's robe for a rancher's outfit, was a hearty, forgiving soul, and he joked with Billy about what the young outlaw had done with that latest haul of eight of his prize horses. Maybe the boy would leave him alone from now on. While he plagued him he saw that Billy's plate was kept well filled. He could have used such a boy.

At four that Christmas afternoon Pat herded his prisoners back to their wagon. A bitter, snow-flecked wind was blowing, and a few hours later the wagon broke down. A fire was built along the trail while two men on horseback hurried to Captain Clancy's for a replacement. Then they pushed on through the night. It was breakfast time when they drew up at Hay's ranch, eighteen miles below Las Vegas.

At two that afternoon of December 26th the driver whipped up his mules and clattered into Las Vegas. Word of the arrest had proceeded their arrival and men who had been waiting in the hotels and bars lined up in the street to welcome the historic caravan. There were cheers mixed with shouts of derision.

For a moment Garrett was worried about the crowd: Rudebaugh having had a part in the murder of the local jailer warned Pat that the native New Mexican element might try to lynch him. Pat not only promised Rudebaugh that he would deliver him safely to the Vegas jail but that he would take him along with the Kid and Billie Wilson to Santa Fe.

To the Kid it apparently seemed little more than some wild and deadly adventure that had failed rather miserably. He was cutting quite a figure, and he knew it. He was both the villain and the hero to this crowd which was partly friendly and partly hostile. It was all the same to him.

Yesterday was yesterday to his stout heart. Tomorrow would be another day.

For him there would always be a *mañana.*

19

Frontier journalism, from the days of Mark Twain and his Virginia City *Territorial Enterprise*, is rich with hidden bits of genius. Tramp reporters, who often could set their own pieces in type, wrote their little gems and then moved on to new adventures. Editors, too, were of a special breed of talented men prone to hide their light under a broad-brimmed, western hat.

It might have been the editor of the Vegas *Gazette*, the versatile J. H. Koogler, who wrote the interview with the Kid on the morning after his arrival at the jail. The alert *Gazette* had already secured the story of the capture from Pat Garrett and the others involved and had hustled out an Extra. The interview with the Kid himself was obtained that same morning and published a day after the Extra, in the regular edition of December 28, 1880.

Somehow, of all the contemporary accounts of Billy this alone seems to penetrate the boy's inner heart and to give him the breath of life and the faithful touch of reality. It is a priceless part of the authentic literature on this extraordinary boy. It is quoted in full:

> With its accustomed enterprise The Gazette was the first paper to give the story of the capture of Billy Bonney, who has risen to notoriety under the sobri-

253

quet of "the Kid," and Billy Wilson and Tom Pickett. Just at this time everything of interest about the
men is especially interesting, and after damning the
party in general and "the Kid" in particular through
the columns of this paper, we considered it the correct
thing to give him a show.

Through the kindness of Sheriff Romero a representative of the Gazette was admitted to the jail yesterday morning. Mike Cosgrove, the obliging mail
contractor, who often met the boys while on business
down the Pecos, had just gone in with five large bundles. The doors at the entrance stood open and a
large crowd strained their necks to get a glimpse of
the prisoners, who stood in the passageway like children waiting for a Christmas tree distribution. One
by one the bundles were unpacked, disclosing a good
suit for each man. Mr. Cosgrove remarked that he
wanted "to see the boys go away in style."

Billy "the Kid" and Billy Wilson who were shackled together, stood patiently while a blacksmith took
off their shackles and bracelets to allow them an opportunity to make a change of clothing. Both prisoners watched the operation which was to set them free
for a short while, but Wilson scarcely raised his eyes
and spoke but once or twice to his *compadres*. Bonney, on the other hand, was light and chipper and
was very communicative, laughing, joking and chat-
ting with the by-standers.

"You appear to take it easy," the reporter said.

"Yes! What's the use of looking on the gloomy
side of everything? The laugh's on me this time," he
said. Then, looking around the *placita*, he asked, "Is
the jail at Santa Fe any better than this?"

This seemed to trouble him considerably, for, as
he explained, "this is a terrible place to put a fellow
in." He put the same question to every one who
came near him and when he learned that there was
nothing better in store for him, he shrugged his
shoulders and said something about putting up with
what he had to.

He was the attraction of the show, and as he stood
there, lightly kicking the toes of his boots on the
stone pavement to keep his feet warm, one would

scarcely mistrust that he was the hero of the "Forty Thieves" romance which this paper has been running in serial form for six weeks or more.

"There was a big crowd gazing at me, wasn't there," he exclaimed, and then smilingly continued, "well, perhaps some of them will think me half a man now; everyone seems to think I was some kind of animal."

He did look human, indeed, but there was nothing very mannish about him in appearance, for he looked and acted a mere boy. He is about five feet, eight or nine inches tall, slightly built and lithe, weighing about 140; a frank and open countenance, looking like a school boy, with the traditional silky fuzz on his upper lip; clear blue eyes, with a roguish snap about them; light hair and complexion. He is, in all, quite a handsome looking fellow, the imperfection being two prominent front teeth, slightly protruding like squirrels' teeth, and he has agreeable and winning ways.

A cloud came over his face when he made some allusion to his being made the hero of fabulous yarns, and something like indignation was expressed when he said that our Extra misrepresented him in saying that he called his associates cowards. "I never said any such thing," he pouted, "I know they ain't cowards."

Billy Wilson was glum and sober, but from underneath his broad-brimmed hat, we saw a face that had a by no means bad look. He is light complexioned, light hair, bluish grey eyes, is a little stouter than Bonney, and far quieter. He appears ashamed and is not in very good spirits.

A final stroke of the hammer cut the last rivet in the bracelets, and they clanked on the pavement as they fell.

Bonney straightened up and then rubbing his wrists, where the sharp edged irons had chaffed him, said; "I don't suppose you fellows would believe it, but this is the first time I ever had bracelets on. But many another better fellow had them on, too."

With Wilson he walked towards the little hole in the wall to the place which is no "sell" on a place of confinement. Just before entering he turned and looked back and explained; "They say, a fool for luck and a poor man for children—Garrett takes them all in."

We saw them again at the depot when the crowd presented a really war-like appearance. Standing by the car, out of one of the windows of which he was leaning, he talked freely with us of the whole affair.

"I don't blame you for writing of me as you have. You had to believe others' stories, but then I don't know as anyone would believe anything good of me, anyway," he said. "I wasn't the leader of any gang. I was for Billy all the time. About that Portales business, I owned the ranch with Charlie Bowdre. I took it up and was holding it because I knew that sometime a stage line would run by there, and I wanted to keep it for a station. But I found there were certain men who wouldn't let me live in the country so I was going to leave.

"We had all our grub in the house when they took us in, and we were going to a place about six miles away in the morning to cook it and then light out. I haven't stolen any stock. I made my living by gambling but that was the only way I could live. They wouldn't let me settle down; if they had I wouldn't be here today," he held up his right arm on which was the bracelet. "Chisum got me into all this trouble and then wouldn't help me out. I went to Lincoln to stand my trial on the warrant that was out for me, but the Territory took a change of venue to Dona Ana, and I knew that I had no show, and so I skinned out. When I was up to White Oaks the last time, I went there to consult with a lawyer, who had sent for me to come up. But I knew I couldn't stay there either."

The conversation then drifted to the question of the final round-up of the party. Billy's story is the same as that given in our Extra, issued at midnight on Sunday.

"If it hadn't been for the dead horse in the doorway I wouldn't be here. I would have ridden out on my bay mare and taken my chances at escaping," said he. "But I couldn't jump over that, for she would have jumped back, and I would have got it in the head. We could have staid in the house but there wouldn't have been anything gained by that for they would have starved us out. I thought it was better to come out and get a square meal—don't you?"

The prospects of a fight (at the train) exhilarated him, and he bitterly bemoaned being chained. "If I only had my Winchester, I'd lick the whole crowd," was his confident comment on the strength of the attack party. He sighed and sighed again for a chance to take a hand in the fight, and the burden of his desire was to be set free to fight on the side of his captors as soon as he should smell powder.

As the train rolled out, he lifted his hat and invited us to call and see him in Santa Fe, calling out *"Adios!"*

2

The affair at the station alluded to by Billy might very easily have turned into a mob riot if Pat Garrett and his three deputies had for a moment shown the white feather. On the morning that Billy had given the newspaper interview, Pat proceeded to the jail to get his three prisoners.

The Kid and Wilson were promptly turned over to him, handcuffed and leg-ironed together. Tom Pickett he knew was being retained on a minor charge and soon would be released on bail by a justice of peace. [In Billy's coldly appraising eyes Tom Pickett must have always seemed a tinhorn gambler and phony badman. Shortly after the Kid was taken to Santa Fe Pickett was arraigned before a J.P. and released on $300 bail, with the proviso that he must appear for examination at the next term of court. For a time he hung out around Las Vegas, posing as a former member of Billy the Kid's gang. Finally he drifted over to northern Arizona where he worked for the famous Hash Knife outfit, later joining the Graham side in the deadly Graham-Tewksbury feud of Pleasant Valley. He lasted long enough to collect a Tewksbury bullet in his leg. When he could ride again he went back to punching cattle. At thirty he married a pretty Irish girl named

Catherine Kelly, whose mother ran a boarding house in Holbrook. The roving Pickett had never before known such happiness, but a year later his sparkling young wife died in childbirth, along with the baby. Pickett was heartbroken and wandered like a lost soul through the west, dealing monte, prospecting, working cattle, tending bar. During the Woodrow Wilson administration he was appointed a Deputy U. S. Marshal in Nevada, having secured a full pardon from Texas on five old cattle-stealing counts. Finally he had his leg amputated and, still dreaming of the bright-eyed Kitty Kelly, he returned to northern Arizona. On May 14, 1934, at the age of 76, he died at Pinetop and was buried at Winslow. He was one of the few of all the boys and men who rode with the Kid to pass the biblical three score and ten and die with his boots off.]

When Pat appeared at the jail in Las Vegas and asked the jailer to bring out Rudebaugh he was told that Dave was being held on a charge of murder and could not be turned over to him. Both Pat and the Texan, Frank Stewart, held Deputy U. S. Marshal warrants and insisted that their claims for Rudebaugh on a federal charge of robbing the mails had precedence over any local county indictment, even for murder. After a hot argument Rudebaugh was reluctantly produced.

Neither Pat nor his deputies, Frank Stewart and Barney Mason, had ever been in Santa Fe, and Garrett asked Mike Cosgrove, the kindhearted mail contractor who had given each of the prisoners a new suit of clothes and knew his way about in the capital, to go along as a special officer. The three prisoners were driven to the station in a hack and placed in the regular day coach.

The passengers already seated were advised to go into the forward coach, because of the danger of an attack by the mob. Two prospectors bound for the gold mines offered their services to Pat and he accepted. Already a considerable crowd had gathered with many of the native New Mexicans heavily armed. It was evident that the mob hoped to take Rudebaugh from his guards and hang him.

Pat had Dave sit on the floor of the coach so that he could not be seen by the mob. Then Garrett and one of his men stood guard at one door of the coach while Frank Stewart and the third deputy took their post at the other end. The brother of Sheriff Romero, who had caused some little trouble when he had met Garrett at Puerto de Luna to relieve him of the captured Webb and Davis, now climbed up to the rear platform of the coach with several of his followers, all armed. He threateningly demanded Rudebaugh.

"If you want him you'll have to take him from us," Pat answered quietly. He was grim as he cocked his Winchester. Romero and his friends slipped off the platform. They wanted none of these stern Anglos. Up ahead several men had pulled the engineer and fireman off the locomotive and were holding them.

The Kid's eyes were dancing merrily when Pat told him that if the mob did attack the coach he would turn him and his two companions loose and arm them.

"All right, Pat," Billy answered. "All I want is a six-shooter."

He looked out of the open window and studied the shouting crowd. "But there ain't no danger, Pat," he concluded. "Those fellows won't fight."

He was right. It was a milling, threatening mob, but it lacked a leader. For almost an hour the train was delayed, despite the fact that Chief Engineer Robinson and Trainmaster Rogers explained to the members of the mob that they could be held criminally responsible for delaying the U. S. mails.

Finally J. F. Moley, a postoffice inspector who had once had some railway experience, climbed up into the cab of the engine and pulled open the throttle. The engine wheels spun and then took hold, and the little train lurched ahead. The engineer and fireman broke loose from their captors and swung aboard a coach.

The Kid raised his hat with a manacled hand, smiled and called out, "*Adios!*" to his new friend the *Gazette* reporter. He was off for Santa Fe.

He had not been in the ancient capital city since shortly after March 1st, 1873, almost eight years earlier. On that date he had signed his own name of Henry McCarty as a witness to the marriage of his mother, Catherine McCarty, and William H. Antrim. Almost at once the little family had moved south to the new mining town of Silver City.

A good many things had happened to Billy in these eight short years since he had roamed the streets and alleys

of this ancient Spanish town—an unknown boy with a forgotten name. It may well be that on this present tragic
day of 1880, he was thankful that his dear mother could
not know of the evils that had befallen him.

3

Deputy U. S. Marshal Charles Conklin was at the station
at the capital when the train pulled in. A crowd of sensa-
tion-seekers were on hand to get a look at Billy and Rudebaugh. Wilson was of minor interest, since the only indictment they had against him was for horse stealing and
possibly for passing counterfeit money in Mesilla and
Santa Fe.

Once Garrett had delivered his prize prisoners to Sheriff
Silva, he and his three assistants adjourned to the famous
old Exchange Hotel at the corner of the *plaza* for refreshments and congratulations. Pat had clearly won the Governor's award of $500, but he had to wait two weeks before
Tom Catron's law partner, W. T. Thornton, and several
other interested citizens advanced the money which was held
up by some legal technicality.

The offer had been for the capture and delivery of the
Kid to the sheriff of Lincoln County; the rub was that
Garrett was still actually a deputy sheriff and would not
become sheriff until January 1st, 1881, still five days away.
There was also some question as to the legality of the re-
ward. A local enthusiast sweetened the kitty by a gift of
five $20 gold pieces, and later the enterprising citizens of
Las Vegas raised a purse of several hundred dollars for
Pat and his aides.

That first night Garrett was the toast of the town. What
happened to the Kid and his mates is best told in an item
in the *New Mexican* of Thursday, December 30th:

> The Kid, Wilson and Rudebaugh were jailed in
> Santa Fe at about 7:30 Monday evening. Tuesday
> morning at 11 o'clock when Pat Garrett and his men
> went to see them, it was discovered that they had not
> had a mouthful to eat since they were put in the jail.
> Whereupon one of the posse went to the keeper of the
> restaurant who had a contract for feeding the U. S.

prisoners and asked why he had not sent down meals
to the three.

The man said he had done so, and after a little examination it was discovered that Jailer Silva, or some
of his henchmen, had eaten the grub themselves. It's
pretty rough on prisoners when their jailers eat the
meals sent to them.

But this was only a taste of the stern treatment that was
handed out to Billy. There is a story that for a period he
was chained to the floor of a stone cell, with little or no
light. And there is an additional legend that in February
he and Rudebaugh and one or two others attempted to
dig themselves out and that the plot was foiled.

The Kid had neither money, friends, nor a lawyer.
Rudebaugh was different. Former members of the old
Dodge City Gang, who were still operating in Las Vegas,
apparently raised a purse and hired a brilliant young
criminal lawyer named Edgar Caypless to defend him.

Caypless, born in Auburn, New York, on June 8th,
1855, had journeyed to London following the study of
law and had there met officials of the Maxwell Land Grant
Company. The company hired him as a sort of watchdog
for its headquarters in Cimarron, New Mexico. The
young man accepted the job but, being both smart and
ambitious, he soon resigned and opened a law office in
Santa Fe.

Touched by Billy's complete isolation and neglect, Caypless apparently tried to do a little something for him.
Eventually the young lawyer filed at Las Vegas a repleven
suit for the Kid's mare that had become the booty of Frank
Stewart, one of Garrett's posse. Partly as a gesture of un-
concern the Kid had given the mare to Stewart, who had
ridden her to Las Vegas and presented the valuable animal to Mrs. Scott Moore, wife of the proprietor of the
Hot Springs Hotel, five miles out of town. The mare was
all the worldly goods the Kid could possibly claim as his
own.

Along about the time the Kid had fallen into Garrett's
hands at Stinking Springs, Governor Lew Wallace asked
for and received a twenty-day leave of absence to journey
to Washington on territorial business. As a matter of fact,

the Governor actually left Santa Fe the morning before Billy's arrival there.

Billy, however, had no knowledge of the Governor's movements, and five days after he was jailed he asked for writing material. On a small ruled sheet he wrote out the following in black ink:

SANTA FE
Gov. Lew Wallace   JAN. 1ST 1881
Dear Sir
    I would like to See You for a few moments if You can Spare time

Yours Respect.
Wm. H. Bonney

Since the Governor was gone there was naturally no reply. Billy waited until Wallace had been back in Santa Fe for some time before he wrote him again. The note read:

SANTA FE, N. MEX.
MARCH 2D 1881
Gov. Lew Wallace
Dear Sir
    I wish You would come down to the jail and see me. it will be much to your interest to come and see me. I have some letters which date back two years and there are Parties who are very anxious to get them but I will not dispose of them until I see you. that is if you will come imediatly

Yours respect
Wm. H. Bonney

Billy must have been disturbed and impatient. Apparently he still retained some slight spark of hope that the Governor might remember and live up to the agreement he had made with the Kid at Squire Wilson's house in Lincoln on the night of March 17th, 1879. Once Colonel Rynerson, the prosecuting attorney from Mesilla, had refused the Governor's request to quash the indictment against the Kid, the Governor had turned his back on the whole affair.

When two anxious days now went by and there was still no word from the Governor, Billy again sent off a letter:

SANTA FE
IN JAIL
MARCH 4TH 1881

Gov Lew Wallace
Dear Sir

I wrote You a little note the day before yesterday,
but have received no answer. I Expect you have forgotten what you promised me, this Month two Years
ago. but I have not, and I think You had ought to
have come and seen me as I requested you to. I have
done everything that I promised you I would, and
You have done nothing that You promised me.

I think when You think The matter over, You will
come down and See me, and I can then Explain
Everything to You.

Judge Leonard, Passed through here on his way
East, in January and promised to come and See me
on his way back but he did not fulfill his Promise.
it looks to me like I am getting left in the Cold. I am
not treated right by Sherman. he lets Every Stranger
that comes to See me through Curiosity in to See me,
but will not let a Single one of my friends in, not
Even an Attorney

I guess they mean to Send me up without giving
me any Show. but they will have a nice time doing it.
I am not intirely without friends

I shall Expect to See you Sometime today
Patiently Waiting
I am Very truly Yours, Respt.

Wm. H. Bonney

Some years later Wallace was quoted as saying that he
had realized that the letters Billy referred to in his note of
March 2nd had to do with the 1879 correspondence between himself and the Kid, and he arranged to protect
himself.

I proceeded to forestall any move on his part by giving them to the newspapers myself, with an account
of just how I had come to make the promises therein.
When this material appeared in print, I sent a copy
to the Kid. I heard nothing further from him, and
I presume he understood that the door of my clemency was shut.

The great success of Lew Wallace's novel *Ben Hur,* which he had completed in Santa Fe, may have slightly affected the keen memory of the Hoosier statesman, for a careful search of the local territorial journals of the period reveal no such use of the letters nor anything pertaining to them. But even had the Governor published them it certainly might be considered somewhat less than a generous gesture towards a friendless boy, who already had most of his little world against him.

In a very few days the spring term of court would open at Mesilla, two or three hundred miles on down the Rio Grande. Here the Kid would face a federal indictment for the murder of Buckshot Roberts at the Mescalero Apache Indian Agency in March, 1878. There was also a territorial indictment against him for the murder of Sheriff Brady, and possibly other charges that could be dug up if necessary.

There is a mixture of pathos and defiance in the final appeal the boy made. The note was hurriedly written by pencil on a sheet of ruled paper, six by eight inches in size, and read:

SANTA FE NEW MEXICO
MARCH 27 '81

Gov Lew Wallace
Dear Sir
    for the *last time* I ask, Will you keep Your promise.
I start below tomorrow Send Answer by bearer
Yours respt
W Bonney

4

It was on a Sunday when Billy sent the futile note. That morning W. T. Thornton, Catron's partner and one of the members of the Santa Fe Ring, boarded the train for Mesilla. Thornton always attended the various District Court sessions, so that there could be no slip-up in legal matters in which the Ring was concerned.

The richest cream in the milking of the Territory—the profits from the great Spanish grants—had long ago been skimmed off, but there was still money to be made by the Ring and its political power. Lincoln County had finally fallen into the business hands of the pro-Ring groups, and Catron and Rynerson had large investments there. They now had this troublesome boy Billy where they wanted him, and they proposed to finish him off for keeps.

At Rincon, where at the time passengers left the train to board stages for the last leg of the trip to Mesilla and on down the Rio Grande, Thornton found a gathering of some thirty people awaiting the train. They had been told the Kid would arrive this day, and Thornton was not certain whether they were planning to lynch the boy or rescue him. He informed them that he was not certain when Billy would leave Santa Fe.

It was several days later when the Kid actually started on the journey to Mesilla. Wilson, facing no more serious charge than horse stealing and passing counterfeit money, was to be tried in Dona Ana County and was taken along as a prisoner.

The Kid must have had mixed feelings when he waved his manacled hands in a good-by gesture and shouted a farewell to Dave Rudebaugh as he was led past the cell. Dave was a most unusual man, and the true reason behind his friendship with the Kid will always be a matter of controversy. [Back on February 16th, some weeks before Billy's departure, Rudebaugh had been tried in the Federal Court in Santa Fe and convicted of robbing the mails of both a train and stagecoach, and he was sentenced to twenty years on each charge. San Miguel County, however, demanded that he be turned over to Las Vegas on the old murder charge of killing the jailer there, and he was transferred soon after Billy left Santa Fe. When he arrived at Las Vegas he found his friend John Joshua Webb still in jail, following his recapture by Pat Garrett back in early December of 1880. On the following December 3rd of this year of 1881, Rudebaugh engineered a jailbreak by digging his way out through a tunnel, taking Webb and five men with him. Rudebaugh managed to escape to Arizona and finally reached Old Mexico. There are many versions of what happened to him from there on: one is that he was killed at the age of forty-five by an angry mob in a small town in Sonora, where he had been riding high on a wave of terror. The gruesome story concluded with the poetic touch that his head was severed from his body, stuck on a pike and paraded around the *plaza*. A second version, which is less sensational, appeared in the *New Mexico Historical Review* of April, 1948: according to that, after breaking jail in Las Vegas he hid out for a time at the home of a friend who helped him get into Mexico. After hiding out there for a year or two he recrossed the border and joined up with a trail herd bound for the Niobrara River country, and shortly moved on to Montana. For years he worked as a top hand, eventually acquiring a small ranch of his own. He married a sympathetic quarter-blood Indian who presented him with three daughters. When his wife died Dave started drinking heavily, lost his ranch, and skidded down the grade. Later, penniless and almost beyond redemption, he went to live with a married daughter in Oregon, and died there in 1928. Whichever version is correct, the unfortunate Rudebaugh might have found at the end some little solace in the ancient Spanish saying, *"La via esta duro, amigo"*—The road is hard, friend.]

On his train ride to Mesilla the Kid was in the charge of Deputy U. S. Marshal Tony Neis. There is some uncertainty as to whether it was the Santa Fe Chief of Police, Frank Chavez, or Bob Ollinger, Garrett's deputy and the Kid's sworn enemy, who went along as assistant guard. It is a matter of small consequence, but in his story, *Frontier Doctor*, Dr. H. F. Hoyt, Billy's friend from the Tascosa days, claims it was Ollinger who accompanied Neis.

It was some years after the event when Dr. Hoyt put down his own little sidelight on history. He wrote that he was awaiting the arrival of the down-train at Bernanillo, just north of Albuquerque, and when it pulled in he saw the Kid through the window of the rear car. He hurried inside and found Billy shackled with handcuffs and leg irons, placed on one side of a double seat. Opposite him sat Neis and Bob Ollinger. Bob had a double-barreled, sawed-off shotgun across his knees. The boy was not the slightest embarrassed when he greeted his old friend. Dr. Hoyt asked Billy if there was anything he could do for him.

"Sure, Doc," Billy said with a chuckle. "Just grab Bob's gun and hand it to me for a moment."

Ollinger had a wry grin when he remarked: "My boy,

you had better tell your friend good-by. Your days are short."

"I don't know," Billy answered cheerfully. "There's many a slip 'twixt the cup and the lip."

The engine bell was ringing and the conductor was shouting, "All aboard!" when the frontier doctor patted Billy on the back, wished him good luck, and hustled down the aisle.

He would never see the Kid again.

5

The courtroom at Mesilla was housed in a single-story adobe structure at the southeast corner of the plaza, across the dirt road from the one-time Butterfield stage-stop and hotel that was now used as the lock-up. It was here that Billy was confined. There is a stubborn rumor that the actual court proceedings were held in an open patio of the temporary courthouse in the pleasant shade of a large tree.

Judge Bristol, presiding over the federal district court, called Billy's case on Wednesday, April 6th. Judge Leonard was promptly appointed by the court to act as Billy's attorney in the federal case, as the boy was utterly without funds. Judge Leonard immediately asked that the court quash the federal indictment against the Kid for the murder of Roberts, because the killing had not occurred on Indian agency ground but on property belonging to Dr. Blazer. Judge Bristol sustained the motion. The Kid was then immediately arrested on a Lincoln County indictment.

Two days later Judge Bristol, who served also as a judge of the Third Territorial District, heard the case of Lincoln County against the Kid for the murder of Sheriff Brady. Colonel Rynerson, arch enemy of the boy and financially interested with Jimmy Dolan in the old Tunstall cattle ranch, was no longer Territorial Prosecuting Attorney. But that made little difference in the obvious plan to deny any fair chance at justice for the Kid, since S. B. Newcomb, close friend and co-worker of the bitter Rynerson, had taken his place as prosecutor.

Frank Angel, the original investigator sent out from Washington three years before, once described Judge

Bristol as fair in all matters except those involving Lincoln County. Judge Bristol had always been anti-McSween, and his violent prejudice against the Kid was well known. The Sheriff of Dona Ana County, who would certainly have hand-picked the panel for the jury, was a willing tool of the local members of the Santa Fe Ring. So it was a sure-fire set-up: a prejudiced Judge, a one-sided prosecuting attorney, a pliant sheriff, and a hand-picked native jury.

Judge Bristol appointed Colonel A. J. Fountain and John D. Bail to defend the boy who undoubtedly was as conscious as his unpaid attorneys as to how blind Justice would be in this court. There is no evidence that the Kid even took the stand. Nor is it known that he produced a single witness; most of the men who were with him on that tragic day of April 1st, 1878, had been killed off.

It is generally held that young Bonnie Baca, who may possibly have been related by the democracy of nature's laws to the late Major Murphy, once principal owner of the great store in Lincoln, appeared as a witness for the State. And J. W. Mathews, who had been with Sheriff Brady the morning he was killed and is generally credited with having wounded the Kid, almost certainly took the stand, as did one or two others brought over from Lincoln. The whole case was swiftly railroaded through, and on the second day it was given to the all-native jury.

The slender hope that sustained the defense was embodied in the argument that, in order to find the Kid guilty of first-degree murder, the jury must be convinced that he had actually fired the shots, premeditatedly, or had actually assisted in firing the shots. Yet Judge Bristol in his charge made it clear in almost so many words that the boy's presence as a member of a gang, which he may have encouraged, made him guilty of murder in the first degree. It was the crux of the State's case, emphasized in the Judge's charge to the pliant jury.

Over and over again the Judge repeated his premise that the jury must bring in a verdict of murder in the first degree if it were convinced of one definite point:

> . . . that such fatal wound was either inflicted by
> the defendant from a premeditated design to effect
> his death or that he was present at the time and place

of the killing of Brady and from a premeditated design to effect his death, he then and there encouraged, incited, aided or abetted, advised or commanded such killing.

If he was so present, encouraging, inciting, aiding in, abetting, advising or commanding this killing of Brady, he was as much guilty as though he fired the fatal shot.

I have charged you that to justify you in finding the defendant guilty of murder in the first degree, you should be satisfied from this evidence to the exclusion of every reasonable doubt that the defendant is actually guilty. As to what should be a reasonable doubt of guilt, I charge you that belief in the guilt of the defendant to the exclusion of every reasonable doubt does not require you to believe absolutely and to a mathematical certainty. That is, to justify a verdict of guilty it is not necessary for you to be as certain that the defendant is guilty as you are that two and two are four or that two and three are five. Merely a vague conjecture or bare probability that the defendant may be innocent is not sufficient to raise a reasonable doubt of his guilt.

Judge Bristol had already defined the word "premeditated" in a way that to the ordinary layman would seem completely unfair to the defendant:

As I have already instructed you, to constitute murder in the first degree it is necessary that the killing should have been perpetrated from a premeditated design to effect the death of the person killed. As to this premeditated design, I charge you that to render a design to kill premeditated, it is not necessary that such design to kill should exist in the mind for any considerable length of time before the killing. If the design to kill is completely formed in the mind but for a moment before inflicting the fatal wound, it would be premeditated, and in law the effect would be the same as though the design to kill had existed for a long time.

The jury was out but a few minutes when it dutifully brought in a verdict of murder in the first degree. The verdict carried a mandatory sentence of hanging within thirty days from the date of the pronouncement of the sentence.

On Wednesday, April 13th, Judge Bristol read the sentence. William Bonney (spelled Bonny in the clerk's formal papers) alias Kid, alias William Antrim, was to be delivered to the Sheriff of Lincoln County and confined in prison until May 13th. The order continued:

> That on the day aforesaid, between the hours of nine of the clock in the forenoon and three of the clock in the afternoon, he, the said William Bonny, alias Kid, alias William Antrim, be taken from such prison to some suitable and convenient place of execution within said County of Lincoln, by the Sheriff of said County, and then and there on that day and between the aforesaid hours thereof by the Sheriff of said County of Lincoln, he, the said William Bonny, alias Kid, alias William Antrim, be hanged by the neck until his body be dead.

The entire trial appeared to be but a thinly veiled travesty of justice, and any shrewd and determined lawyer supplied with $50 for court costs could probably have secured a retrial. But Billy didn't have the $50. He didn't have fifty cents. And he was as bereft of influential friends as he was of money.

Had he stood in with the court and been properly backed he would have been granted a new trial and let out on a fake "straw" bail furnished by some professional native New Mexican. As it was, he alone of all the men involved in the Lincoln County War had now been tried and convicted and sentenced to death. Friendless and penniless, he must pay the supreme penalty.

He had fought John Chisum's battles against Murphy and Dolan and Catron and the Santa Fe Ring. And Chisum had turned against him, using his great influence with Captain Lea and the post traders at Fort Stanton and the other men of means in Lincoln County to hire Pat Garrett to capture or kill the Kid or run him off. That his liquidation would now be achieved by legal execution was even better for Chisum and Lea and Catron and all the others. It gave a slightly sanctimonious touch to the

disposal of the boy; a split-second of torture at the end of
a rope and it would be over almost as quickly as a lead
slug could do the job. And hanging was safer and more
sure, since it would eliminate any chance of some possible
slip-up.

The Kid stood in the way of progress. These men of
prominence and compelling ambition were slightly uneasy
as long as this avenging night-rider was loose. He had to
go. It was the higher law.

There is a legend that the boy made a smart-aleck reply
to the Judge when, at the end of the pronouncing of his
sentence, he was asked if he had anything to say. But there
is no whit of evidence to sustain the myth. It would have
been out of character. It was not his way.

There is a much greater probability that he dropped
some humorous pleasantry with a sheriff's deputy or a
court attendant as they led him back to his cell.

6

Two days after Judge Bristol pronounced the sentence of
death, the Kid made his final effort to raise the money for
a new trial. Attorney Caypless of Santa Fe had already
filed a suit of repleven to recover the boy's bay mare, still
in the hands of Mrs. Scott Moore of Las Vegas.

The letter Billy wrote laid bare a stout heart and a will
that could never be broken. There was no whimpering; he
was simply stating the desperation of his situation. The
note as it now survives has apparently been put into
slightly better spelling and punctuation than the Kid
would have used:

> I would have written before this but I could get no
> paper. My United States case was thrown out of
> court and I was rushed to trial on my Territorial
> charge. Was convicted of murder in the first degree
> and am to be hanged on the 13th of May. Mr. A. J.
> Fountain was appointed to defend me, and has done
> the best he could for me. He is willing to carry the
> case further if I can raise the money to bear his ex-
> penses. The mare is about all I can depend on at
> present, so I hope you will settle that case right away
> and give him the money you get from her. If you do

not settle the matter with Scott Moore, and have to
go to court about it, either give him (Fountain) the
mare or sell her at auction and give him the money.
Please do as he wishes you to do in this matter. I
know you will do the best you can for me in this.

I shall be taken to Lincoln tomorrow. Please write
and direct care Garrett, Sheriff. Excuse bad writing.
I have my handcuffs on.

I remain as ever

Very respectfully
William Bonney.

It was perhaps a day later that the Kid was interviewed
in his cell by a reporter from the Mesilla *News*. The account shows how Editor Newman of the opposition paper
evidently had aroused Billy's anger:

Shortly after sentence was passed upon the Kid, a
reporter of the Mesilla *News* interviewed him with
the following effect. Said the Kid, after considerable
delay:

"Well, I had intended at one time not to say a
word in my own behalf, because people would say,
'Oh, he lied'; Newman gave me a rough deal; has
created prejudice against me, and is trying to incite
a mob to lynch me. He sent me a paper which shows
it; I think it is a dirty, mean advantage to take of me,
considering my situation and knowing that I could
not defend myself by word or act. But I suppose he
thought he would give me a kick down hill, Newman
came to see me the other day; I refused to talk to
him or tell him anything; but I believe the *News*
is always willing to give its readers both sides of a
question.

"If mob law is going to rule, better dismiss judge,
sheriff, etc., and let all take chances alike. I expect
to be lynched in going to Lincoln. Advise people
never to engage in killing."

Editor—"Think you will be taken through safe?
Do you expect a pardon from the Governor?"

"Considering the active part Wallace took on our
side and the friendly relations that existed between
him and me, I think he ought to pardon me. Don't

know that he will do it. When I was arrested for that murder, he let me out and gave me the freedom of the town and let me go about with arms. When I got ready to go I left. Think it hard that I should be the only one to suffer the extreme penalties of the law."

Here the sheriff led us away and said we had talked long enough.

Final arrangements for the transfer of Billy from Mesilla to Lincoln were made between Pat Garrett and the Sheriff of Dona Ana County. Among the guards assigned were Bob Ollinger, a regular deputy of Pat Garrett's who probably had been in Mesilla since the trial began; one Kinney, who apparently is the same notorious John Kinney whose Rio Grande desperadoes had been sent to Lincoln by Colonel Rynerson to assist the Dolan side; and J. W. Mathews, Brady's deputy who had been walking a short distance behind Brady when he was killed and who shot and wounded the Kid. [A number of years later Mrs. Susan McSween, well versed in the Lincoln happenings, explained to Governor Miguel Otero that the Kid would have been acquitted of the killing of Brady at any fair trial; it was unquestionably Mathews whom he had tried to kill and not the sheriff.]

There were rumors and threats that a gang of toughs from the mining town of White Oaks, seeking revenge for their own humiliation at his hands, were all set to take the Kid from his guards and hang him. A second rumor also was circulated that Billy's friends might try to rescue him on the 150-mile journey to Lincoln. [Billie Wilson, a dapper and rather precise man of medium size, must have felt pretty blue on this evening when they led the Kid past his cell and on out of the vile Mesilla jail. The court had already convicted Wilson of horse stealing, but he had his own plans about serving the sentence. In a matter of weeks after he said good-by to the Kid he dug his way out of the old jail, mounted a horse that some confederate had tied up for him, and rode hard for Texas. He crossed into Old Mexico and disappeared for several years. Eventually he returned to Texas, and with a brand-new mustache passed himself off as Doc Anderson. Later on he showed up at El Paso to appear as a witness in a suit for damage to cattle in a train wreck and, according to the late Maury Kemp, a distinguished and picturesque attorney, Pat Garrett recognized him as the same Billie Wilson he had captured with the Kid at Stinking Springs. Pat still carried the gun he had taken from Wilson. Upon investigation he discovered that the erstwhile Billie Wilson was now happily married, with a family of children, and had long been leading an honorable and useful life. At this time Billie was sheriff of Terrell County, Texas. Pat, now Teddy Roosevelt's Collector of the Port of Santa Fe, arranged for him to come alone to Santa Fe and secretly appear before the Governor. He walked out with a full pardon for his old crime and jailbreak. Wilson as Doc Anderson was a kindly, decent man, despite his wild youth. About 1911, while he was still sheriff in Texas, he was called to the railroad station to arrest a drunken cowboy who was brandishing a gun and raising a disturbance. It was a hot day, and Wilson appeared in shirtsleeves and without a gun. The cowboy was holed-up in a shed and the sheriff was warned that he'd better get a six-shooter and prepare for trouble. He answered that he knew the boy and that he could handle him all right. He walked straight to the thin, wooden door, identified himself and called to the boy to come on out. Instead, the cowboy shot through the door and killed Wilson.]

7

It was 10 o'clock at night on April 18th, 1881, when the little party started from the Mesilla jail on the first leg of the long journey by horseback and Dougherty wagon to Lincoln.

It takes little imagination to picture the scene: the awed crowd, the quiet business of lifting the handcuffed and leg-ironed Kid to the hack, and chaining him to the seat. The heavily armed men taking their places. It was all as deadly serious as if the slight, twenty-one-year-old boy had been a 500-pound gorilla that could kill a man with one blow of his paw.

A reporter writing for *Newman's Semi-Weekly* most accurately conveys the grim mood of the departure:

> He was handcuffed and shackled and chained to the back seat of the ambulance. Kinney was beside him.

Ollinger on the seat facing him. Mathews facing Kinney, Lockhart driving, and Reade, Woods and Williams riding along on horseback on each side and behind. The whole party were armed to the teeth, and anyone who knows the men of whom it was composed, will admit that a rescue would be a hazardous enterprise.

He appeared cheerful and remarked that he wanted to stay with the boys until the whiskey gave out anyway. Said he was sure his guard would not hurt him unless a rescue should be attempted, and he was sure that would not be done, unless perhaps "those fellows over at White Oaks come to take me," meaning to kill him. It was a stand-off whether he was hanged or killed in the wagon.

The Mesilla jail was the worst he had ever struck. The sheriff wanted him to say something good about it when he left, but he had not done so. He wanted to say something about John Chisum, and it would be some satisfaction to know that some men would be punished after he had been hung.

Nothing could quite break through the inherent cheerfulness and good humor of the Kid. Of all the men present he was probably the only one who was completely at ease.

It was a familiar route that the little party took: across the Rio Grande ford, the long, fifteen-mile pull up the west slope of the Organs to the San Agustin Pass, then the downhill ride to Shedd's ranch and the springs below the massive fortress-like house. Dawn probably was breaking when they pulled up their tired horses for water and feed.

They planned to wait there until early afternoon when the sting would be gone out of the April sun and then start on the fifty-mile journey across the desert sands of the Tularosa Basin.

Billy must have thought back to a fall day almost four years past, when he had ridden down this same eastern slope of the Organs to Shedd's ranch and the springs. It was twilight when he had topped the San Agustin Pass and caught his first glimpse of the vast, fearsome Basin, stretching on below, filled with lights and colors and a frightening beauty that was hardly of this world.

He had been a wild young adventurer then; this time he was a convicted murderer going to his death, hand-cuffed and shackled.

But a man must never give up hope.

8

Buried among the half-truths that cling like cockleburrs to the myths and legends of the Kid, is a little story in-volving a stop made at the end of the third day of the long trek to Lincoln:

The party put up for the night at a house near Blazer's Mill on the Tularosa, in the midst of the great cedar forests that cover the sides of the high, green mountains of the Apache Reservation. There was a young mother here with a baby in her arms. While supper was being prepared the Kid, still wearing steel bracelets and leg-irons, asked the mother if he might hold the baby for a minute or two. The kindhearted young woman gladly set the child in the boy's lap, and the two had a great time playing with the bright handcuffs. It was something a little new in the line of toys for the baby. Billy seemed utterly unconscious of his guards as he entertained the tot. Bob Ollinger tried constantly to plague the unfortu-nate boy, and during supper kept referring to the fact that Billy wouldn't have many more meals coming to him and that he better enjoy this one.

Finally the young mother turned to the revengeful dep-uty sheriff: "You shouldn't talk that way, Mr. Ollinger. How'd you like to be in Billy's place? He's only a poor boy, with everything against him."

But no matter how hard he tried, Ollinger couldn't get the Kid's goat, as the saying went at that time. When they set out around dawn on the cut-off for Fort Stanton, the Kid was the only gay one in the party. Despite his three and a half months in prison and the pallor that had re-placed his sun tan, he still had great endurance and re-serve, and he could stand physical punishment from the elements that would have exhausted most men.

Pat Garrett was waiting at Fort Stanton when the little

caravan arrived. He took charge now, and the Rio Grande men turned their horses around and headed back for Mesilla.

It was April 21st, 1881. The Kid was scheduled to be hanged on the 13th of the following month.

20

By late afternoon the Kid was well settled in the corner room on the second floor of the old Murphy-Dolan store. It had only recently been purchased from Catron for use as a courthouse by the Lincoln County Commissioners.

The Lincoln jail leaked prisoners like a sieve. Therefore Garrett arranged to hold the Kid in this large northeast room under the day and night guard of either Bob Ollinger or J. W. Bell. The scar-faced Bell was a member of the posse which had tangled with the Kid in the little fight at Coyote Springs near White Oaks. Ollinger had been against the Kid from the start. He was a big, husky, part Cherokee in his middle thirties, and his face was deeply pitted with smallpox.

The substantial adobe building, now turned into the courthouse and special jail, had been built by Major Murphy and Colonel Fritz in 1873. Aside from the government buildings at the army post at Fort Stanton, it was the largest structure in the county. It was two stories high. Facing the single street of the village was an overhanging upper balcony, thirty feet or more long. A high wall surrounded the yard in the rear of the main structure enclosing several smaller buildings. One of these served as a home for the caretaker, Old Man Gauss, and his roommate, the proprietor of the Wortley Hotel across the wide

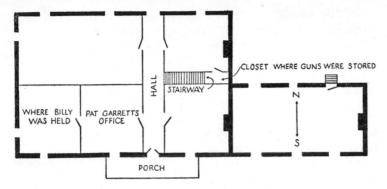

dirt road. On the east side of the big building was a path that led from the street gate on back to the doorway in the rear of the structure. On this east side was a good-sized vegetable garden.

The main part of the second story was traversed north and south by a wide hall. A door to the right near the front of this corridor opened into Pat Garrett's office. Straight on through this inner room lay the large, square chamber where Billy was closely guarded. To the south down the hall and below the stairway, was a room on the west with a closet which served as an armory. Here the spare weapons and ammunition belonging to the sheriff's office were stored.

A door at the front or north end of the middle hall led to the overhanging balcony. It was surrounded by a railing, but there were no stairs to the street.

Billy's cell-room had a cot and a small table and two or three plain chairs placed near the east wall. A chalk line was drawn north and south down the middle of the large room, and the Kid was informed that to cross this line without proper authorization meant instant death. There was a chair or two and a table on the west side of the prison chamber for the guards, who took turns night and day in guarding their valuable and deadly prize.

From the start of his imprisonment the Kid was always handcuffed and wore leg irons. After a day or two Garrett decided that the short leg irons hurt the boy when his guard took him up and down the stairs to the outhouse in the rear, so he had the village blacksmith rivet on a longer chain.

Shortly before the Kid had arrived a fabulous cowboy named Charlie Wall and his Anglo partner who were trying irrigated farming over near Tularosa, dashed up to the courthouse entrance on horses covered with sweat. They shouted to Garrett for help. The tall Charlie Wall had been severely wounded, and when the sheriff opened the front door he almost fell into Garrett's arms.

Charlie had hardly been admitted to the building when a half dozen heavily armed native New Mexicans rode up, angrily demanding that the two men be handed over to them. In a fight over water rights Wall and his partner had killed four natives out of hand. Charlie had been wounded and the two Anglos had barely succeeded in getting to their horses and making the long run for the safety of the Lincoln County courthouse.

The shooting had occurred in Dona Ana County and was definitely outside of Garrett's jurisdiction, but when he had heard Charlie's side of the story Pat refused to give up his volunteer prisoners. Secure in this generous protection Charlie settled back while his wounds healed, filling the role of a sort of jail trusty. Once or twice he made his way to the Kid's room while Bell was on duty, and the guard let him sit there for an hour or so and spin yarns to the condemned boy. It was an art Billy had never cultivated, but he enjoyed the tall tales that Charlie recounted. Like many men who had lived close to death, the cowhand genuinely felt sorry for the doomed lad.

One could easily believe that deep in his heart Bell also had hidden sympathy for Billy. Certainly Bell was quite different from Bob Ollinger, who never missed a chance to poke fun at the boy and remind him how swiftly the days were passing. Bob had nailed a large calendar on the west wall, and each morning he seemed to take special delight in having the Kid watch him while he X'd out the day that had passed. Then he would turn the sheet and point to the date of May 13th, which had a circle drawn around it. Fortunately it was a type of torture which apparently did not bother the boy.

2

There is ample evidence that Bob Ollinger had arranged to rent from the Widow Casey her very fine irrigated farm

on the Hondo, some twenty miles below Lincoln. But
along with the purely business side of the transaction he
was interested in Lilly Casey, the vivacious young daughter. He was much older than she and in later years when
Lilly referred to him she invariably dignified him by using
his full name of Robert Ameridth Ollinger.

An appealing bit of testimony, involving Ollinger and
concerning the deep affection that many residents had for
the Kid, comes to light in a short unpublished autobiog-
raphy of Lilly's brother, Ad Casey, taken down in 1937 by
the Southwest historian, J. Fvetts Haley. It bears complete authenticity and is of the very stuff of warm, human
history. One page reads:

> I knowed Bob Ollinger. When Billy the Kid was held
> up there in Lincoln this place had been rented by
> my mother to Bob Ollinger for three thousand dol-
> lars a year, and he was to move down here and com-
> mence work on it as soon as they got rid of Billy
> the Kid, but he had to stay up there and take care
> of him. He was guarding him then. It was getting
> late and mother got uneasy and wanted him to com-
> mence on the place. Finally she says, "Ad, I want you
> to go to Lincoln tomorrow." That was Sunday.
>
> We fixed up and started and we got to where the
> Hondo store is now, and we met the mail in a buck-
> board coming down. I was acquainted with the mail
> driver, and Bob was on it coming down to our place.
> He'd come down most every Sunday.
>
> Bob says to the driver, "Stop and let me out. I
> want to get in that wagon." Jack Wilson was driving
> the mail buckboard. He says, "Ad, get out and ride
> with me." I did, and that left Bob and mother in
> our wagon.
>
> We come on down here, and there was two Mex-
> ican women—Siquio Sanchez' wife was one of them—
> and she had come down to get some information. I
> was nothing but a kid about seventeen years old, and
> this other one was single—Josefita Analla. They was
> entertaining the women folks, and I come around to
> where they was, and this girl asked me if the law
> in New Mexico wasn't like it was in Old Mexico. I
> says "I don't know."

She says, "The law in Old Mexico is that when a person is sentenced to be hung and a girl asks for him to marry her, they have got to reverse the sentence and give him to that girl."

I had never heard of any such law. I laughed and she cried. Her sister, Mrs. Sanchez, says, "They'll never hang him. We have got fourteen men now to take him out, and that's a-plenty, but we'll get more, and they'll not hang him."

So I went to Bob Ollinger and told him right that very day. I says, "You want to watch out up there. This is Siquio Sanchez' wife, and he's a son-of-a-gun, and he's one of the Kid's main friends." He was an expert with a six-shooter. He was a bugger. Bob, he lets off a whole lot of steam and blowed and said that forty men couldn't get to that corral. I dropped the subject right there.

In a way, Ollinger must have been a blowhard. He was a great big man. They called him The Big Indian. He was from Oklahoma.

The information that young Casey gave to Ollinger was passed on to Pat Garrett: it ended most of the visits from native New Mexicans and even the Anglos, but the kind-hearted Bell did permit Sam Corbett, one-time clerk at the Tunstall store and now married to Teresita Baca, to pay the Kid a visit and shake hands with him. Bell also allowed the old German, Godfrey Gauss, to enter the prison room. Gauss had been the cook at the Feliz ranch in the days of John Tunstall and was now the janitor of the courthouse premises, living in the small adobe building in the rear.

Billy had plenty of spare time on his manacled hands these hot July days, and he and Gauss soon discovered that when Bell was on watch the old German could hang around the doorway of Billy's cell-room as much as he wished.

The Kid liked to listen to the broken English of the wise old German who would stand in the hallway and talk to him. Billy had been away from Lincoln for almost two years and he was now able to catch up on the gossip concerning a number of the people who had fought either with or against him in the war days. For instance, Gauss

told him that Susan McSween was now married to a
surveyor named George B. Barber of Lincoln, but that
it didn't look as if it would last too long. She hadn't done
too badly at that: she'd been made administratrix of both
the Tunstall and Brewer estates, as well as her own husband's. She had collected around $8,000 from the $20,000
investment of the senior Tunstall, but not one dollar of
it ever found its way back to London. When it came to
the $10,000 Fritz insurance policy, she got the two heirs
to take the old Baca house, valued at $3,000, for a settle
ment in full. She was now building up a considerable
cattle ranch west of the White Mountains at Three Rivers,
and John Chisum had sent her 400 head of fine bred-up
heifers as foundation stock for her herd; gossip had it that
she had some sort of an Indian sign on old Uncle John.
Looked like he was mighty soft in any business deal where
she was concerned.

Billy and Old Gauss kept going back to Jimmy Dolan
in their talks. Billy always looked upon Dolan as being as
much of an enemy of his as was Colonel Rynerson of
Mesilla. Gauss told him that Jimmy had married Caro-
line, the oldest daughter of Charlie Fritz, on July 3rd,
1879, after the Santa Fe Ring had got him acquitted at
Socorro of second degree murder in the killing of the one
armed Chapman. Jimmy was now a partner of Colonel
Rynerson in operating the former Tunstall ranch on the
Rio Feliz, and well on the way to a new fortune. [Long
before Dolan died, wealthy and highly respected, on February 26th, 1889, at fifty-three, he had fully justified Doc
Blazer's observation that on the frontier "many bad young
men turn out to be good old men."]

From both Gauss and the visit he had with Sam Corbett
Billy next learned about his old side-kick John Middleton,
who had been shot through the lung by Buckshot Roberts
in the fight at Blazer's Mill, and who eventually had
pulled out for the Texas Panhandle with Fred Waite and
Henry Brown. For a while Frank ran a small grocery
store at Sun City, Barber County, Kansas; then he married
the fifteen-year-old Colcard girl whose brother became
one of the wealthiest men in Oklahoma City. The marriage lasted only a few months, and before long John
drifted down to the Texas Panhandle where he died as a
result of his old gunshot wound.

Gauss had some hot news to tell the Kid regarding Henry Brown who had ridden off from Tascosa that same day in early December, 1878. Henry became Deputy Marshal in the tough town of Caldwell, Kansas. He was an odd sort of character who neither drank, smoked, nor gambled. A year after he left Billy, when he was twenty-six and had just married a young lady named Alice Levagood, Henry suddenly turned bad, joined a little band of outlaws, rode into Medicine Lodge, Kansas, and attempted to rob the bank there. After they killed two of the bank officials the gang was captured, but a mob took them from the jail and hung them without benefit of clergy.

When Billy and Old Gauss got around to discussing Sally Chisum, niece of Old John, it was Billy who had the latest information; Sally had married a bookkeeper named Robert in Anton Chico, and Uncle John made him a sort of business manager of his interests. [Within four years Old John would be dead of cancer of the throat, and within ten years the considerable ranch fortune would be squandered and the good-natured and romantic Sally would be divorced from Robert. Always throughout the long years of her life she held a warm spot in her heart for the boy who had brought her the little presents when she was riding north with the remnants of the Chisum herds, on up the Pecos into the beautiful country of the Canadian River.]

Among the other people whom the Kid and Gauss discussed in their quiet conversations in the prison room on the second floor was the elusive figure of Bob Widenmann, the young man from Ann Arbor, Michigan, who had been educated in Germany, had wandered down to Santa Fe and had fallen in with John Tunstall. Bob had been under indictment in connection with the Lincoln County War, and following the killing of McSween he simply pulled out for the far places. Later he visited John Tunstall's parents in London, and finally returned to the States and a successful business career in New York. He was obviously an unusual and rather talented man. [It was years later that Widenmann disclosed his own views of the sinister background of the Lincoln County conflict and the affairs of New Mexico in a letter he wrote to his sister-in-law, Mrs. R. H. Kempf, on February 3rd, 1927. It

commented on a book concerning the Kid which had just
been published. Part of the letter read:

> None of the parties to that fight—if any of them are
> still alive—dare to open up the whole matter and
> give the real causes. On our side there were only four
> men who knew the real facts. They were President
> Hayes, Carl Shurtz, Tunstall and myself. On the
> other side the reopening of the discussion of the
> whole trouble down to the real fundamentals, would
> involve and ruin the reputation of an Ex-President,
> several senators and congressmen and the then-time
> high officials, besides a number of the higher officers
> of the army. It would also involve digging into the
> records of the Departments of War and Interior and
> the Bureau of Indian Affairs. Besides, one of the
> Secretaries of War was in it up over his head.
>
> At one time I thought of writing a full account of
> the whole matter and really had begun it when it
> struck me that I had better consult those still living,
> and I wrote to Hayes who advised strongly against it.
> Then I went up to Lake George and spent a whole
> week with Carl Shurtz. Shurtz told me that he was
> convinced that most of the records appertaining to
> the case in the War Department as well as those in
> the Dept. of the Interior and the Bureau of Indian
> Affairs, had been removed by the Secy. of War in the
> term of Pres. Garfield, David Elkins.
>
> An investigation quietly undertaken after that con-
> ference established the truth of Shurtz' supposition,
> and when Shurtz and I went over the case again we
> were both of the opinion that to publish the facts
> then would lead to a whale of a fight, in which cer-
> tain documents and proofs needed by us could not be
> produced, because they had been destroyed by our
> opponents. . . .
>
> I must add to the above, that until the Cleveland
> administration came in, Shurtz and I were under a
> close system of espionage we well knew, and had we
> made any move we would, undoubtedly have been
> put out of the way. . . .
>
> I told Cleveland of the whole situation during his
> second administration; then Elkins died and we were

not bothered any more after that, though the effects of what those scoundrels did still showed a long time after that.]

When John Tunstall's name came up Gauss told the Kid about a letter he had written John's father regarding the wages that were due him. The Kid could sympathize with that; he himself had never received a red cent, save a few dollars' worth of stuff charged against him at Tunstall's and later at the Ellis store. Nor had John Chisum or McSween or his wife ever paid him a penny. When he was in desperate need of money during and after his trial and conviction in Mesilla, none of them had sent him as much as $50 which might have paid the court costs for a new trial. He had fought their battles, and now he was to be hanged for it.

3

April 28th was a Thursday, and Billy had now been in close confinement at Lincoln exactly one week. Bob Ollinger's big calendar showed that he had fifteen more days on this bright, sunny earth, before May 13th rolled around.

Early on Wednesday morning Pat Garrett had checked in at the prison room. He'd be riding over to Los Tablos to collect taxes and the next day he'd jog on west to White Oaks. He told Ollinger and Bell that he supposed he might as well order the lumber for the scaffold while he was at the Oaks. Certainly he had no heart to go through with the hanging. It was grim business to be a sheriff. He'd be back along about Saturday: that was three days off.

It was the first time that Pat had left Lincoln during the six days that Billy had been held a prisoner. He had treated the boy with every consideration, but he made no bones about warning the two guards that they must be constantly on the alert. They must never let the Kid see the back of their shirts. There was nothing intentionally mean in Pat's warnings to his deputies: he wasn't trying to rub it in on the Kid. Actually he probably had a soft spot in his heart for the boy.

After Pat rode off Ollinger took his double-barrel breech-loading shotgun from the armory in the closet near

the head of the stairs on the second floor and brought it
into the room where Billy was held. He thumbed the lever
that opened the breech of the valuable gun and put in
two brass shells.

"There's nine buckshot in each of them shells, Billy,"
he remarked. "The man that gets one of them loads will
feel it."

Billy grinned over at him when he answered: "You better take care you don't get a load of them buckshot yourself, Bob."

Ollinger patted the shiny gun and set it in the far corner of the room by the north wall. It was well within the
prohibited territory that Billy could enter only on threat
of instant death.

Nothing unusual happened the rest of that Wednesday
or during the long morning or early afternoon of Thursday, the 28th. Late April is probably the loveliest time of
the year in this high country of central New Mexico. But
the boy, sitting in his chair by the open window, handcuffed and wearing leg irons, was hardly thinking about
the warm, bright day and the friendly street noises. He
was thinking about freedom. That fatal day of May 13th
was approaching pretty fast.

Just about now Garrett would be ordering the lumber
for the scaffold. Ollinger told Billy in great detail just how
high the drop was, and how it would be erected in the
open space behind the courthouse. The hanging was even
going to be a public affair.

Billy had been extra quiet all day. Things had come out
exactly as he had hoped. It meant a good deal that Garrett
was a full day's ride away.

It was mid-afternoon when Bob Ollinger called to the
three or four minor prisoners who were jailed in the room
across from the wide, central hall. He motioned them to
march on down the stairs to the back door and then on
across the street for their dinner at Wortley's Hotel. From
the open window the Kid could look down on the path
that led to the street. He watched Charlie Wall limping
along behind Ollinger. Charlie's wounds were almost
healed.

The Kid waited for a few minutes, then he asked Bell
if he'd mind taking him down to the privy. There was

nothing unusual about the request. Bell told him sure he would: lead the way. The Kid shuffled from his chair on through the adjoining room to the wide hall and down to the far end, and then he turned to the right and slowly clanked down the stairs.

Bell patiently waited outside in the warm sun while the Kid went inside the outhouse. It was too nice a day for anything to happen. By rights a man should be taking a little siesta along about this time. He could sure use one on this quiet, hot afternoon, when there wasn't even the suspicion of a breeze.

Ollinger and the prisoners were across the street eating their dinner; Pat Garrett was a good forty miles away; and here at hand Bell was daydreaming. This was the moment.

4

There are many versions as to what happened during the next sixty seconds. Over a period of three decades Lt. Col. Maurice G. Fulton, long Professor of English at the New Mexico Military Institute at Roswell, explored every possible angle that might lead to the solution of the drama that now swiftly unfolded. A year or two before his death in 1955, the distinguished scholar arrived at what he was certain was the accurate sequence of the deadly happenings. His conclusion can be accepted either as completely factual or as near the truth as will ever be ascertained.

The day before, when Sam Corbett had shaken hands with Billy on his visit to his prison room on the southeast corner of the second floor, he had managed to slip into the Kid's manacled hands a tightly folded note. The doomed boy patiently waited his chance to read it and then probably swallowed the paper. He learned that a six-shooter wrapped in an old newspaper would that night be tucked under the wooden *vegas,* or round poles which supported the dirt roof of the adobe privy.

So on the afternoon of the following day when Ollinger and his prisoners were well along with their meal at Wortley's Hotel, the Kid asked Bell to take him downstairs to the outhouse. And the easy-going Bell remained outside. In the hot, lazy sunlight there was no need to be concerned over the boy.

The Kid located the gun wrapped in the newspaper and concealed under a *vega* near the door. It had been placed there some time during the night by Jose M. Aguayo, a high-class young New Mexican who had been friendly to the McSween faction but had been too young to take an active part in the terrible feud of three years before.

The Kid reached up his arms and pulled down the bundle. He took out the six-shooter and saw that the gun was fully loaded. He managed to stick it under the waistband of his trousers, the butt concealed by his manacled hands. He waited a plausible length of time and then pushed open the door and stepped out into the bright light.

When he reached a spot three or four feet away from Bell, he jerked out the six-shooter and pointed it at Bell's middle. Unquestionably he disarmed him at once. The Kid did not raise his voice as he spoke to the guard. Bell was to march through the rear door and then up the stairs. He'd have to kill Bell if he shouted for help or did not do exactly as he was told.

Bell led the way, the Kid walking a pace or two behind him. Bell made straight for the back door, then up the three stairs to the landing and turned up the longer series of steps that led to the upstairs hall. It is probable that the Kid's intentions were to march the guard either to the room at the right of the stairs, or to another room where Bell could be held while the Kid made his next move. Billy might have figured on forcing Bell to unlock his handcuffs and his leg irons.

In the hall not far from the top landing Bell suddenly turned and made a break for the stairs, possibly following a tussle with the Kid. Billy, holding his gun in his manacled hands, managed to shoot when Bell was halfway down. He missed, but the slug careened off the left-hand wall of the stairway and entered the guard's body just below his left armpit. It plowed its way through to his right side.

Bell managed to keep his feet and lunged around the lower platform into the downstairs room. Then, calling on some subconscious reserve force, he staggered through the rear door.

He fell into the arms of Old Man Gauss and was dead by the time he was laid on the ground.

5

Swift as a kangaroo the Kid leaped in short jumps down the hall and into the room of his confinement. He grabbed Ollinger's shotgun and crossed to the window that looked down on the pathway that followed the east side of the building and ran on out through the little gate to the street.

Ollinger was at that moment coming through the gate, his drawn six-shooter in his right hand. He had heard the single shot and, as he had hurried from the eating house, he had remarked that Bell must have had to kill the Kid.

"Hello, Bob," the Kid shouted down when the deputy was directly under the open window.

When Ollinger looked up the Kid, awkwardly holding the long heavy gun in his manacled hands, pulled the trigger. The buckshot felled Ollinger like a bolt of lightning.

The Kid swiftly hobbled across his prison room and through the sheriff's office to the hall. Turning to the right he crossed to the front balcony and in short jumps reached its east end. He could see Ollinger lying inside the gate and a little beyond the east corner of the building. He laid the shotgun over the railing, pointed it downward, and managed to pull the left-hand trigger. Then he tossed the gun at the dead figure of the hated Ollinger.

"Take this, too, damn you!" he shouted. "You won't follow me any more with that gun."

He could see the men under the porch of the hotel across the street, and he shouted for them to stay where they were. Swiftly he returned to the hall, sped down it to the room on the right in the rear. He crossed to the closet at the northwest corner and tried the flimsy door. It was locked, but he threw his weight against it and the lock gave way.

Two or three Winchesters rested, butts down, in the rear corners of the closet. Several Colt revolvers hung from scabbards and gunbelts on hooks screwed in the back wall. The Kid picked out a Winchester, examined it, and then chose a Colt with its belt filled with shells.

He hobbled out of the room and turned to the right and the open window at the bottom end of the hall. He

saw Old Man Gauss on below and ordered him to throw
up a file, that if Gauss did as he was told there'd be no
trouble.

The Kid now made his way up the corridor and out to
the front balcony. Charlie Wall and two or three of the
prisoners were still standing under the overhanging porch
of the Wortley Hotel. One man, consumed with curiosity,
started across the dirt street just as the Kid stepped up to
the railing.

He shouted for him to go back. No one must cross the
street or come near the building. He'd kill anyone who
did.

There is no certainty as to just how the boy got shed of
his handcuffs. He had large wrists and it is barely possible
that he managed to pull his small hands through the
steel cuffs. It is far more likely that he forced Gauss to
search Bell's pockets and when he found the keys to the
handcuffs to come upstairs and remove them from his
wrists.

According to Gauss' story, he was told to locate a file
but the best he could do was to find a prospector's pick-
axe, with a steel point on the long shank, and he tossed it up
through the open rear window to the Kid.

The Kid finally succeeded in loosening the rivets on one
of the iron shackles, thus freeing one foot. Time was fleet-
ing and he decided to tie the loose anklet and the chain
to his belt.

He was now fully mobile, although he was still somewhat handicapped when he walked. The sound of the
dangling chain links clanking as he walked must have
sounded like the happy music of jingling spurs to his ears.
It meant that he was going somewhere.

He was free. He wouldn't have to hang on May 13th.
He had outwitted them all.

6

Never did the Kid betray the names of the loyal friends
who had slipped him the note and planted the six-shooter
for him. Nor did he ever describe the details of how he
freed his hands from his steel bracelets and loosened the
one anklet of his leg irons. Even Pat Garrett's report, published a year and a half later in his own book on the Kid's

life, seems jumbled and unsound, as if Pat had deliberately attempted to cover up the tragic carelessness of Bell.

Almost ten years after the spectacular event occurred, the old German janitor wrote out his own account for the Lincoln County *Leader* of White Oaks, and it was published in the issue of March 1st, 1890. Despite its apparent frankness, there is a suspicion that Gauss did not quite tell all the truth: possibly he held back certain details in order to protect some accomplice of the Kid's, or even to conceal the full story of his own assistance:

> That memorable day I came out of my room whence I had gone to light my pipe, and was crossing the yard behind the courthouse when I heard a shot fired, then a tussle up stairs in the courthouse, somebody hurrying down stairs, and deputy sheriff Bell emerging from the door running towards me.
>
> When I arrived at the garden gate leading to the street, in front of the court house, I saw the other deputy sheriff, Ollinger, coming out of the hotel opposite, with four or five county prisoners where they had taken their dinner. I called to him to come quick. He did so, leaving his prisoners in front of the hotel. When he had come close up to me, and while standing not more than a yard apart, I told him that I was just after laying Bell dead in the yard behind, and before he could reply he was struck by a well directed shot fired from the window above us, and fell dead at my feet.
>
> I ran for my life to reach my room and safety, when Billy the Kid called to me: "Don't run, I wouldn't hurt you—I am alone and master, not only of the court house but also of the town, for I will allow nobody to come near me. You go," he said, "and saddle one of Judge Leonard's horses and I will clear out as soon as I can have the shackles loosened from my legs."
>
> With a little prospecting pick I had thrown to him through the window he was working for at least an hour, and could not accomplish more than to free one leg, and he came to the conclusion to await a better chance, tie one shackle to his waistbelt, and start. Meanwhile I had saddled a small skittish pony

belonging to Billy Burt, as there was no other horse
available, and had also, by Billy's command, tied a
pair of red blankets behind the saddle. I came near
forgetting to say that whilst I was busy saddling, and
Mr. Billy the Kid trying to get his shackles off, my
partner, Mr. Sam Wortley appeared at the gate leading from the garden where he had been at work, and
that when he saw the two sheriffs lying dead he did
not know whether to go in or retreat, but on the assurance of Billy the Kid that he would not hurt him,
he went in and made himself generally useful.

When Billy went down stairs at last, on passing the
body of Bell he said, "I'm sorry I had to kill him,
but couldn't help it." On passing the body of Ollinger he gave him a tip with his boot, saying,
"You're not going to round me up again."

We went out together to where I had tied up the
pony, and he told me to tell the owner of the same,
Billy Burt, that he would send it back next day. I, for
my part, didn't much believe in his promise, but sure
enough, the pony arrived safe and sound, trailing a
long lariat, at the court house in Lincoln.

And so, Billy the Kid started out that evening,
after he had shaken hands with everybody around
and after having a little difficulty in mounting on account of the shackle on his leg, he went on his way
rejoicing. . . .

Who will blame Billy the Kid for killing his two
guards at the time of his escape from Lincoln, whilst
he himself was to be hanged the week following?
This is the only murder I know of Billy ever commit-
ting. I did not blame him then—I do not blame him
now. Life is sweet.

7

It was a good hour after he had killed his guards before
Billy was ready to pull out. He was in no hurry. He knew
that no informer had ridden up the single street of Lincoln and on to the west in front of the courthouse, to carry
word to Pat Garrett; he had seen to that himself.

Pat was still forty miles away. That meant that at the

very earliest he couldn't be on his trail until the following evening, probably not until the second day.

In the opposite direction, to the east, no deputy sheriff or law officer lived within fifty miles: that would be on the Pecos near Roswell. Everything had broken in his favor. He'd have at least a twenty-four-hour start.

He filled two cartridge belts with .44 shells that would fit either a rifle or a six-shooter. There is a legend that he now strapped on a pair of revolvers—although all his life he had held two-gun men in contempt.

The pony was a little frightened when Billy, with his rifle held in one hand and with his leg chains jingling, swung on board. Before he could get his feet firmly in the stirrups Collie bucked him off.

After Billy had been thrown, Gauss caught the pony and led him up for a second try. This time Billy had the old German hold his rifle until he had mounted and quieted the horse. Then he reached down and took the rifle in his right hand.

Across the street, under the porch of Wortley's Hotel, the crowd watched the performance. A few years later Charlie Wall told a young cowboy, who eventually became the great cattleman and founder of the Arizona Rangers, "Cap" Burton C. Mossman of Roswell, that he could easily have picked off the Kid with a six-shooter—but that he was on the boy's side. So were almost all the people there. They hoped he'd have luck and make it safely out of the country.

Billy waved his rifle at the friendly crowd. Then he let out a yell and touched his pony's flank with his iron shackle. Collie threw up his tail and started off at a gallop.

The Kid took the west road on up the Canyon of the Rio Bonito. He was as wildly joyous as an eagle suddenly freed from its cage.

No one moved until he was well out of sight.

PART FOUR

The Hunted

21

Billy must have been concerned about Pat Garrett as he rode at a high gallop on westward up the river road. Luck had surely been with him. He had accomplished the impossible. But his life would still be forfeit for the slightest error or miscalculation.

Fort Stanton was only eight miles southwest up this road, on the left-hand fork. There were two or three troops of the Ninth Cavalry there. He wasn't afraid of them; he'd never had the slightest trouble hiding out from these troopers even when he was almost under their very noses. But on below the post and some fifteen miles away was the Mescalero Indian Agency. The Apaches there were famous trailers. In covering every angle of his escape the Kid would have to consider the possibility of Garrett's bringing in two or three of these tireless and almost uncanny scouts and turning them loose like bloodhounds on a fresh scent.

Obviously he must get off this main road as quickly as

possible. He took the first used-trail that led to the right and wound its way through a gap in the Capitans to the gently rolling hills to the north. It was country he knew well. Some of his trusted friends lived here at the tiny springs and water holes that lay in the foothills. One of them was Jose Cordova. He rode there now in the gathering twilight.

Cordova sent a boy for his neighbor Sepio Salazar, and together they knocked off the heads of the rivets of Billy's leg shackles with a chisel. A woman brought him a plate of boiled black beans and chili and a stack of hot *tortillas,* while the men worked at his leg irons.

It was growing dark when he thanked them and rode to the home of his old friend, Ygenio Salazar, who had been wounded and left for dead in the Big Fight when McSween was killed almost three years before this. Ygenio would die before he would betray his *amigo Beelie.*

Apparently it was this Salazar who that night helped the boy get Andy Richardson's prize bay horse Don at the Three Block Ranch. The animal had sufficient mustang in him to be durable and enough quarter-blood and thoroughbred to make him swift and greathearted. He was short-coupled and fairly heavy-boned and weighed close to a thousand pounds. There was a white star on his forehead, and he was of gentle disposition. In all of New Mexico there wasn't a better horse to serve Billy's present needs.

There have been a number of recorded instances where men, aided by special provisions for feed and water, have ridden one horse a distance of a hundred miles between sunup and sundown. But Billy certainly wasn't thinking of any record when he mounted Don some time that next morning after he had shot his way to freedom. He was thinking only of reaching the safety of the country and friends around isolated Fort Sumner. Pat Garrett had trapped him once in this area. The Kid would need to be more alert this time. He'd take no chances. He'd keep on the move until he decided just what he wanted to do.

Old Mexico offered him his only hope of permanent safety. As long as he remained within the borders of the United States he would be in constant danger of arrest. Governor Wallace would be offering a new reward for his capture. You could be dead sure of that.

But strange desires helped make up the Kid's mind.

There was the girl Celsa; and Fort Sumner was home—or as near home as he had ever known; and there was pride, too—he wasn't running away from Pat Garrett.

2

When he swung up on Don old Salazar almost certainly handed him a little bundle of food tucked in a flour sack partly filled with oats. The jerked beef and cold *tortillas* would last him until he reached Fort Sumner, a hundred miles away. He did not push the bay as long as the hot April sun beat down. Finally twilight closed in on the high, barren mesa and the whole limitless horizon suddenly seemed lost in a great burst of color. The air was cool and bracing when Billy spoke to Don and touched him lightly in his flanks. The gallant animal did not hesitate. He took up a little faster trot. When the moon rose he was still checking off the miles.

There were one or two water holes the Kid knew of and he cautiously let Don drink. He fed him sparingly of his tiny store of oats, while he ate of his own jerky and *tortillas*.

It was almost morning when Billy made out the sand hills and familiar landscape that led down to the Valley of the Pecos. He knew Don was done for as he walked him up to an adobe hut and tiny corral and spring hidden in a depression. It could not be seen from the valley road yet was only a few miles from the outskirts of the one-time army reservation.

He called out a name and an old native New Mexican answered, "*Quien es?*" (Who is it?)

"*Beelie! Beelie. Su amigo.*" (Billy. Your friend.)

Billy slipped out of his saddle. From the sound of Don's breathing he was sure he had winded the brave animal. [It is known from the written testimony of Colonel Jack Porter, long a resident of Sumner, that on the Kid's first secret visit to Pete Maxwell he asked Pete to settle for Don with Richardson, manager of the Three Block Ranch, and to promise to look after the pony as long as he lived. Pete, who fortunately had more heart than brains, gave his word. He adopted the brave little horse as his own until the Maxwell ranch was sold out three years later. Pete then got Jack Porter, range boss of the new outfit, to pledge he would care for Don as long as the horse was alive. Porter kept him in his personal *remuda* and rode him sparingly until years later the noble old pony crossed to the other side of the big river where the pasture is always green and the water cool and sweet.]

3

It was late on the night of Friday, April 29th, a good thirty hours after the event, when the first word of Billy's escape reached Pat Garrett at White Oaks. Pat was new to Lincoln, and the town was largely on the Kid's side. No one had bothered to gallop west that first night; the Kid might be waiting with that deadly rifle of his behind some boulder at a point where the canyon narrowed.

So it was Friday morning when John C. Delaney, post trader at Fort Stanton, got the news and hurried off a messenger with a letter to Pat. It was what the tall sheriff had feared all along.

Garrett waited for Saturday dawn before he mounted up, then pushed hard on the reins as he rode the forty miles east to Lincoln. He found that no one at the county seat had made the slightest effort to try to follow the Kid's escape route.

He picked up one or two men and rode back west and then north through the Capitan Gap. But the trail was cold and he could cut no sign. The natives he interviewed only shrugged their shoulders: they had seen nor heard nothing. *Es la verdad, señor.* (It is the truth, mister.)

It was this same afternoon that the black pony Collie came in dragging a tie rope. A day or two later someone rode in from the Three Block Ranch with the news that Andy Richardson's best mount had disappeared.

Pat was severely criticized when he made no serious move to run down the Kid. Instead of being alert and active, he seemed almost negligent in his obvious duty. He spent most of the time at his ranch on the Pecos. It was almost as if he were caught in some deadly grip of indecision, some enervating spell of vacillation. His whole reputation and his future were at stake, yet he seemed incapable of shaking off the lethargy that held him.

Days went by and he still made no move towards meet-

'ing the terrible challenge. It seemed logical to many that if the Kid hadn't already pulled out for Old Mexico, he'd soon do so. There was open talk that Pat didn't want to close with him; that he was giving him plenty of time to make his get-away.

At least one authenticated fact had come to Pat the day after his escape: the Kid had started directly for Fort Sumner on the Richardson horse and there had picked up a pony belonging to one Montgomery Bell, who happened to be visiting at the abandoned army post from his ranch some fifty miles to the north. Bell hired Barney Mason and a man named Curington at Sumner to try to follow up his horse, on the surmise that it had been stolen by some New Mexican.

Barney Mason, carrying a Winchester and six-shooter, rode into a sheep camp, with the unarmed Curington at his side. Suddenly Billy stepped out from the hut with a rifle in his hand, his sense of humor getting the best of his good judgment. Mason, whom the Kid despised, did exactly what Billy was sure he would do; he jerked his mount around and disappeared in a cloud of dust. In Pat Garrett's own words, "He wore a new pair of spurs."

The Kid talked pleasantly with the unarmed Curington, and told him to report to the rancher that he would either return the horse to him or pay for it—when he got the money.

When Curington was out of sight Billy quietly mounted his borrowed horse and turned to the south. It would be best to leave the Fort Sumner country for a spell. Maybe it had been a terrible mistake to come here instead of heading for Mexico.

But he'd had to see Celsa. And how could you blame a fellow for that when he'd been penned up for four months and had just escaped from hanging?

4

There are many stories of what the Kid did or did not do during these days and weeks that followed. Certainly Pat was constantly on his mind.

Even Billy's gay disposition could hardly have dissipated the cold facts of his danger. He held no illusions about the capabilities of this able officer who was ten years his senior. He fully realized that Pat knew the country and his hide-outs in Sumner and in the friendly sheep camps almost as well as the Kid himself did.

Billy apparently was bothered with neither hate nor fear in considering this professional enemy. He must have tried calmly to figure out how Pat would operate against him. Here at the start he surely realized that his own best chances lay in cautiously moving about the country by night and hiding in little out-of-the-way spots by day.

One of the most reliable sources of contemporary evidence concerning the Kid's actions is the same John P. Meadows who had first met Billy in Fort Sumner when Meadows arrived there from the Texas plains early in 1879, his face blistered from sunburn. At the Old-Timers' gathering in Roswell many years later, when Meadows described this first meeting with the Kid, he also told of the last time he saw the young outlaw. John was batching at the time with Tom Norris in a cabin on the Rio Peñasco, southwest of Roswell. He had not even heard of Billy's escape when the boy dropped in on him out of the sky:

> The Kid come to my place three or four days after he made his escape from the jail, and Tom and me was in the cabin cooking some supper and the Kid come around the corner of the house and saw nobody there but us, and stepped in and said, Well, I got you, haven't I. And I said, Well, you have, so what are you going to do with us. He says, I'm going to eat supper with you. I says, That's all right as long as you can stand them beans. He sat there and told me about his arrest at Stinking Springs, at Las Vegas and all the way around. . . .
>
> We talked until eleven that night. He said, if I was laying out there in the arroyo and Pat Garrett rode by and didn't see me, he would be the last man I would kill. I wouldn't hurt a hair on his head; he worked pretty rough to capture us, but he treated me good after he got me; he treated us humane and friendly and was good to us after he did get us captured, I have ever such a good feeling for Pat Garrett.
>
> I said, What kind of a feeling do you have for Bob

Ollinger. He says, I expressed that a day or so ago.
That was the first time I heard of it.

I said, when I was sick and down and out, you befriended me, and there is two things I have never
done, I have never kissed the hand that slapped me
nor went back on a friend. Nor I never did. And I
said, Anyway, I'm going to befriend you now. I have
got fourteen head of old Indian ponies, some of them
ain't very much, but you go out and look 'em over,
and if one of them does you any good, take it and you
are welcome to them all, But don't go back to Fort
Sumner for if you do, Garrett will get you sure as
you do, or else you will have to kill him.

He said, I haven't any money, what would I do in
Mexico with no money? I'll have to go back and get
a little before I go. Sure as you do, I said, Garrett will
get you. He said, I have got too many friends up
there and I don't believe he will get me, and I can
stay there a while and get money enough and then go
to Mexico. I said, You'd better go while the going is
good, you go back up there and you will get killed or
Garrett. He went back to Sumner.

Meadows was a wise old man of unquestioned integrity
in 1931 when he thus reached deep down into the reser-
voir of his memories. Garrett and the Kid had been on his
mind all the years since he had first met the two men at
Fort Sumner back in 1879. His conclusions are worth recording:

There is a terrible big difference between them. Garrett was raised in Louisiana in civilization and the
Kid was raised in Silver City in the dance hall and
gambling hall and the bar room. The Kid didn't have
as good a chance as Garrett had, but there is something about the Kid that makes me think he was
pretty well bred. I believe the Kid did have some
pretty good feeling, he was pretty well bred and was
an expert at what he tried to do. He was an expert at
both shooting monte and six-shooting. He had that
humane feeling that most of us have. . . . I feel
good towards him. He was a creature of circumstances.

5

The Kid made his way on north to Fort Sumner after his visit with Meadows on the Peñasco. He spent most of his days and nights at one or another of the little sheep camps where he was always welcome. Now and again he'd slip into Sumner late at night and make his way to the doorway of the rooms where Celsa lived and always seemed to be awaiting him. He'd be gone before daybreak. He could not forget how Garrett had outwitted him the night when Tom O'Folliard was killed just outside the old Indian hospital at the edge of Sumner.

No one can ever know for certain why the Kid did not at least try to make his way the two or three hundred miles on south through the thinly populated mountainous country to the safety of Old Mexico. He promised his friend John Meadows he would do just that as soon as he got together a little money. But day after day he delayed the going.

It was as if the boy could not quite down his pride nor betray the romantic figure he had created in his own mind and in the eyes of the loyal little people who were helping him. Nor had he ever been able to disavow or forget the sustaining ideal that John Tunstall had created for him. Somehow, it seemed that he must stay on and face his pursuers, just as the brave young Englishman had done on that late February afternoon three years ago, in the wooded hills below the Ruidoso.

So it wasn't only the kind and tender Celsa whom he could not abandon; it was his own projected vision of himself as a valiant boy on horseback, fighting his lone battles seemingly against insurmountable odds. It was almost as if he did not care to escape his rendezvous with Fate.

To himself and to these gentle, uncomplaining natives he had become a champion, a bright, smiling symbol of revolt lighting up their own dreary and eternal struggles with life. He was a true part of this lonely, mystical land and these neglected people. And he was touched by their overpowering sense of God's will, their ageless acceptance of destiny. He was their happy warrior, for these were his people and here was his land. And even for life itself he could not leave it now.

He wanted nothing for himself—except to live out his own little adventurous life; to gamble and race his pony and be with his sweetheart; to sing a little and dance a little, and to love a little—and maybe steal a little to get even with his unfair past. Unwittingly he represented a subconscious dream that has appealed to many men throughout time; the right to live without ambition, without drive, without hurry. He was an idealist, even though his ideal seemed not quite an accepted one.

Pat Garrett represented in a way everything that was the opposite. He wanted wealth, power, fame, recognition. And he had wanted it strongly enough to hire out his pistol to the highest bidder. He was now a tool of something called progress, or civilization, or materialism—or maybe it was just dollars and cents.

Apparently there wasn't room in this tiny world along the Pecos—or the Mississippi—or the Hudson—or along any river in this silly, spinning globe—for these conflicting ideas to exist together. One of them had to give way.

Yet Pat, too, was a dreamer in his own way: he, too, was only a poor little mortal fighting the tides of his Fate. It was of infinite pathos that this tall, brave man from the buffalo ranges, and this slender boy from nowhere who could talk the beautiful Spanish, seemed doomed to meet in deadly conflict—and let Death make its choice.

The only question was where and when and how the terrible ordeal would come—for one of them must kill the other.

22

Even the publication of the Governor's offer of reward on May 4th did not stir Pat Garrett into any genuine activity.

Altogether he had won more than a thousand dollars from his original capture of the Kid. The money had come in handy in the development of his 1,200-acre ranch four or five miles north of the little settlement of Roswell. He had had generous financial backing from Captain Lea and John Chisum and the other big men who had induced him to come to Lincoln County and take over the sheriff's job.

Probably the Kid enjoyed the idea that his escape must have brought considerable qualms of fear to some of these men who had once been his friends. They would think him desperate and revengeful now. John Chisum would figure that his own backing of Garrett against the Kid had put him high on the list of accounts to be settled which the young outlaw might make out. The chances are that Old John made tracks for Santa Fe or Las Vegas the minute he heard the Kid had broken jail.

Billy probably wondered, too, whether Governor Wallace might possibly have pardoned him at the last minute if he had not taken matters into his own hands and killed his guards. But he'd had his lesson from Wallace, and he was not surprised when, immediately after the news of his

escape reached Santa Fe, the Governor announced a reward in the *Daily New Mexican:*

BILLY THE KID
$500 REWARD

I will pay $500 to any person or persons who will
capture William Bonny, alias the Kid, and deliver
him to any sheriff of New Mexico. Satisfactory proof
of identity will be required.

Lew. Wallace
Governor of New Mexico.

The announcement ran for ten days. It was only one of
several such awards offered, in line with a fresh outbreak
of lawlessness that spread over the Territory. Governor
Wallace threw up his hands in disgust. Before long he was
appointed Minister to Turkey by the new President Gar-
field, and from this moment on New Mexico and the Kid
were far away and long ago in his mind.

Speaking of the frustrations that would ultimately come
to his successor in Santa Fe, Wallace remarked with rare
cynicism: "Of course he will do as I did, have the same
ideas, make the same effort, soon cool in zeal, then finally
say, 'All right, let her drift.' Every calculation based on experience elsewhere fails in New Mexico. In six years I will
be sixty. I have spent enough time in this place."

On May 30th the Governor left the Territory for the
last time. The Kid, in hiding in the country near Fort
Sumner, must have had rather jumbled reactions when he
read in some worn, dog-eared newspaper of Wallace's departure. His deal with the Governor simply hadn't worked
out. He and Tom O'Folliard would have been far better
off if they had ridden on to Old Mexico as they had
planned instead of going into Lincoln on the Governor's
assurance of protection and pardon. All his troubles since
then, he probably told himself, had stemmed from the subsequent inability of the Governor to make good his side
of the bargain.

But even at this dangerous hour the Kid made no effort
to shake himself loose from his lethargy and pull out.
There is some evidence that he crossed the high mesas to
White Oaks, riding at night and hiding out during the
day. He still had friends there: Sam Dedrick and West at

the livery stable, and other men who would never think of betraying him.

There was a new deputy of Garrett's now at the Oaks. He was a heavy-shouldered, quiet, highly intelligent Kentuckian of thirty who had migrated to the buffalo ranges around Fort Griffin in 1870. His name was John Poe, and it was claimed that he had killed 20,000 buffalo as a professional hunter. When the buffalo ran out Poe became marshal of tough Fort Griffin, and later deputy sheriff of Oldham County in the Panhandle. His election as sheriff there had seemed so certain that some of his best friends had not even bothered to go to the polls. When he was beaten by one vote he was so disgusted that he took the job of replacing Frank Stewart as the New Mexican representative of the Canadian River Cattlemen's Association, with headquarters at White Oaks. Stewart, it will be remembered, had had a considerable part in the Kid's capture.

Poe held a commission as a Deputy U. S. Marshal, and when Garrett contacted him in April of 1881 he accepted appointment as deputy sheriff of Lincoln County. He and Garrett arranged to work hand in glove in running down cattle rustlers and in breaking up the traffic in stolen Panhandle steers. News of the newcomer's arrival was passed on to the Kid, but it meant nothing to him. Pat had always had a deputy at the Oaks. This new one wouldn't even know the country or his way around.

Pat still made no real move. The Kid must have wondered if it meant that Garrett, maybe for old times' sake, was giving him plenty of time to make his get-away.

May drifted into June. It was bad now when the merciless noon sun beat down through a cloudless sky. Billy had long ago learned to live with this sun, but it was never easy. He still spent most of his days over in the Pecos country. For hours he'd lie stretched out on a hilltop searching the skyline with his glasses.

Nights were different. It was cool and lovely then. He could quietly ride up to the tiny stone or adobe hut of some friendly sheep camp, and rest under the stars, or lie back against a wall in the soft moonlight. From way off would come the whining, baby-like cry of a coyote, and then from across the magic horizon the answering call would float in like an echo—plaintive, searching, mystical.

The herder's woman might fix him a dish of beans and lamb stew and a little stack of warmed-over *tortillas*.

For an hour or two he could shake off the deadly fear that forever pursued him. He might even close his eyes and sleep while his host kept watch, his dog ready to give the alarm at first suspicion of an approaching stranger. But these bits of relaxation were never long. Always there was present the shadow of a tall, lean, deadly man, who could move as silently as the dropping of night or the coming of dawn.

Sleeplessness was the price of vigilance, and eternal vigilance was the price of life. Billy took his snatches of sleep with one eye open. Some day Pat would come for him. That he knew for a certainty.

And so, as June slipped into July, a great weariness must have come over the boy. He was still alert and ever conscious of his danger, but the sharp edge of his awareness and his once-perfect reflexes could hardly have kept from being dulled. Long ago he had mastered the science of self-preservation. The art was still with him, but the complete co-ordination of all his faculties must have become slightly blurred.

He still held fast to his inner sense of life. He could still laugh and joke, but the sparkle and the humor were gone. He had worn out his resilience. An hour or two of sleep could no longer recharge his batteries. He was near the end of his road.

Every time he saw Celsa she tried to make him promise he would leave. Some of his old native friends at the sheep ranches where he stopped were likewise quietly urging him not to wait any longer. It was dangerous. He must go now—*pronto—esta noche* (soon—this night). He must not delay! Billy would thank them and promise he'd go soon. It was always that way. It was as if something bigger than he was kept holding him back.

2

It was getting into the second week of July. John Poe, at White Oaks, was preparing to leave for Tombstone, Arizona, on the trail of a little herd of stolen Texas steers. The day before the date of his departure a barroom hanger-on, who had once been a respectable citizen and friend of Poe's in the Panhandle country, came to his hotel room at the Oaks.

Swearing him to secrecy, the man told Poe that he had been sleeping in a small room next the office of the Dedrick & West livery stable, and that through the thin partition he had overheard a conversation regarding the Kid: the young outlaw was still around Fort Sumner and had actually made two visits to White Oaks during the past few weeks.

It was hard for Poe to believe that the Kid had not gone to Mexico, but he put so much confidence in the tip that he rode off at once for Lincoln to give the information to Sheriff Garrett. Garrett had just started for his ranch on the Pecos, and Poe followed him there.

At first Pat was skeptical. However, he had received a note from Brazil, at whose ranch the Kid and his gang had stopped immediately before their capture, containing the information that the boy was still around the neighborhood of Fort Sumner. Brazil, fearful that the Kid might seek revenge on him for his part in his capture, offered to do anything to help Pat run him to earth.

For a full ten weeks Pat Garrett had taken things quietly. Lately he'd been getting quite a bit of prodding from Captain Lea and other friends. Seventy days had gone by since he had made his first and only move: at best that had been nothing more than a perfunctory ride through the Capitan Pass in a futile gesture of trying to cut sign on the Kid's trail. Seventy days was a long time to face criticism which was now turning into open bitter talk.

The strangest part of all was that the Kid himself seemed to be under the same spell of inaction and indecision. Day after day Pat's paralysis seemed matched by the Kid's own hesitancy to take advantage of this incomparable opportunity to escape. It was as if both were guilty of an unaccountable lapse in self-discipline. Yet always before each one had been swift in reactions to danger and certain of ability to meet any crisis.

Garrett himself was a complicated man who could never quite fit himself into any definite pattern of life. He had taken up with big men of property and ambition, and he wanted wealth and power for himself; but he also wanted to play poker and drink good bourbon and loaf around

barrooms. He, too, had a kindly feeling for native *gente;*
he had fallen in love and married two of them.

Yet some force within him kept urging him on to try
big things. He dreamed of a great irrigation project
around Roswell, but he sold out his share in the enterprise before the big profits started rolling in; he dreamed
of a vast cattle ranch in Lincoln County, but he disposed
of it to the first Englishman with money who came along;
he dreamed of raising quarter-horses at Uvalde, Texas,
but abandoned the venture before his first colts were long
yearlings. Always it was to be that way.

He was not quite hard enough and self-centered enough
for this demanding thing called success: again and again
he found himself touched and softened and even handicapped by some futile sense of the easy-going and the romantic. [Apparently it was only strong-willed men, determined to have wealth and power, who could sustain and
drive through their ambitions. It took such men as Tom
Catron and Dave Elkins to form a Ring and win a Territory; each ended up a U. S. Senator, Elkins elected from
West Virginia, while Tom Catron shared with Albert C.
Fall the honor of being the first elected from the new
State of New Mexico in 1912. Captain Lea would become
the father of a city; but not even Old John Chisum was
hard enough to win and hold his empire of grass. And
when the halo of fame tarnished for the tall, lonely dreamer, his money gone and himself old and tired out at 57,
Garrett died from a bullet in the back of his head and was
buried in an unmarked grave near the banks of the Rio
Grande. *La via esta duro, amigo!* (The road is hard,
friend.)]

3

John Poe quietly prodded Pat to make the big try. His
tip was too important to be put aside, and Pat had to
move at last. He could delay no longer.

Finally he sent for his deputy, Tip McKinney, an amiable man from Uvalde, Texas. They saddled up and pulled
out on the night of July 10th. Pat sent a messenger ahead
to request Wilcox to meet him at the mouth of Taiban
Arroyo, five miles below Sumner.

Shortly after dark on July 13th the party of three arrived at the point where the arroyo gave off into the Pecos. Wilcox was not there. Garrett and McKinney waited two hours and then rode on north to within a mile or two of Fort Sumner.

They slept until dawn on their horse-blankets, with their saddles as pillows. Then they carefully concealed themselves in the hills to the east.

Both Pat and Tip McKinney were well known in Sumner. Therefore in mid-forenoon it was decided that Poe, pretending to be a disgusted miner returning from White Oaks to Texas, should jog on into the village. But he found nothing, and when he cautiously mentioned the Kid's name he gained only suspicious looks. His instructions were to ride on north to a trail-crossing near the Pecos known as Sunnyside. Here he was to contact a man named Rudolph, who had been a minor member of the party which had captured the Kid.

Rudolph appeared very much disturbed when he was asked what he knew about the Kid's whereabouts. He explained to Poe that Billy had pulled out, but he was not at all certain where or when.

Poe had arranged to meet Garrett and McKinney at moonrise at a point four miles north of Sumner called by the lovely name of *La Punta de la Glorietta*. He finished his supper, thanked his host, and was approaching the designated spot when he saw his two companions riding up. It was perfect timing.

When Garrett heard Poe's report he figured his last remaining chance of getting any reliable information was for him to call on Pete Maxwell who, with his mother, owned the one-time army post. Pete would be reluctant about giving away the Kid, but Pat did not believe that he would lie to him.

The three men mounted and quietly rode south. A short distance from the darkened village they ran into a man camped alone by a fire. They pulled up and discovered that, oddly enough, he was an old Texas friend of Poe's. The trio were glad to share in a pot of hot coffee and a yarn. They unsaddled their horses and staked them out to graze.

A short distance away was a peach orchard, and before long the three searchers walked through the trees towards a row of adobe buildings, part of which were used by

native families. Pat knew that some of the Kid's friends
lived here, and that there was just a possibility that Billy
might show up or that they could overhear something
about his movements. The Maxwell house, which had
been converted into a residence from one of the group of
officers' quarters, was not more than 400 feet away from
the west end of this little orchard. (Turn to Map, page 313)

For two hours the three men lay quietly among the
trees, their eyes and ears alert to every sound and movement. After a long wait they heard voices over by the row
of single-story buildings, and through the deep shadows
of the peach trees they caught sight of the figure of a man
who rose to his feet and walked towards another group
of buildings on to the south of the Maxwell home. The
light was uncertain but he seemed to be in his shirtsleeves.

For a second time their search had proven fruitless. The
one possibility which now remained was for Garrett to
confer privately with Pete Maxwell. The three men silently circled the orchard on foot, coming up to the Maxwell house from the opposite direction.

A lawn stretched out to the south in front of the wide
porch of the residence, and a white picket fence ran close
to the east side. There was a gate here and a little walk
that led on to the steps of the porch. Down at the lower
or southern end of the lawn was a second small gate that
opened onto a dirt street. Across the road stretched a row
of adobe rooms that had once been used as storehouses.

Garrett knew that Pete's bedroom was at the east corner
of the former officers' quarters and that it had a window
and a door opening on the wide porch. He whispered for
Poe and McKinney to wait here in the shadow of the
fence, while he tiptoed to the porch and then turned into
Pete's room for his talk.

A bright moon was shining and the two men left outside gave way to complete relaxation. It had been a long,
hard trip, with very little chance for rest.

4

It must have been well before moonrise when the Kid
slipped out from a sheep camp a few miles to the east of
Fort Sumner and racked into the village. This might well
be his last visit. The old man at the camp where he'd been

for two or three days was urging him again, and Billy had half promised to leave for Mexico the following night. But he had to see Celsa once more.

He stabled his horse at one of the several abandoned structures at the edge of the post. It was a perfect midsummer night, and he left his coat tied on the back of the cantle of his saddle. He dropped off to have a little talk with some friends in the row of adobe houses next the peach orchard. The fragrance of the pink blossoms had long since gone, but it was safe and peaceful here. They talked in monotones, for always there was the possibility of some chance spy.

It was growing late when Billy rose from among his little group of trusted friends lounging in one of the doorways. In low tones they bade him *"Adios"* and wished him good luck. *"Vaya con Dios!"* (Go with God!) they repeated.

Slowly he made his way on past the Maxwell home to the dirt road below. He followed the fence that ran along the south end of the lawn.

He had now been on the dodge exactly seventy-eight days. He was not only physically tired from the endless strain but utterly spent in mind and body. He had worn thin the last reserves of his inner being. It was almost as if he no longer had the energy to care much what happened to him. Anything was better than this silent, neverending torture. Two months and a half had been too long to live on snatches of sleep and half rations.

A little way on beyond the corner of the fence he turned in at one of the two rooms where his Celsa lived. She was sitting on the steps of the open doorway waiting for him. She rose and put her arms around him, and she did her best to keep from crying. Only this afternoon she had talked in low tones to her brother about the tall Sheriff Garrett who now lived in Lincoln and whose duty it was to run down "Beelie." He'd be showing up any time now with his deadly guns.

"Beelie" must go away, now, at once. He must promise. Mexico would be the best. She would try to get money for him from her brother and her family, but they had so little. He must take off his boots and rest for a while. But he must start this night.

She would build a fire at once and cook him something

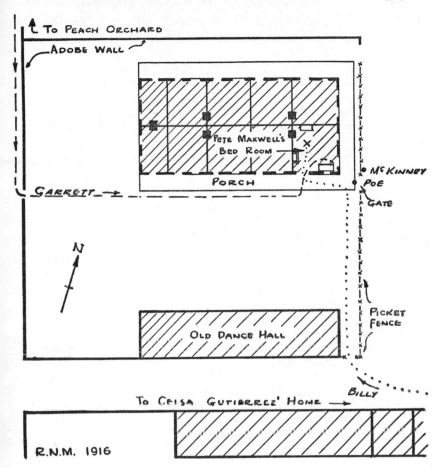

hot and nourishing. She was sorry she had no meat at
hand. But Don Pedro Maxwell had killed a yearling heifer
that morning. If "Beelie" would walk across the patio to
Pete's room and get the key from him for the meat house
at the far end of the porch, he could cut off a nice steak
and she would fry it for him. He joked with her and
asked for a butcher knife. He unbuckled his heavy gun
belt and pulled out his .41 calibre, double-action Colt
from its holster, and stuck it in the waistband of his
trousers.

In his stocking feet he walked along the inside of the
picket fence, with the bright moonlight streaming down

on him. He had crossed the lawn and was almost on the porch when he heard a suspicious noise on the right by the gate.

He jerked out his six-shooter. His eyes took in two men. One had half-slipped to his knees when a spur caught on the steps as he tried to get to his feet. Billy couldn't make out who they were or what they were doing here.

They were speaking in English; one of them said for him not to get excited since they wouldn't hurt him.

"*Quien es?*" (Who is it?) Billy repeated his excited question—"*Quien es?*"

It would have been easy for him to kill both men. Neither of them had pulled a gun: neither had seen him until he was almost on them. But maybe they were Pete's friends, he thought. He couldn't take the chance of shooting them down.

He turned quickly, crossed the porch and darted into Pete's bedroom. The overhanging porch made it dark in here, but he knew the exact spot where Pete's bed stood in the corner, at the right of the doorway. He slipped up to it in his stocking feet, still deeply worried about those two strangers outside on the porch.

"*Quien son estos hombres afuerta, Pedro?*" (Who are those men outside, Pete?)

He was close to the bed when he repeated the excited inquiry. "*Quien son?*" (Who are they?)

Then he made out a figure seated on the bed close to Pete's head. The Kid's six-shooter was hardly a foot away from the face of this man here.

"*Quien es?*" he begged. (Who is it? Who is this third man here?)

It was dangerous to wait longer. But he couldn't quite pull the trigger. The visitor might be a friend of Pete's, or even Pete himself.

What was the matter with him? Why didn't he fire? Had he turned soft? Why take this awful chance?

He backed off towards the center of the room, again pleading, "*Quien es?*" (Who is it?)

My God! wouldn't someone tell him who this stranger was?

Garrett did not have to ask "*Quien es?*" for he knew the voice. It was the one.

The break was Pat's—the priceless second of hesitation,

the decent second the Kid gave this man-hunter rather
than kill him without giving him a chance to draw his
gun.

Garrett swung his body to the left in one swift move,
pulling his gun and firing as he bent down. The flash of
powder blinded him as he took his second shot.

It went wild, but the first one had found its mark. It
was enough. There was a short cry. Then the thud of a
body crumpling up on the floor.

Pete Maxwell jumped from the bed and with the bed-
clothes clinging to him made for the door. Only luck kept
the two deputies outside from killing him as he rushed by
them.

Garrett followed, shouting, "I've killed the Kid! I've
killed the Kid."

The household was awake and terrified. Dulvenia, the
old Navajo, in her long nightgown and bare feet and with
a candle in her hand, waddled out of her room far down
the porch. The others had fled from the room of death,
but without fear she walked into the silent chamber.

The boy lay face up on the wooden floor. There was a
splotch of blood on the left side of his shirt where the
bullet had entered just below the heart.

Garrett and the others pressed back into the room, their
pistols drawn and cocked. The flickering light of the single
candle cast weird, moving shadows as they bent down over
the boy.

The old Navajo woman cried out that they had killed
her *pobrecito* her poor little one. Then she turned on Pat
and showered him with filthy words in Spanish.

5

Most of that night two men worked on the pine coffin, and
dawn had come when they lifted the body into the crude
box and set it on two wooden carpenter-horses. Dona Luz
Maxwell brought out her tall, solid-silver candlesticks and
placed them on stools at the head and feet.

They tried to count the boy's exact years and days: 21
years, 7 months and 22 days in all. And they told in low,
awed tones of his deeds and his many acts of thoughtful-
ness.

It was close to twelve noon when they carried him on

their shoulders to the old military grounds and laid him beside the open grave between his two dear friends, Tom O'Folliard and Charlie Bowdre. There was no priest in the little community to say the final words.

There had been a delay until a coroner's jury of five natives, with young Rudolph Milnor of Sunnyside as foreman, heard the few witnesses and then wrote out the findings in Spanish. At the bottom of the sheet the five men solemnly made their marks and Milnor set down their names and then his own signature. The hand of Pat F. Garrett was duly certified as the one that had fired the bullet which brought death to the boy, and the document added, "He deserves to be rewarded."

Some of the women in the little crowd were weeping as they watched the men lower the rough coffin into the grave.

For many years to come Billy would be remembered with affection by these humble people. And they would tell stories of his valor and his kindness to them.

It is almost unaccountable that in the end he alone of all the men of his time was to gain the immortality of a deathless legend.

He alone, of all those he had encountered on the hard road, would live on.